van
lliams®
CE 1783

CKY'S **1**ST DISTILLER

ntucky
TRAIGHT
urbon
HISKEY

KY, BOTTLED BY OLD EVAN WILLIAMS
WN, KENTUCKY 40004 • 43% ALC/VOL

GENUINE SOUR MASH

American Whiskey, Bourbon & Rye

A Guide to the Nation's Favorite Spirit

Clay Risen

A Scott & Nix Edition

STERLING EPICURE
New York

To Poppy, who introduced me to bourbon, and
Michael, who made sure I stayed friends with it.

STERLING EPICURE
New York

An Imprint of Sterling Publishing
387 Park Avenue South
New York, NY 10016

STERLING EPICURE is a trademark of Sterling Publishing, Co., Inc.
The distinctive Sterling logo is a registered trademark
of Sterling Publishing, Co,, Inc

Produced by
Scott & Nix, Inc.
150 West 28th Street, Suite 1900
New York, NY 10001
www.scottandnix.com
whiskey@scottandnix.com

ISBN 978-1-4027-9840-5

Distributed in Canada by Sterling Publishing
c/o CanadiaManda Group 165 Dufferin Street
Toronto, Ontario, Canada M6K 3H6
Distributed in the United Kingdom by GMC Services
Castle Place, 166 High Street, Lewes, East Sussex, England BN7 1XU
Distributed in Australia by Capricorn Link (Australia) Pty. Ltd.,
P.O. Box 704, Windsor, NSW 2756, Australia

For information about custom editions, special sales, and
premium corporate purchases, please contact Sterling Special Sales
at 800-805-5489 or specialsales@sterlingpublishing.com.

Manufactured in China

10   9   8   7   6   5   4   3   2

www.sterlingpublishing.com

Contents

Introduction

When I told a friend I was writing a book about American whiskey, he joked that my next topic should be Canadian tequila. Without offending his age or patriotism, I should note that my friend came of age in an era when, if not exactly an oxymoron, "American whiskey" struck many a refined palate as a gross insult. What had once been a vital, aggressive drink had, over the course of the twentieth century, been tamed, trimmed, thinned, and coddled, in the same way mankind took the wild wolf and produced the teacup poodle. As Kingsley Amis, who knew his bourbon, having been a visiting professor at Vanderbilt, wrote, "American whiskeys are second to none in smoothness, blandness, everything that goes to make a fine spirit." While this book is dedicated in part to my paternal grandfather, who introduced me to bourbon, I offer a second dedication to my sarcastic friend, and all the countless scotch devotees like him, who still believe that American whiskey is best found in Manhattans, mint juleps, or nothing at all.

There is nothing boring about American whiskey today. Hardly a week passes without a new distillery opening. After decades of hidebound tradition, innovation is rampant. And the days of hunting for a decent shot are over—there is hardly a major city in America without a good whiskey bar.

But this embarrassment of riches presents a new problem: how do you know what to drink—and what not to drink? To the newcomer, it's all brown liquor. What's the difference between bourbon and rye? What does proof mean? Overproof? Straight? Sour mash? Blended? And unless you have a trust fund or a horde of gold bullion, exploring the wide world of American whiskey isn't cheap: while it may be the best deal in the liquor store, who wants to spend forty dollars just to find out if a bottle is any good? It may be the best of times for American whiskey, but it can also seem like the most frustrating. This book, I hope, will cut through some of that fog and show just how diverse and exciting American whiskey is today.

Whiskey, and bourbon in particular, is tremendously versatile. It is great by itself or in cocktails. You can cook with it. It goes equally well as an aperitif or a digestif. Whiskey is, I believe, the most enjoyable, approachable, diverse liquor in the world.

American whiskey, the subject of this book, is simply grain alcohol distilled in America under 190 proof. Most of it is made from corn; some of it is not. Indeed, any grain will do; Koval, a distillery in Chicago, makes a whiskey out of a form of wheat popular in Central Europe called spelt. There are rules for categories of whiskey, to be sure—very strict rules, in the case of bourbon. But it doesn't have to meet any of those standards to be called plain old whiskey.

American whiskey sat on the bottom shelf for the better part of the late twentieth century, and except for a few expressions like Maker's Mark and Eagle Rare, it deserved to be there. There is a belief that Prohibition killed off whiskey culture in this country. That's only partly true. It actually died a slow death. Prohibition did knock out a lot of producers, and it caused a lot of drinkers used to aged liquor to switch to more readily made products like gin. But some distilleries survived Prohibition and came roaring back in the 1930s. Except that, of course, the 1930s weren't a great time to be selling anything other than basement-priced liquor, which meant that while sales might have increased overall, there was hardly a golden age of whiskey innovation and expansion around the corner.

Whiskey—and liquor production in general—took another hit during World War II. Not only did domestic rationing limit how much people spent on liquor, but the necessities of war-related manufacturing and the explosive demand for industrial-grade alcohol drove most distillers to switch away from consumer production entirely.

The first few decades of the postwar era saw a moderate return in domestic whiskey production. Though the expansion of middle-class incomes had a perverse impact: scotch, with its cosmopolitan image, took over a big chunk of the market. Meanwhile Canadian distilleries, which had done quite well during Prohibition as one of the few sources of quality whiskey, retained a sizable share of the American market. The writers of *Mad Men* have Don Draper drinking Canadian Club for a reason: that's what everyone drank.

Then came the 1960s and 1970s, and the shift in consumer tastes toward clearer, cleaner-looking liquor (which is strange, given the popularity of outlaw country and *Hee Haw* and *The Dukes of Hazard*). White wine and vodka were in; whiskey, an old man's drink, was out. The decline created a vicious cycle: weakened brands, some with amazingly long traditions and unique flavor profiles, were either shuttered or bought up by ever-larger, multinational distilling concerns. In turn, they reoriented their expanded profiles toward an increasingly downmarket clientele.

Four Roses is a case in point. A distillery with roots in the early nineteenth century, it enjoyed a solid reputation throughout the prewar era. In 1943 it was bought by Seagram, which already had a whiskey portfolio, but wanted a brand with strong name recognition that it could sell off the bottom shelf. By the late 1970s, the name Four Roses was synonymous with winos and boozy uncles.

Then something strange happened: American drinkers started asking for American whiskey. Maker's Mark, Jack Daniel's—by the late 1980s, the small hesitant shoots of a domestic whiskey revival were poking through the snow. Cocktail culture, the boom in single-malt scotch, and the retro trend made people take a second look—or, if they were young enough, a first look—at American whiskeys.

The last decade, and in particular the last five years, has seen a renaissance in American liquor, particularly whiskey. On the consumer side, demand has grown precipitously. So too has output: not only are the big distillers expanding production, but they're also widening their portfolios, offering new mash bills and flavor profiles alongside limited-release, experimental expressions. Even more exciting is the proliferation of craft distillers across the country, some of whom promise to become the venerable brands of the next half-century.

This book, then, comes at a critical time, but also a rapidly changing one. I have tried my best to describe the outline of the contemporary American whiskey market, and fill in as much as possible. I have reviewed most, though probably not all, of the whiskeys you will find on your liquor-store shelves. There will inevitably be missing entries, either because they are too rarified, too small in their distribution, or too new to have made this edition. Future editions, drawing on reader feedback, will attempt to fill in the gaps.

What You'll Find in This Book

I've written *American Whiskey, Bourbon and Rye* to be a robust companion to the world of whiskey, useful for anyone new to the spirit or already casually acquainted with it. The first section is this introduction: the characteristics of American whiskey, its history, how it's made, and how it's consumed.

The second portion is a nearly encyclopedic review of more than 200 American whiskeys of all types, from bourbon to single malt and everything in between. I've included all the big producers and as many of the small, craft distillers as I could get my hands on. The reviews are grouped by producer and/or brand, with a brief introduction to the story behind the label and its maker. Each expression is then reviewed individually, with a general commentary followed by detailed tasting notes and a rating. All these notes are the results of my own tasting, though in many cases I had the help of a panel of trusted confederates who tasted the whiskeys with me and added their own thoughts. The decision on how to review and rate them, however, was my own.

The goal of the book is simple: to provide an entertaining and informative guide to the neophyte and intermediate drinker of American whiskey. It is not necessarily intended for the connoisseur, who does not need a guide to tell her or him what to drink.

What You Won't Find in This Book

Despite the breadth of this book, there is much about American whiskey that I've decided to leave out, for reasons I'll explain—though mostly for the brute fact that there is too much material for any one book to cover effectively, and boundaries have to be drawn somewhere.

The first thing a knowing reader might notice is that I have left out unaged whiskey, alternately called "new make," "white whiskey," "white dog," and even, incorrectly, "moonshine." Everything reviewed in this book has sat in barrels long enough to have at least a tinge of brown to it. I excluded the white whiskeys because, while there are some decent ones available, by and large I consider them a novelty. I've seen far too many liquor cabinets with a dusty, almost-full bottle of unaged spirit in the corner to believe that many actually enjoy the stuff. And while I've had a few drinkable cocktails made with unaged whiskey in place of aged, most of them are pale impressions of the real thing. In ten years, I predict, you'll have a hard time finding many unaged whiskeys on the market.

I've also left out flavored whiskeys, despite their widespread popularity. I am not a fan of cherry-flavored or honey-infused whiskeys, but I know people who are, and I admit that it makes an inter-esting cocktail ingredient. But even though they are whiskey-based, they are different drinks, with different flavor profiles, different noses, and different standards. There is no way of comparing standard straight bourbon and Jim Beam's Red Stag. Nor is there any need to: If you're looking for a cherry-flavored liquor, you're probably not interested in its "mouthfeel" or subtle undertones on the palate. You're looking for something intoxicating that tastes like cherry.

Nor will you find cocktail recipes in this book. I think recipes in drink books are often padding—there are hundreds of places to find cocktail recipes online and books dedicated to the subject. It would be arbitrary to the point of uselessness for me to select ten or twenty for this book. More to the point, I wouldn't be a particularly good guide to cocktails, since they're not really my thing. I've had some astounding concoctions in my life, and I appreciate the creative energy buzzing around today's well-stocked cocktail bar. I like to drink whiskey by itself because I believe there is more than enough going on inside the glass to keep me interested. True, there are some whiskeys that aren't good for much else than mixing, and that's fine, the world needs them. But while a cocktail might complement a fine whiskey, it will inevitably detract from the full appreciation of it. A glass of Woodford Reserve is, to a large extent, about admiring the craftsmanship of Brown-Forman's master distiller, Chris Morris. If you mixed it into a fancy cocktail, it would be less about Morris's craft.

I've also left out many of the smallest distilleries, though not all. By and large, if a whiskey is only sold at its distillery or in a very small market, I probably didn't cover it. I won't pretend to have a bright-line test for how small a producer has to be to get skipped; we can argue whether it was fair for me to cover Chicago's Few Spirits but not Zeppelin Bend from Michigan. There was no method to my madness; I tried to gather as many whiskeys as I could acquire in a reasonable amount of time and review them. Some were small enough to fall through the cracks, and their absence is no comment on their quality or potential.

Finally, I have left off many, though not all, vintage and limited-edition whiskeys. These change from year to year in important ways, so my comments would need to be limited and general. And really, if you know you want a bottle of 2010 George T. Stagg, there's not a lot that I can tell you that you don't already know. More to the point, in the sense that there is a decision to be made between depth and breadth of coverage, I opted for the latter, hoping to introduce readers to as many different whiskeys as possible, without overwhelming them with the arcane, but very real, distinctions among different vintage years.

My hope is that, with all these exceptions aside,

American Whiskey, Bourbon & Rye will cover most anything you are likely to encounter at your better local liquor store, wherever you are in the country. If I've left something out that you'd like to see reviewed in the next edition, feel free to email me at *whiskey@scottandnix.com*.

What Is Whiskey?

Making whiskey is in theory a very simple proposition: combine milled grain and water, let yeast convert the grain's sugars into alcohol, and distill the whole thing. If you want, you can let it sit in wood barrels for a while. Or not. As far as the American federal government is concerned, that's more or less all you need to call it whiskey. (Even the spelling can vary: while Scottish whiskey is uniformly spelled "whisky," its American cousin can go with or without the "e"—though it's usually spelled "whiskey.")

This makes whiskey a rather broad category: single malt, bourbon, rye, corn, Tennessee, scotch, Irish, Canadian—they're all variations on that same basic idea. The complexities come in what sets them apart. Some distinctions are required by law; bourbon, among other things, has to be made from fifty-one percent or more corn, while Tennessee whiskey has to be made in Tennessee (bourbon, contrary to what the guy next to you at the bar says, does not have to be made in Bourbon County, Kentucky; it doesn't even have to be made in Kentucky). But that broad definition doesn't help much when you're staring at a bar full of brown liquor. So what, exactly, is it?

There are several types of grain spirits, of which whiskey is one. Grain vodka is another (potato vodka is, obviously, not). What sets whiskey and vodka apart from each other, at the most fundamental level, is that vodka is distilled several times until it's at least 95 percent alcohol, or 190 proof (a liquor's proof is simply twice its alcohol percentage). Since the goal of vodka is to be completely without character, distillers usually filter it through charcoal to remove any distinctive color, aroma, or flavor. It is then cut with water to make it potable,

though it can't be bottled at less than 80 proof.
Vodka is, therefore, alcohol and water and nothing
else. Apparently, this is a very attractive thing to
drink—vodka far outsells whiskey.

Whiskey, on the other hand, is distilled from
grain at less than 190 proof, bottled at no less than
80 proof, and, according to the maddeningly
circular definition of the federal government's
Alcohol and Tobacco Tax and Trade Bureau (TTB),
which regulates alcoholic beverages has, "the taste,
aroma and characteristics generally attributed to
whisky." What those tastes, aromas, and characteristics are goes unsaid, though it stands to reason
that the TTB is thinking of grain-derived notes,
typically floral, citrus, vanilla, and pepper.

There is no restriction on which grains are used
to make whiskey, but they tend to bo bailey, corn,
wheat, and rye (though these days it's possible to
find exotic grains like spelt and quinoa). Single-malt
scotch must he 100 percent barley, but most
whiskeys are a blend of grains. Different combinations produce different flavor profiles, and some
distillers guard their grain formulas, called "mash
bills," jealously.

In the United States, in order to identify a
whiskey by a grain name—for example, to call
something a rye whiskey—it has to be made with at
least fifty-one percent of that grain (things are
different in Canada, where rye whiskeys usually
contain just enough rye to give them flavor, the rest
being other grains and grain neutral spirit). All
bourbon is at least fifty-one percent corn, though its
"small grains," that is, the smaller portions of other
grains, can be whatever the distiller fancies. Rye
is typically the second-"largest" grain in a bourbon-
mash bill, because it brings complementary
floral and spice notes. There's almost always a
third grain, usually barley. There are also popular
"wheated" bourbons—Maker's Mark, Pappy van
Winkle, and W.L. Weller are all wheated bourbons—
which simply means that wheat, rather than
rye, is the second grain.

A note on nomenclature: scotch is a whiskey
(spelled without an "e") from Scotland distilled
according to British laws, of which there are many,
the most important being that it has to come from a

pure barley mash, "to which only whole grains of other cereals may be added," and aged for at least three years. Most scotch is made by blending whiskeys from a variety of distilleries (including some of the most prestigious, like Johnny Walker). A single malt, in contrast, is whiskey made in a pot still by a single distillery, e.g., Laphroig or the Balvenie, using exclusively malted barley.

All scotch must be made in Scotland. Anything made according to "the scotch style" outside Scotland has to be called something else—Japanese or Indian whiskeys, which copy the scotch style very closely, can't use the name; the same goes for American products like McCarthy's or Wasmund's. You can have an American single malt, but not an American scotch.

The king of America whiskey is bourbon. According to U.S. regulations overseen by the TTB, any spirit labeled bourbon must meet the following requirements:

- Bourbon must be produced in the United States.
- The spirit produced from distillation may not exceed 160 proof (80 percent alcohol by volume).
- Bourbon must be distilled from a fermented mash of not less than 51 percent corn.
- The whiskey must be stored at no more than 125 proof (62.5 percent alcohol by volume) in charred new oak containers.

There's no rule on how long it has to stay in the barrel, but given that the barrel has to be new, and full-size barrels cost upwards of one-hundred dollars each, it's rare to find a bourbon younger than a year. To be a "straight" bourbon, it has to be stored for at least two years. Again, contrary to what your trivia night buddy says, bourbon can be made anywhere in the United States.

Bourbon isn't the only corn whiskey. In fact, the best-selling American liquor in the world isn't bourbon, but "Tennessee" whiskey, thanks almost entirely to the global alcoholic juggernaut that is Jack Daniel's, made in Lynchburg, Tennessee. In addition to all the steps required to call something bourbon, Tennessee whiskeys are traditionally filtered through sugar maple charcoal before going into a barrel, the so-called Lincoln County Process.

Unlike bourbon, Tennessee whiskeys do have a geographic requirement; you can make a bourbon in Tennessee, but you can't make a Tennessee whiskey in Kentucky—or anywhere else outside the Volunteer State. (To make things more confusing, while the federal government recognizes that the Lincoln County Process is part of what distinguishes Tennessee and bourbon whiskey, it is not required in order to call your whiskey "Tennessee," and there are a few craft whiskeys around the state, like Prichard's, that produce a non-charcoal-filtered Tennessee whiskey. As a corollary, use of the Lincoln County Process doesn't prevent a whiskey from being labeled a bourbon; assuming it has met all the other requirements, it could be both a bourbon and a Tennessee whiskey.)

There is no specific method for applying the Lincoln County Process: Jack Daniel's passes its whiskey through a tall column packed with charcoal; George Dickel, another Tennessee whiskey company, steeps its whiskey in a charcoal-filled vat. Both distilleries claim that the process gives the whiskey a cleaner, smoother taste, like a piece of sandpaper working down the rough edges of a wood block. It also gives the whiskey an ever-so-slight sootiness. Critics divide between those who think the process takes away too much, leaving behind a sweet, overly smooth drink, and those who think the whole thing is mostly marketing.

When it comes to identifying whiskey, it's useful to pay close attention to the label—not just what it says, but how it says it. Anything labeled simply "corn whiskey," for example, is made with at least eighty percent corn in the mash bill and, if it's been aged, has been put in new or used uncharred oak barrels. And if you see the word "blend," that means the stuff inside is a combination of alcohols—probably some bourbon, mixed with cheaper corn whiskey, as well as grain neutral spirits. Unlike in Scotland, where blending is a high art, American blended whiskey is almost always found on the bottom shelf, because it's made from lower-grade materials. It's simply a different meaning of the word "blend." Interestingly, a number of startup craft operations have released highly-respected whiskeys blended in the Scottish style—that is, they're combinations of premium whiskeys bought from other distilleries and mixed to achieve a certain flavor profile.

I've overheard more than a few conversations in which the answer to "What sort of bourbon do you like?" is "Sour mash." Roughly speaking, that's like saying you're partial to baked bread, as opposed all the other kinds of bread on the shelf. Almost all American whiskey, in practice, is sour mash. Much like sourdough bread, sour mash whiskey involves setting a portion of a mash batch (usually twenty percent) aside before distilling. That portion, called the backset, is added to the next batch, from which another twenty percent is set aside, and so on.

Why? For one thing, it ensures the consistency of the yeast strain, a critical source of flavor. Every distiller has his or her own proprietary yeast, which they carefully preserve, convinced that theirs is the best. But just because they love their yeast doesn't mean it will dominate the bubbling, nutrient-rich ecosystem of a whiskey mash. Other, naturally occurring yeasts and bacteria are in fierce competition. So saving some of the spent mash that is already fine-tuned for that yeast strain to thrive for the next batch gives the next dollop of yeast an advantage. Adding backset also makes production more efficient by increasing the pH level, which helps yeast grow.

The sour mash process was first used in Kentucky in the 1800s, though who first decided to do it is lost to history. We do know that the first person to make it a fixed part of a commercial process was a Scottish immigrant and chemist named James Crow, who codified many of the early principles of bourbon while working at the Old Oscar Pepper Distillery in the 1830s.

The opposite of sour mash is called sweet mash. It is rarely used today. A few years ago, Woodford Reserve trotted out a limited edition sweet mash bourbon; it received a mixed reception, but it was a fun experiment. (Also, sour mash shouldn't be confused with "sour yeast mash," which refers to a mash to which lactobacillus, as well as the distiller's standard yeast, has been added. Lactobacillus generates lactic acid, which lowers pH levels in the mash, achieving a similar effect as adding backset.)

Finally, what does it mean to call a bourbon or rye "straight"? Any bourbon or rye under two years old has to have its age written on the label. If it's between two and four years old, it can be called straight, but it still has to have its age listed. Anything over four years can simply read "straight." Thus, if the label doesn't say straight or give an age, you know it's at least two years old.

For all the innovations and technological advances in whiskey making over the centuries, the fundamentals have remained strikingly the same. The distiller starts with a few basic ingredients: water, grain, and yeast. Kentuckians will tell you that it's the water that separates their product from the rest; and, indeed, Kentucky sits atop a vast stretch of limestone, through which the water drawn for whiskey making percolates. The limestone naturally removes iron, which inhibits yeast development, and deposits magnesium and calcium, both of which make the water taste sweet. But water is far from the most important ingredient.

Even more important is the grain. In the case of rye or barley, the grain is first malted—that is, it's mixed with water and allowed to germinate, which releases sugars. Corn is never malted, because its kernels don't germinate, and in any case, corn has a lot of sugar to begin with. The grain is then milled, mixed with water, cooked, and allowed to cool, creating a sugary goop, after which yeast is added. The yeast eat the sugar and produce ethyl alcohol, carbon dioxide, and congeners, a class of more than a hundred compounds, including fusel alcohols, esters, and aldehydes, many of which contribute to a whiskey's flavor and aroma. Each yeast strain produces different ratios of compounds, which will ultimately produce different flavor and aroma profiles. Eventually, most of the sugar is gone and the yeasts die off, poisoned by their own alcoholic waste.

Ask distillers what the single most important variable is in making a specific whiskey, and they will almost always tell you it's the yeast. Ask the average person at the bar what sets one whiskey apart from another, and I doubt one in two-hundred will say the same. Poor, underappreciated yeast. For thousands of years, people didn't understand why a warm barrel of watery, sugary grain mash began to bubble and ferment, producing a boozy slop that, if filtered, gave them beer, or, if distilled gave them liquor. Even after it was discovered that naturally occurring yeasts, floating on the air in through the distillery's window and settling into the mash for a nice snack, were responsible for fermentation, distillers and scientists didn't know precisely how the process worked. Thus, they were unable to isolate the particular yeasts involved. That only happened after Louis Pasteur discovered the chemistry behind fermentation in the mid-nineteenth century, after which there was an explosion in yeast cultivation in Europe.

The techniques quickly spread to the other side of the Atlantic, and by the latter part of the century, any decent distiller kept his own strain of yeast, often in a jug tucked away in a cold spot somewhere. Distillers soon realized that different strains produced different flavor profiles, even after the rigors of distillation and aging. And so while some were willing to share their yeast strains with friends, most kept them secret, often the most secret part of their operations. Even today distillers will swear by their yeast strains, passed on in some cases for several generations of makers.

Knowing how much yeast to add, and when, is one of the most important skills of the master distiller. Adding too little yeast to a mash risks it being overwhelmed by errant bacteria, which also likes a hearty meal of sugary grains. Adding too much, however, risks killing off the fermentation before it starts, without enough time to produce the alcohol and congeners needed for a good whiskey.

The yeast and mash aren't put together all at once. Rather, a dollop of yeast culture is added to a bit of grain in what's called a dona tub, where it is allowed to propagate. Once the fermentation gets going smoothly, the distiller adds the starter batch to the main batch. In the past, the fermentation process took place in giant wooden vats, usually made of cypress; a few distilleries still have some of these in use for demonstration purposes only. Most distilleries today use stainless steel vats instead.

The fermenting mash sits in the vats for a few days, after which it is filtered to remove the spent mash. The goop is usually sold to nearby farmers, who use it to feed their cattle. It sounds like an exercise in eco-friendly trendiness, but selling spent mash has long been a cash cow for distillers; it's why the Whiskey Trust, a massive enterprise that nearly cornered the whiskey market in the late nineteenth century, was formally called the Distilling and Cattle Feeding Company.

The liquid, now bereft of its solid component, is often called the "beer" or distiller's beer," and, strictly speaking, it is a beer, just not one you'd want to drink (it's unhopped and largely flavorless). Now it's ready for the still.

There are, in basic terms, two types of stills: the pot still and the column still (the latter is also called a "continuous" still.). The pot still is a direct descendant of the alembic, the most traditional form of distilling device, used by alchemists since ancient Greece. It is essentially a metal bulb sitting neck up above a fire, with the tip bent to the side. Liquid sits in the bulb, and as it boils, the vaporized water and alcohol rise through the neck of the bulb. The further the vapors get from the heat, the cooler they get; eventually they condense and drip, at the end of the bent neck, into a collecting vessel. Because water and alcohol boil at different temperatures, a practiced distiller can separate the two as they come through the neck of the still.

Of course, nothing's perfect, nor should it be—no distiller wants to separate the two liquids entirely, in large part because the two carry with them all sorts of oils and chemicals, including the trace compounds that give liquors their individual flavor. What a distiller does want to separate out, however, are the poisonous alcohols and other toxic compounds that evaporate first and last from the batch. These portions are called the "heads" and "tails," which a distiller collects and tosses back in the pot to redistill, hoping to squeeze out just a little more of the boozy goodness from the poisonous liquid chaff.

Eventually distillers added the distinctive, spiraled

copper neck (often identified with backwoods moonshine, but which is actually quite sophisticated). The coil further helps separate the water, ethanol and other chemicals: among other things, the copper reacts with unwanted compounds and elements like sulphur, creating a deposit called "grunge," which falls away as it circles through the neck.

Pot stills are still used today, most frequently in Scotland and Ireland, and in many American distilleries as well. But since the first alembics, the principle remains the same, so that if you drink a pot-distilled whiskey, you're drinking something very close to what imbibers 200 years ago would have consumed. The problem with the pot still is that, well, it's a pot, and after each use it has to be cleaned—a major task when you're dealing with a 1,000 gallon still.

The modern liquor industry has many fathers (and a few mothers), but probably no one has a better paternity claim than an Irish-born excise officer and inventor named Aeneas Coffey. In 1831 he patented a device he called the column still, also sometimes called a patent or continuous still. Instead of a pot that is set out to boil, Coffey's still is a wide, tall tube—today they can be several stories high, and up to five feet in diameter—with perforated plates along the inside, stepped in a zigzag pattern. The distiller's beer is pumped in through the middle, dripping down from plate to plate. At the same time, steam is pumped from the bottom. As the steam rises, it heats the beer and pulls out the alcohol, which evaporates at a lower temperature than water. The steam and alcohol rise to the top, where, like in a pot still, they pass through a curved neck and down through a copper cooling tube, where they condense back into liquid.

The column still has two advantages over the pot still. As its alternate name implies, it can run continuously—aside from routine cleaning every few days, it can go as long as the distiller wants. It is also more efficient at stripping out impurities from the beer, producing a more pure alcohol and water mix—which is why industrial distillers love them, and why some purists say they produce characterless whiskey. Most whiskeys are at least double distilled, using two different stills. The first is called the "analyzer," the

The standard-bearer for Tennessee whiskey, Jack Daniel's, carries no age statement. The company proclaims "It'll be ready when it's ready." Almost all modern American whiskeys are sour mash, but few proclaim it as boldly on the label as Old No. 7.

Most whiskeys do not tout their mash bills, but this one carries it on the front of the label: "Pot-distilled from 100% New York corn." This whiskey also states that it is "Aged under 4 yrs in American oak."

second the "rectifier" or "doubler." The latter is sometimes replaced with a pot still, which lets a distiller create a more robust, "dirtier" whiskey. Some distillers also replace the doubler with what's called a thumper, into which the distillate enters in vapor form; as the vapor expands and contracts in the still, it produces a knocking noise against the metal walls, hence the still's nickname.

What comes off the doubler goes by many names: white dog, high wines, new make. White dog has a clean, fruity and floral nose, with hints of banana and citrus, and a surprisingly pleasant taste—though, at a typical 160 proof, a little bit goes a long way. Call it white dog, call it new make— the one thing it is not is moonshine. This term is used to denote illicitly made liquor. Most moonshine isn't even whiskey, but applejack or a crude form of rum. If it's made legally, it's not moonshine, and no amount of slick marketing can make it otherwise.

Most distillers look at unaged distillate directly from the still the way barbecue chefs look at raw pork: an essential product, but just a step in the process. It takes a well-made white dog to make a good whiskey, but to leave it at that excludes the most important step in the whiskey-making process: barrel-aging.

Barreling begins with barrel-making, or coopering. Once a major American industry, today coopering is a rarely practiced art. Though a few "artisanal" cooperages have opened recently, almost all barrels are made by just a handful of operations. Brown-Forman is the only distiller that owns its own cooperages. Most other barrels come from the Independent Stave Company of Lebanon, Missouri. Whether intended for bourbon or not, almost all barrels are made from American oak, with either an American or French oak head (that is, the round pieces at the ends of the barrel). The bungs, which are the plugs that seal up the barrel, are usually made of poplar, a soft, malleable wood. The wood mostly comes from trees in far northern states, such as Minnesota, where cold tempera-tures force trees to grow tighter, denser grains, thus reducing the amount of liquid that over time can seep through and escape. After it is milled, the wood is stacked outdoors and allowed to air dry for well over a year. Drying, which can also be done in about a month in a temperature-controlled room, brings the water content of the wood down from about forty percent to twelve percent. The oak wood is then cut into staves, steamed, and formed into barrels.

For bourbon, rye, wheat, and malt whiskeys, the interior of the barrel has to be charred, which both seals the interior and caramelizes the surface of the wood. This process makes it easier for the whiskey to extract the many aromas and flavors locked inside the staves. The wood is often toasted first, holding the barrel over a gentle flame to warm it, which starts the process of turning the starches in the surface of the wood into sugars. Coopers then char their barrels by inserting an open flame inside them for up to a minute; the longer the exposure to the flame, the deeper the char. There are four standard grades of char, ascending in depth from one to four; most whiskey uses a three or a four.

In the case of bourbon, the barrels can only be used once, creating a robust market in used barrels. Most go to Scotland and other centers of distilling, where barrels can be used and reused repeatedly—malted barley mash is more delicate than corn or rye, and works better with used barrels.

Once the barrels are filled with whiskey, they go into a warehouse, often called a rickhouse. The houses stand several stories tall, and each floor hold stacks for two or three barrels. Traditionally, rickhouses are not climate controlled, so the barrels inside experience the full swing of the seasons' temperatures. That's another advantage of Kentucky: bitterly cold winters are matched by equally uncomfortable summers. As the tempera-ture climbs, the wood expands and soaks up some of the whiskey; as it falls, the wood contracts, expelling the whiskey back into the barrel, along with all sorts of wonderful chemical compounds that give whiskey its color, aroma, and flavor.

A barrel full of aging whiskey might not be too exciting to look at, but three critical things are happening inside. First, the alcohol and the water in

Wild Turkey is a prototypical Kentucky straight bourbon. The word straight means that it is at least two years old. And because any whiskey labeled straight that is less than four years old has to give its age, the lack of an age statement implies that it is at least four years old. (In fact, Wild Turkey 81 is a blend of six-, seven-, and eight-year-old whiskeys.)

Barrel proof means this whiskey, unlike most, has not been diluted before going into the bottle. Because the contents of each barrel will have slightly different alcohol levels, distillers usually handwrite the proof on each bottle, rather than print new labels for each new barrel.

the whiskey are mingling inside of the barrel, pulling in all sorts of chemical compounds. Those compounds then interact with the various chemicals in the whiskey, breaking down and reforming as new compounds. Second, the whiskey is pulling in oxygen through the wood (which, no matter how tight the grain, is still porous); oxygen is highly reactive, and it likewise interacts with the chemical compounds in the whiskey and wood. Finally, the wood is also absorbing alcohol and water and expelling it outside the barrel into the rickhouse. That loss is called the "angel's share," and can average up to four or five percent a year, so that after a decade, a once-full barrel might be half-empty.

Each of these steps is dynamically related to the other, so that the whiskey inside changes significantly from year to year. Indeed, a barreled whiskey may taste almost "ready" one year, then immature the next, only to be perfect the following year.

Generally speaking, though, the longer the whiskey is in the barrel, the more of these qualities it takes on, though in some cases, after ten years or so (in the case of bourbon) the whiskey can take on too much woodiness, so that it tastes like sucking on a table leg. On the other hand, too little aging means the compounds in the whiskey don't have time to blend and mellow, producing a whiskey that tastes too much like the underlying grains—like Chex Mix in a blender.

One interesting consequence of an unheated rickhouse is that since hot air rises, the barrels on the higher floors will experience more intense summers than the ones at the bottom, which will experience colder winters. Over the years, whiskey made from the same ingredients and left to age in identical barrels for the same period of time will taste radically different. Some distillers regularly rotate their barrels to get a consistent flavor (though some don't, preferring the range of flavors created by keeping barrels at different levels). Master distillers know how to work with these variations to produce complex but consistent flavor profiles.

In many modern rickhouses, the aging process may be accelerated to some extent by using temperature controls; since the bulk of the aging process happens during warmer months, swings that once took a year to complete may now be achieved over several weeks. Temperature-controlled rickhouses may also obviate the need to rotate barrels. Since barrels on the top floors of a traditional rickhouse will experience much hotter summers than those at the bottom, some distillers regularly rotate their barrels to get a consistent flavor (though some don't, preferring the range of flavors created by keeping barrels at different levels).

There's no fixed time at which the whiskey has to come out of the barrel; it's up to the master distiller to monitor his charges and decide when each is ready, a judgment that can vary widely even between two adjacent barrels. If you've ever seen a photograph of a full whiskey barrel, you may have noticed the long, thin stains drooling down from a small, plugged hole. The puncture is there thanks to a small drill, which the master distiller and his team will use to remove a bit of the whiskey inside for tasting. In the past, when power drills were too bulky to make such precise holes, distillers would have to climb on top of the barrel, remove the bung and insert a whiskey thief—basically a cup on a long, thin stick. The drill method seems less artful and more wasteful, but it's actually more efficient, since it doesn't open the barrel completely and risk losing vaporized whiskey inside.

The master distiller decides when a barrel is ready based not only on how it tastes individually, but how he imagines it will taste when combined with whiskeys from other barrels. Unless the whiskey is going into a single-barrel release, the contents of any given barrel are just a component of the whiskey that the distiller is trying to build. Of course, the larger the production, the more leeway there is in selecting barrels: a single person could not examine every single barrel, repeatedly, at a mega-distillery like Jim Beam. But in smaller, higher-premium releases, that's exactly what happens, and this is why master distillers get paid the big bucks. There's simply no substitution for a well-honed nose and palate.

This label includes an age statement (10 years) and, around the neck, details about the barrel and warehouse numbers (indicating that the contents come from a single barrel). What the label doesn't tell you is that Michter's does not actually distill its own whiskey. Rather, it purchases selected stocks of whiskey from a distillery and bottles it under its own label.

Instead of an age statement, Evan Williams Single Barrel comes labeled with a vintage date. In this case, the whiskey was put into oak barrels in 2002. This expression is the seventeenth in a series of vintage releases from Evan Williams.

Once the whiskey is dumped from the barrel, blended, and cut with water to the bottling proof, it is usually filtered to remove fine particulates that can cause a whiskey to "cloud" when it's chilled or poured over ice. (Higher proof whiskeys don't cloud over ice, so they don't need filtering.) There are two common methods for filtering: charcoal and chill filtering. There's constant debate over which is better, and some look down on filtering by any method. But it's not a mark of quality one way or the other—Pappy Van Winkle and Buffalo Trace chill filter their whiskeys, while Maker's Mark does not. All three are excellent whiskeys. Charcoal-filtered whiskey, like Johnny Drum or Jack Daniel's, tends to be smoother, but lacks some of the funky depth of trace particulates acquired during the aging process.

Chill filtering involves lowering the temperature of the aged whiskey to a few degrees below freezing, which solidifies certain esters and other compounds. The whiskey is then passed through a silk cloth to remove them. For some, this is preferable to charcoal filtering, but again, others abjure filtering entirely. In any case, the particulates in question, and the clouding they can produce, are largely cosmetic—there's no significant change in aroma or taste, just a cloudiness that some find off-putting.

Whiskey is not like wine; once it's in the bottle, it no longer develops. All things being equal, a whiskey that has sat in a bottle for a year will taste the same after it's been there for forty years. Of course, all things are not equal. Bottled whiskey can stand a wider swing in temperature, light and humidity than wine or beer, but those are still factors. If you buy whiskey to store, make sure it's left in a dark, cool space, with as little swing in temperature as possible. And make sure to store the whiskey standing upright: whiskey can eat away at a cork stopper. Still, evaporation is a given, and even the best-sealed, best-protected bottle will lose some of its content over enough time. After my grandfather died, my brother moved into his house in Nashville; while going through the dining room closet, he found an unopened bottle of Lem

Motlow's, a whiskey once made by Jack Daniel's. We figured it to be about thirty years old—and almost a third of it was gone.

Before diving into the incredibly diverse world of whiskey today, a brief history of American whiskey is in order. Many excellent books have used a whiskey bottle as a prism to admire the reflected light of early American trade, culture, politics, and law. I have listed several in the reference section at the end of this book. What follows is a summary of the major periods from pre-colonial days to the present.

In bourbon lingo, a batch is a set of barrels filled and dumped on the same days, and located in similar parts of the warehouse. A small batch will have less variation and more distinct character. However, there is no standard definition of "small batch," and at a big company, it could be a very large batch by any objective standard, even if it's smaller than what the distillery usually produces.

A Brief History of American Whiskey

Early American Spirits

Partisans of scotch will tell you that American whiskey is nothing more than an imported deriva- tive of their hallowed drink. But with apologies to Caledonia, the Scots neither invented distilling nor had much influence on its early development in the New World.

People were distilling long before they knew anything about why it worked the way it did. While the historical record is unclear on precisely who first thought to take a fermented grain beverage and vaporize it to remove impurities and concentrate the alcohol, it's likely that the technology emerged independently almost 2,000 years ago in China and the Middle East. In any case, by the ninth century A.D. Egyptian Arabs were using a predeces- sor of the alembic, or pot still, to distill alcohol for medicinal purposes. The word alembic itself derives from the Greek word *ambix*, which means a vase with a small opening; the word changed into *al ambiq* in Arabic. (Some posit that St. Patrick brought distilling to Ireland as early as the fifth century; then again, many believe he kicked out the snakes, too.)

As Muslims extended their political control into Europe, their cultural and technological prowess came with them; as their power receded, they left behind, like flotsam on the beach, things like the *ambiq*, which, as it spread across the continent, became known as an alembic. It's unknown when the Scots began distilling grains, but the earliest evidence is from a 1495 mention in the royal finance records, known as the exchequer rolls, which noted "eight bolls of malt to Friar John Cor wherewith to make aqua vitae." The good friar's *aqua vitae* translates from Latin to "water of life." Indeed, across Europe, many of the local terms for a distilled alcoholic liquid reflect its similarity to water, whether it's vodka ("little water" in Russian) or *uisge beatha* ("water of life" in Celtic). *Uisge beatha* eventually transmuted into the word whiskey, though it wasn't until much later that Scottish distillers began to age it regularly in barrels.

By the time distilling practices were being regularized and regulated in Scotland, distilling had already jumped the Atlantic and taken root in the early colonies. Alcohol was a necessity to the first settlers, not only for pleasure but also for health: water was notoriously unhealthy, particularly in settled areas where waste and drinking water intermingled, and even small children drank mildly alcoholic "thin" beer instead. Some of the earliest dispatches back home from English colonists include reports on successful distillations; in 1620 Capt. James Thorpe wrote from Virginia that he had managed to distill alcohol from corn, a native crop.

These early accounts record a wide variety of ingredients, not surprising given the poor performance of European grapes in American soil and the rich bounty of local plants. Everything from wild berries to pumpkins went into the still. Applejack was particularly popular, as was pear brandy, and metheglin, a type of mead flavored with cinnamon, chamomile, and other herbs and spices.

For the first decades of the seventeenth century, colonists either brewed or distilled their own alcohol for personal use or imported it. It wasn't until 1640 that William Kieft, the director general of the Dutch New Netherland colony, opened the continent's first commercial distillery, on Staten Island. Records show that his master distiller, Wilhelm Hendriksen, used corn and rye, among other things, to produce his liquor, making him the first known whiskey distiller in the colonies.

As the East Coast grew denser and colonial society more settled in the eighteenth century, a defined culture of alcohol production and consumption emerged. How much and how often you drank depended largely on where you lived and to what social class you belonged. Farmers had more or less ready access to grain alcohol: surplus crops had to go somewhere, and it was easier, and more lucrative, to store and transport liquor distilled from grain than it was to store and move the bulky grain itself. But because of the poor transportation networks linking rural and urban communities, a high percentage of that liquor stayed close to home, used as barter to pay labor or to buy supplies for subsequent seasons.

In contrast, urban centers preferred imported quaffs, particularly brandy and fortified wines like Madeira. The most popular drink, however, was rum, much of which was distilled in New England from molasses imported from British colonies in the Caribbean. The earliest record of rum distilling in the future United States shows an operation at New London, Connecticut, in 1654, and by the end of the seventeenth century the region was flush with scores of rum producers. Centered in the Massachusetts cities of Salem, Medford, and Boston, in 1750 there were sixty-three distilleries in that state alone. Molasses was easier to transport than raw sugar cane, and it became a staple in the "triangle trade," in which slaves, cash crops, agricultural products, and manufactured goods circulated among the Western Hemisphere, Britain, and West Africa.

Despite its popularity (or perhaps because of it), commercially produced and imported liquor was too expensive for most colonists, who, though hardly dry, had to make do with weak brews where they could find them. Access to distilled drinks was further limited by social control over tavern licensing; in much of the colonies, clergy and other self-appointed moral guardians had more or less veto power over who got to sell liquor and who got to buy it. The higher the social standing, the looser the rules were applied, so that tavern life, and public drinking in general, was largely a function of class. As the historian W.J. Rorabaugh notes in *The Alcoholic Republic,* drinking among the upper classes wasn't just tolerated—it was practically required. When a Maryland doctor, gimlet eyed in more ways than one, traveled to New York, Rorabaugh notes, he found that "a reputation for hearty drinking was essential for admission to the best society."

Social control over alcohol consumption rested in large part on high prices for high-power liquor; as those fell during the course of the eighteenth century, so too did the barriers to the working classes. By the eve of the Revolution, molasses and rum imports constituted a full twenty percent of all inbound trade. Cheap booze flooded the market, and thirsty colonists soaked it up. A new, egalitarian ethos took hold: by the end of the century democracy was on the loose, from the ballot box to the bar. "Upper class patriots," Rorabaugh writes, "found it difficult after the Revolution to attack the popular sentiment that elite control of taverns was analogous to English control of America."

War with Britain, and the continued bad blood even after the fighting stopped, meant that the flow of molasses into New England had essentially dried up by the start of the nineteenth century. This was aided by Congressionally imposed import duties, the expansion of distilling industries in the Caribbean, British bans on American rum, and the ban on slave trading. In 1770, the 2.1 million American colonists consumed some 8 million gallons of rum; twenty years later, a population that had nearly doubled, to 3.9 million, drank only 7 million gallons.

That doesn't mean Americans were drinking less alcohol. Quite the contrary. As rum consumption sank, whiskey consumption shot up; by 1810 whiskey far outpaced rum as the national drink. At first much of the whiskey was based on rye, which was easier to grow in the East. George Washington ranked among the large rye distillers at the end of the eighteenth century. Consumers did not, however, ask for "George Washington's rye whiskey" by name; individual bottling, let alone branding, didn't exist. Drinkers would gather at a tavern and take cups from a barrel, or they would fill up their own jugs to take home; in either case, they'd ask for whiskey based on its place of origin, which served as a proxy for recipe, flavor, and potency. Thus, the most popular and widespread whiskeys, both ryes, were from Maryland, made in distilleries near and around Baltimore, and Monongahela, made in western Pennsylvania.

The explosion in whiskey production was the timely and happy confluence of several factors. An influx of German, Scottish, and Irish immigrants, born in national cultures steeped in grain-distilling traditions, brought a new set of techniques and tastes to the country's nascent distilling industry.

Geographic shifts helped. Growing populations along the coast pushed people inland, and the resulting rapid expansion of farmland brought a flood of cheap corn and rye to the market, the surplus of which was easily converted to whiskey. In 1776 the Commonwealth of Virginia, which held claim to what is now Kentucky, offered up to 400 acres to any settler west of the Appalachians, who built a cabin and maintained a farm—what became known as "corn patch and cabin rights." Tens of thousands, and eventually millions, took up the offer or followed in their footsteps.

Jacob Beam (born Jacob Boehm) was the son of German immigrants (or a German immigrant himself, no one knows for sure) and the progenitor of the Beam distilling dynasty. He was among the many who trekked west, pulling up stakes in Maryland in 1787 and moving to Kentucky. Like his fellow migrants, he took with him his knowledge of farmhouse distilling, as well as his precious distilling equipment. In Kentucky he and others found fertile soil practically ready made for growing corn. Liquor, once too expensive for most people, was suddenly cheap and abundant. While much colonial liquor was either imported or commercially produced, the new wave of whiskey was homegrown; stills were as common as barns, and as important to the agricultural economy.

But the biggest change was in the fabric of

American life. A new, crudely democratic ethos lifted whatever social constraints might have kept the average new American from the bottle. Attempts by the coastal elites to control and profit from whiskey backfired. Western Pennsylvania farmers rose up against a federally imposed excise tax and started the 1791 Whiskey Rebellion. A levy of eleven cents a gallon on whiskey had been enacted to cover 45 million dollars in war debts. Though the tax was reduced twice, the revolt continued on principle, and President George Washington, at the instigation of Treasury Secretary Alexander Hamilton, sent in troops in August 1794. The rebellion disintegrated soon after. But although it succeeded in legitimizing government power, it failed as an attempt by easterners, like Hamilton, to control the new masses of the interior. The small farmers of western Pennsylvania, against whom the tax was aimed and who relied on whiskey for barter, simply moved further into the interior or found ways to hide their distilled trove. They did not, as myth has it, move *en masse* to Kentucky to start a new distilling tradition there; though some undoubtedly did move west, whiskey making was already well under way in Kentucky by the time of the Whiskey Rebellion.

Then, after the political revolution, came a more profound social upheaval. Families moved frequently, and men often traveled alone for long periods of time in search of work. By 1810 some fifteen percent of Americans lived west of the Appalachians, "apart from the influences of traditional society," Rorabaugh writes. "It should not be surprising that these isolated and lonely western pioneers had a reputation for drinking." Men who couldn't pair off with women to form families were left to wander. "This anomic existence, lawless and alienated from society, gave rise to acute drinking." Solo binge drinking was a widespread social malady.

By the second decade of the nineteenth century, American alcohol consumption per capita per year had skyrocketed, to some five gallons for every man, woman, and child. That's even more astounding when you consider that drinking in early nineteenth-century America was highly gendered, so this figure is nearly exclusively men over sixteen years old. As one foreign wag noted while traveling across Virginia, "The American stage coach stops every five miles to water the horses, and brandy the gentlemen!"

Eventually, the rest of the country settled the West as well, and consumption dropped to about two gallons, and has gone down more or less steadily from there. By 1830 the Ohio and Mississippi Valleys were dominated by booming urban centers, where factories soaked up excess labor and the forces of social constraint—family, church, and reformist movements—could put a damper on excess drinking. Religious revivalism found loamy soil in which to root. And so the American ideology changed once again; freedom no longer meant the right to excess; rather, it meant the right to control one's body for profit and personal salvation. And that meant controlling what one put into it.

The agricultural sector changed too: better roads and the advent of rail and the steamboat meant that excess grain in its original form could get to market, and didn't need to be converted to alcohol. And whereas thousands of personal stills did that work in the first decades of the century, after 1830 a powerful commercial industry was in place, which concentrated production and once again put a price, and thus, a natural point of control, on liquor.

While overall alcohol consumption decreased, the quality and volume of what we would today recognize as bourbon—corn-based, aged in oak barrels—increased. Like much of early American frontier history, the records on the origins of whiskey production are sparse. In the years leading up to Prohibition, "wets" established the legend that Elijah Craig, a Kentucky pastor, was the first bourbon distiller. Indeed, there was a real Pastor Craig, who really did distill whiskey in Kentucky (and who is today the namesake of a bourbon made by Heaven Hill). But there is almost no basis for deeming Craig the "first," and every reason to suspect the story as a bit of anti-Prohibition propaganda.

Then again, there's little evidence to support anyone else in Craig's place. Over the years, books on American whiskey history have offered a small army of contenders for "first whiskey distiller": Gen. James Wilkinson, Wattie Boone (brother of Daniel), Stephen Ritchie, William Calk, Jacob Myers, Joseph and Samuel Davis, Jacob Spear, Evan Williams, and James Garrard, to name just a few. But none have any more support to their name than Craig. In part that's because many early settlers between the Appalachians and the Mississippi were at best semiliterate, and public functions, let alone record-keeping regulatory bodies, were practically nonexistent.

But trying to locate the first distiller is beside the point, akin to trying to pinpoint who discovered fire. No one invented bourbon because everyone did. As the historian Henry Crowgey writes in *Kentucky Bourbon: The Early Years of Whiskey Making*, "As a matter of fact, any argument as to the identity of Kentucky's first distiller should be considered purely academic. What actually happened was that a people moved in who regarded whiskey as a way of life."

Folk distilling was related to folk remedies, practices that spread through porch-front conversation. Farmers as a matter of course had stills among their most valuable possessions, and any competent migrant brought a still with him to Kentucky and promptly began distilling surplus crops, when he had them. Some stills were as simple as a pot with a cheesecloth over it to capture and condense escaping vapors; the wet rag was then rung out and replaced, hundreds of times, to get a relatively clear distillate.

In time, as roads improved and population densities grew, the average farmer-distiller was able to sell his liquor commercially, alongside his grain and, perhaps, his livestock. Likewise, over time, he would have developed particular recipes and particular techniques that he liked and, if he was commercially minded, would have set apart his whiskey from that of the farmer down river from him. By the end of the 1780s, a distinctive style of Kentucky whiskey, lighter in body and made primarily from corn, was well known through the region, and by the 1810s it was in demand across the Ohio and Mississippi Valleys, all the way to New Orleans. By 1820, some 2,000 barrels were shipped annually out of state through Kentucky's Ohio River ports.

Why Kentucky, though, and not Tennessee or Ohio, or any of the other new, then-western states? Farmer-distillers thrived in those states as well; wherever men set down stakes, they set up stills. But the commercial reputation of Kentucky whiskey flourished. One reason is its abundance of sweet water. Kentucky, and Tennessee to its south, sit on a vast strata of blue limestone from the lower Silurian of the Trenton Period—a fancy way of saying that it's the type of rock that imparts lots of softening calcium and removes hardening iron salts from groundwater. This produces exactly the sort of medium in which yeasts flourish. It helps, too, that the state is riven with waterways that feed directly into the Tennessee, Ohio, and Mississippi Rivers, including the Cumberland, Green, and Licking Rivers—all of which mean that almost every farmer in the state was within a few days' travel of navigable water. And though it only came to matter later, when aging became a critical part of the whiskey-making process, Kentucky is blessed (or cursed, depending on your point of view) with a wide seasonal temperature swing, with hell-hot summers and snow-covered winters. Such swings work wonders for whiskey aging: hot summer air makes barrels expand like a sponge, absorbing whiskey, while chilly winters make it contract, pushing wood-soaked whiskey out. Over the seasons, this produces a whiskey unmatched in color and complexity.

What came off the farms in the early 1800s was not yet, however, bourbon, at least as we know it today. Whiskey at the time was only occasionally aged, and rarely on purpose; much of what people consumed was young, right off the still.

The origins of the name "bourbon" are murky. Many believe it comes from Bourbon County, which initially constituted a huge chunk of central Kentucky but was soon chopped up into smaller, more manageable polities. As commercial demand for Kentucky whiskey grew, farmers began moving it to ports along the Ohio River, particularly Maysville (then known as Limestone), and from there down and sometimes upriver. The whiskey was shipped in barrels labeled "Bourbon," for their county of origin. By the end of its trip, the whiskey might have sat in the same barrel for upward of six months, taking on some of the wood's color and character. Customers grew fond of it, and learned to ask for it by name.

Not everyone agrees with this story. The whiskey historian Michael R. Veach argues that the land around Limestone was a part of Bourbon County for too short a time for its whiskey to become readily associated with that name. Veach posits that it was more likely that bourbon was simply a pleasant-sounding marketing gimmick, chosen by an enterprising wholesaler to give his product an old-world ring. Whatever the case, by the early nineteenth century, bourbon was rapidly gaining a reputation across the interior.

Much of that reputation came thanks to the barrels, and the particular qualities of barrels in use at the time. Nineteenth-century barrels were like the metal shipping containers of today: reusable, and given their price, often reused until they fell apart. A barrel holding whiskey might have once held pigs' hearts. To clean it of residual contaminants, distillers would char the insides, a step that also killed any wood-burrowing pests and singe any remaining splinters. Eventually, consumers and distillers recognized that the brown liquor that came out of charred barrels after several months in transit was sweeter and more complex than the unaged product. Because repeatedly charring a barrel weakened it structurally, distillers came to demand new oak barrels as the optimal choice for aging. As early as 1793, "old" whiskey sold at a premium, and by 1814, aging was a selling point in early newspaper ads, increasingly under regular brand names (though the possibility of buying a sealed bottle off the shelf was still a half century away).

A similar evolution occurred with regards to sour mash, the practice of setting aside, or "back-setting," a portion of one fermented mash and adding it to the next. There was no chemist to tell farmer-distillers why it would work; it just happened, either by accident or by the trial and error of some particularly curious soul. In any case, backsetting produced more alcohol more quickly, and a final product that tasted more balanced than a whiskey distilled *de novo*.

The 1820s also saw major steps toward the standardization and commercialization of the American whiskey industry. What had once been a land of farmer-distillers began to sprout commercial operations, some of them financed by capital from the big cities along the Ohio River, or even from the East Coast. One of the first, and most spectacular, operations was the Hope Distilling Company, founded in 1816 in Louisville with a $100,000 investment from coastal money men. Powered by a forty-five horsepower steam engine, it could produce 1,200 gallons of liquor a day, hundreds of times what even the most efficient small distiller could produce. Within a few years, though, the operation was bankrupt—the victim, some say, of a fatally inferior product, but also doomed as an idea far ahead of its market and time.

Other innovations came later in the decade. In 1825 Alfred Eaton invented the so-called Lincoln County Process, in which distilled whiskey was passed through several feet of charcoal, removing impurities and imparting a subtle sweetness. And in 1831 Aeneas Coffey, an Irish excise official, patented the continuous or column still, which soon jumped the Atlantic to the United States.

While Coffey was perfecting his pathbreaking still design, another scientific Scottish immigrant, James Crow, was perfecting the outlines and under-lying chemistry of Kentucky whiskey—becoming, in as much as anyone can claim the title, the father of bourbon. Working as the master distiller for the Old Oscar Pepper Distillery (on the site of today's Woodford Reserve distillery, near Frankfort), he was the first to explain why sour mash, or backset, whiskey worked the way it did. He was also the first to use tools like the saccharimeter and the litmus paper test to analyze sugar content and acidity. A good Scotsman to the end, Crow (famously fond of the poetry of Robert Burns) died at work in 1856. Though it is long extinct, his whiskey, branded under the Old Crow label, was one of the best-selling bourbons in the country for over 100 years (today's Old Crow is a different drink entirely).

By the middle of the century, bourbon had a national reach, and was, alongside Pennsylvania and Maryland rye, the country's premier tipple. In 1861, during a stop at a military installation on Staten Island, the visiting Prince Napoleon of France (nephew of the deceased Emperor Napoleon) asked a soldier for a sip of his liquor. As a reporter on the scene recorded, the royal, pleased with the stuff, asked was it was. "Old bourbon," replied the soldier, probably unaware that his favorite drink shared a name with the royal dynasty that had returned to power after his uncle's defeat. "Old bourbon, indeed," the prince said. "I did not think I would like anything with that name so much."

The Gilded Age of Whiskey

The Civil War left the heartland of American whiskey production in tatters. Of the 75,760 Kentucky men, black and white, who went to war, 10,770 were killed outright, and multiples more died soon after of their injuries or were rendered partially or wholly incapacitated by physical and psychological wounds. The Confederate invasion in the summer of 1862, during which Rebel forces captured Frankfort and Lexington before being pushed out after the Battle of Perryville, was followed by three years of near constant, destructive raids from Tennessee. Railroads and supply depots were razed, farms were torched, and families were terrorized. Pennsylvania and Maryland saw less direct damage, but still lost tens of thousands of men to the war. Whiskey production was among the least on people's minds.

To pay for the war, in 1862 President Abraham Lincoln reinstituted the whiskey excise tax. Thomas Jefferson had repealed the tax in 1802 and it had only been used once since, between 1813 and 1817, to cover debts from the War of 1812. The tax started at twenty cents per proof gallon (that is, per gallon of 100 proof whiskey), then rose to sixty cents in early 1864 and $1.50 later that year, and, finally, to $2 on January 1, 1865. Whiskey prices climbed steeply, in part because of the tax, but also because of sharply limited supply—corn went to feed troops, young farmers went off to war, and supply lines out of Kentucky were disrupted.

Things were particularly bad in the Confederacy, where access to Kentucky whiskey, or any whiskey at all, was rare. In 1860, whiskey sold for twenty-five cents a gallon; by 1863, it cost $35. Steeply rising prices may explain the reputation Rebel soldiers developed for consuming dangerously caustic substitutes, like cleaning solvent; in a March 1862 dispatch from Virginia, the *Chicago Tribune* reported Southern soldiers drinking "in quantities that would astonish the nerves of a cast iron lamp post and of a quality that would destroy the digestive organs of an ostrich." There was undoubtedly more than a little truth to the report, though it was likely burnished by a modicum of pro-Union bias; in any case, there couldn't have been many ostriches in the Richmond area to verify the statement.

By the end of the war the number of distilleries in Kentucky had been cut nearly in half, from 250 to just under 150. And yet that thinning out allowed the survivors to thrive on the boom in demand that followed the war's end. The period between the end of the war and the beginning of Prohibition was the golden era of the bourbon industry, the age in which many of the "royal" bourbon names—Beam, Dant, Wathen, Stagg, Taylor—rose to prominence. Quality standards were set, reputations were established, and fortunes were built. Paradoxically, whiskey as a whole—industrially produced and completely unregulated—developed a reputation that would fuel increasingly severe restrictions on its distillation and consumption well into the next century.

Bourbon makers got a big boost in 1868, when Congress created a one-year bonding period for aged whiskeys. Up to then, distillers owed the excise tax on whatever came out of the still, as soon as it came out of the still. For a distiller planning to age his whiskey for several years, that meant paying a sizable tax bill long before he would make a penny of profit. Since whiskey evaporates in the barrel at a rate of about 4 percent a year, a distiller would pay tax on 100 percent of his whiskey up front but, after three years, be left with only 85 percent or so of it to sell.

The bonding period revolutionized the aged whiskey industry. But the law also opened the door to corruption and market bubbles. To make sure distillers didn't cheat while their whiskey was in bond, government revenue agents kept the barrels in guarded warehouses. Almost immediately, stories of bribery and kickbacks were rampant, reaching all the way to the administration of Andrew Johnson and, most spectacularly, that of his successor, Ulysses S. Grant. In 1875 news broke that a group of distillers across the Midwest had conspired with Republican politicians in the federal government to withhold taxes on bonded whiskey, then funnel some of the money into the party coffers—the so-called Whiskey Ring scandal. Though there's little evidence that Grant himself was aware of the ring, it left a permanent stain on his reputation, and it marked his two terms as one of the most corrupt periods in American history.

But the bigger, more lasting consequence of the tax and bonding process was economic. Unlike after previous wars, the federal government kept the whiskey excise tax in place, and in fact increased it several times over the subsequent decades. Lacking an income tax, the government was overly reliant on excise taxes, tariffs, and other duties on commerce. As a compromise with the distilling industry, however, Congress refused to make tax increases retroactive on any whiskey already in bonding warehouses. As a result, whenever there was even a rumor of a tax increase, distillers would ramp up production in order to get as much whiskey as possible in bond for the better tax rate ingnoring present demand.

The tendency toward overproduction was made worse by the growing trade in whiskey receipts. A whiskey bond was, literally, a bond—a document stating how much whiskey was in a particular facility and when it would come out. Distillers could take those bonds and sell them to investors, receiving cash they could then pump back into production (or horses, or trips to Europe, or whatever they wanted). The more whiskey they distilled, the more warehouse receipts they could sell. In 1879, there were 14 million gallons of whiskey in bond; by 1881, thanks to a law extending the bond period from one to three years, there were 50 million gallons, already about three times the estimated annual demand. A year later the amount had nearly doubled, to 90 million, almost all of which was owned by speculators and banks. And the government was happy to see it happen: the whiskey excise tax bill in 1882, when the federal government took in about $300 million, was an astounding $81 million.

All of this was, of course, painfully short sighted. The bonding period didn't last forever, though through the last decades of the nineteenth century Congress frequently fought over extending it, first from one to three years and eventually, under the 1897 Bottled in Bond Act, to four (today there is no limit on the bonding period). When the bond elapsed on a particular barrel, tax had to be paid, and distillers were under pressure to sell the product as soon as possible. This meant that waves of whiskey would hit the market regardless of the state of consumer demand; if it came during a recession, or just a temporary turn in consumer preferences, distilleries could be doomed. And not just distilleries: whiskey was one of the country's biggest industries, and its exaggerated boom-and-bust cycle, hitting bottom in sync with the general economy, exacerbated regional economic woes.

The cycle became all the more pronounced as the industry consolidated and modernized. Even in tradition-bound Old Kentucky, as the writer Gerald Carson notes in *The Social History of Bourbon,* "The grist mill operator who did some distilling as a side-line in an open-faced shed was passing from the scene." In his place came businessmen-distillers, who rallied capital from Chicago and New York to build extensive, mechanized plants that could provide whiskey for a thirsty growing nation.

Within a decade of the war's end, whiskey had become a major American industry, covered in minute detail by all the major papers. Whiskey was easily the biggest alcoholic product in the country, representing something like seventy percent of the market. It was consumed in mass quantities, and often prescribed as medicine for a whole host of ailments. An 1889 advertisement in the *Washington Post* noted that Pure Old Rye Berkeley Whisky, "with its recuperative qualities is highly endorsed by the medical profession." Skeptical doctors got extra inducements for prescribing whiskey; a 1901 advertisement in the *American Druggist and Pharmaceutical Record* promised doctors who collected ten coupons from Meredith's Pure Malt Whiskey a "beautifully decorated *jardiner* and pedestal worth exactly $15.00."

Not everyone sold out. One maverick doctor, writing in the *Chicago Tribune* in 1885, had the temerity to criticize his profession's penchant for prescribing whiskey for any and every problem:

> "It is fair to presume that the very learned medical men who thus permit their names to be used in recommending a product of the alcoholic still as a medicine care little for the welfare of the 'patients,' still less of the unfortunate wives of the miserable slaves to drink, and nothing whatever for their offspring."

Quality Kentucky bourbon, however, represented a very small part of the postwar whiskey industry—no more than three to five percent of the market. In much the same way that today's beer market divides into about ninety-five percent mega-brands and five percent craft, post-Civil War whiskey production was dominated by giant distilleries, operating mostly in the northern Ohio Valley states.

But whereas the big beer makers today churn out what is, regardless of quality, a product recognizable as "beer," no one could confuse the output from the two sides of the nineteenth-century whiskey industry. The "craft" side, as it were, made something more or less like today's bourbon: distilled from corn, aged in American oak, and bottled at about 100 proof under often-famous brand names. But the industrial side produced what we'd today call grain neutral spirits: distilled at eye-poppingly high proof, with little flavor, and indistinguishable from one distillery to the next. It was a commodity bought and sold in bulk, no different from Nebraska wheat or Arkansas pork belly—in fact, the *Wall Street Journal* ran daily reports on the latest whiskey prices.

The biggest whiskey state was Illinois, not Kentucky. In 1880 the *Chicago Tribune* bragged, "The state of Illinois may justly be claimed as the Whisky State of the Union. It produces more distilled liquors than any other state. Few people realize the magnitude to which the business has grown in Chicago within the past few years." By the newspaper's count, 11 million gallons were produced in the state in 1879. Production centered in Chicago and, increasingly, in Peoria, whose location on the Illinois River, proximity to grain manufacturers, and access to naturally cooled water from a large spring made it an Eden for whiskey distillers. Though Peoria is best known today as a synonym for Midwestern blandness, in its distilling heyday it was known as a den of iniquity. The writer Gerald Carson, who grew up in Carrolton, Illinois, two hours to the south, said that "Peoria was very nearly a swear word, except that we didn't swear."

Illinois whiskey was then sold to rectifiers, companies that further distilled it and then blended it with coloring, flavoring, and various chemicals to make it look aged. At best, these additives were harmless; at worst, they were poisonous. "A fresh barrel of raw whiskey is taken in hand by the expert, who converts it in a few hours into old rye or bourbon, by a judicious admixture of oak shavings, burned sugar and glycerin," the *New England Farmer and Horticultural Register* reported in 1883. "Sometimes he takes away the crude taste by passing an electric current through it. Much of the highest-priced whiskey sold in the best places is made in the artistic fashion." Those rectifiers then sold the whiskey to wholesalers, who branded the product and sold it to bars.

Fake whiskey was one of the biggest scams in the late nineteenth century. Already by the end of the first full year of post-Civil War peace, the *New York Tribune* could write about the ubiquity of whiskey fraud:

> "It is not to be measured by gallons or barrels, but rather by lakes and rivers of turpentine and bribery. A vast ocean of untaxed and unin-structed whiskey deluges the land; it is not strange that the distillers grow rich and drink Carte d'Or and venue cliquot; that inspectors and assessors can afford French brandy; that the Government does not pay off the blessings of the national debt."

Indeed, whiskey was the perfect symbol for post-Civil War America. The decades after the Civil War saw an explosion in economic growth, but also the emergence of a brutal, everything-goes ethos born of the war's nihilistic mass violence. In his epic history of the era, *Rebirth of a Nation*, the historian Jackson Lears describes postwar America as the contrast between "everyone rolling up his sleeves and getting ready to pitch into an expansive economy" and "a postwar landscape littered with lost souls." Old values fell aside in the face of oppor-tunities to make millions off cheap labor and ill-informed consumers. A rampant, debased form of *laissez-faire* capitalism took over the country, one in which the utterance *caveat emptor* was often sufficient to settle the moral qualms of the few who raised an objection to outright hucksterism and fraud.

Not surprisingly, given whiskey-making's reputa-tion, federal relief for the industry was a tough sell in Congress. In 1879 Representative John G. Carlisle of Kentucky won an extension of the bonding period from one to three years, and the next year secured a tax change that allowed distillers to avoid paying taxes on evaporation; he also pushed for laws to exempt homemade whiskey from taxes. But he was up against the powerful rectifying and bulk whiskey industry, as well as a public that was happy to consume distillers' products but wary of helping a sector branded as sinful by the high moralizers. In 1882 the House Ways and Means Committee unan-imously backed a bill to extend the bond period indefinitely, a move heavily supported by eastern banking interests that had invested in "Kentucky gold." If Congress failed to extend the bond, one banker warned, "the exaction by the government of its pound of flesh will inevitably ruin many banks, and incidentally cripple every branch of industry and every line of trade." The bill passed the House, but the Senate first trimmed it to a two-year extension, then refused to pass the bill at all.

It was something of a surprising turn, given how personally popular whiskey was among congressmen, who consumed it throughout the day and well into the night, on the floor and off. The Capitol cafeteria, reported the *Boston Globe*, served "every species of beverage that the most fastidious could desire." The *Globe* went on to describe one of Congress's most popular employees, Richard, a bartender who was an "artist in determining the exact proportions of each ingredient of a mixed drink." Many men clearly partook of Richard's wares: Missouri Senator Francis Cockerell said "he had known of an appropriation bill to be occasionally delayed because of the intoxication of its members." Maine Senator William Frye noted that in the past "the Senate had been found time and time again without a quorum because more than a quorum was drunk." Though this was by way of defending the current temperance of the two great deliberative bodies, where inebriation was much less common, though hardly unheard of. Eventually, after several high-profile incidents of congressmen and senators falling asleep drunk in hearings or, even worse, getting into alcohol-fueled fights, the Senate decided to act: in 1885 the ban on drinking in the Capitol, already in place for visitors, was extended to elected officials.

As Congress dithered, the industry began making its own moves to stabilize the market. Already in the 1870s, whiskey distillers, particularly the bulk operations north of the Ohio River, were experimenting with cartelization, forming pools into which members paid an assessment based on how much whiskey they produced; the less they produced, the lower their payments. In theory, this should have suppressed production. But because pools were voluntary, there was no legal way to enforce them, and cheating was rampant. Moreover, it was relatively easy to open a distillery, and more than one enterprising businessman made a small fortune off serially opening distilleries, which the pools would then have to pay off to limit production (and, if they didn't, the new operation would benefit from the new, higher whiskey prices). As a result, whiskey pools were short lived; one of the most extensive, high-profile efforts, the Western Export Association, launched in November 1881 and was defunct by May 1882.

Finally, in 1887, the biggest whiskey makers and their investors decided to borrow a page from John D. Rockefeller and form a legally binding trust. The new operation, based in Peoria, would encompass two-thirds of the "high-wine" industry, which made alcohol for consumption as well as industrial and agricultural applications. Rye and bourbon producers were explicitly excluded. In exchange for shares in the trust, some sixty-five distillers and some eighty plants across the country fell under the control of nine trustees, who operated out of a mansion owned by one of the men, Robert G. Ingersoll. Only two large distilleries stayed out, Schufeldt and Calumet, both in Illinois.

The so-called Whiskey Trust, formally named the Distillers and Cattle Feeders Trust, succeeded for a time, thanks in large part to the ruthlessness of its executives. Ernest E. East, a historian of the trust at the Illinois State Archives, later called it "one of the largest and most notorious combines in the industrial history of the United States." After shutting down all but twelve of its distilleries, it created an innovative method for manipulating prices. The trust sold whiskey to any rectifier that wanted its products, but then offered rebates—bribes, really— to wholesalers who bought from particular rectifiers. That way, both rectifiers and wholesalers had an incentive to stay in line.

Almost immediately, the trust came under public and government suspicion. In 1888 the *New York Times* condemned the operation categorically: "All trust organizations deserve condemnation. The methods of this trust are oppressive, and its purpose is to kill competition." It didn't help that soon after it formed, fires began breaking out at distilleries owned by industry holdouts. On February 11, 1891, Chicago police arrested George Gibson, the secretary of the trust, for offering an undercover federal agent $25,000 to blow up Chicago's Shufeldt distillery. It wasn't the first time Schufeldt had faced violence—in 1888 someone tossed dynamite on its roof, which almost fell through a skylight; instead, it caused only minor damage. Despite Gibson's arrest, both Schufeldt and Calumet sold out to the trust later that year (though there was significant evidence against him, Gibson was acquitted, and he remained on the trust's payroll in an advisory role). Nevertheless, the trust didn't last long; unlike oil, alcohol production was simply too easy to break into, and the punishments meted out by the trust too lenient, to make the system work. But as a going concern, the organization—which reorganized multiple times, under multiple names, between 1890 and 1920—was successful in dominating the raw whiskey sector up to Prohibition.

Largely in response, both the Kentucky bourbon distillers and the various rye producers along the East Coast frequently attempted to coordinate distillery stoppages to boost prices, with limited success. Indeed, bourbon distillers suffered greatly during the last few years of the nineteenth century, as rectifiers and blenders became expert at taking a small amount of the good stuff, mixing it with a lot of the cheap stuff, and selling it at a premium to unsuspecting customers. "Cheap Peoria whiskey" became the bane of Bluegrass existence; among the firms to go under were once-famous brands like Monarch Brothers, W.H. Thomas, T.B. Ripy, Batley, and Johnson and Co.

It wasn't all gloom for bourbon distillers, though they might not have seen it at the time. In the 1870s Old Forester, thanks to advances in industrial glass-making, became the first bourbon to be sold in sealed glass bottles directly to consumers. That opened the door to the landmark 1897 Bottled-in-Bond Act, devised by Senator Joseph Blackburn in conjunction with E.H. Taylor, one of the leading

them, and another easy pretense for punishing them—though of course it was advocated as a paternalistic step, to save intemperate blacks who would otherwise descend into crime. "No prohibition law, Georgians say, would ever have been passed if it had not been for the negro," wrote the *New York Tribune* in 1909.

Immigration and the backlash against it was also a factor. As the cities filled with Italians, Irish, and Germans, a division arose in the minds of white, protestant, small-town America between their own right-thinking, sober republicanism and the teeming ethnic hordes that flocked to the bar to drink and the ballot box to vote Democratic. As Theodore Roosevelt wrote in his diary about his Irish-Catholic colleagues in the New York legislature, "They are a stupid, sodden, vicious lot, most of them being equally deficient in brains and virtue." These "hyphenated Americans" not only represented, to men like Roosevelt, the unwashed, besotted masses, but also the corrupt, machine-driven politics that stymied so much of the progressive Republican agenda. Thus, a tripartite alliance was formed against the bottle, one linking progressives, small-town Republicans, and Deep South racists. Ban alcohol, and their problems would all be solved.

Except that when Prohibition did come, nothing was solved. As 1920s wags were wont to say, "Prohibition was better than no liquor at all." The Prohibition Department, part of the Treasury, was never sufficiently staffed, and despite countless high-profile raids across the country, the dragnet against illegal liquor leaked like a sieve. Licenses to make "medicinal" whiskey and constant smuggling along the borders, kept the booze flowing. In 1921, one bootlegger in New Orleans told the *New York Times* that he was sure, "as long as Prohibition lasts, if the risks of detection are eliminated, of a good living, but I'm afraid the legal dry as a bone period is near an end. The basis of my belief is the fact that everybody I come into contact with is against Prohibition.... For selfish reasons I hope Prohibition continues as it is, but I am afraid it is sure to be modified." After falling for a few years in the early 1920s, national alcohol consumption rates actually climbed.

The same held true on the production side. Though the number of distilleries shrank considerably, by 1926 the savvier, better-capitalized whiskey men, seeing the inevitable end of Prohibition on the distant horizon, began accumulating distillery licenses to produce medical whiskey. All the while, they stockpiled for the day when their products would once again be legal for all. By 1926, estimated Emory Buckner, the United States attorney for the Southern District of New York, bootleg liquor took in annual sales of $3.6 billion— astonishingly the same amount, noted the journalist Daniel Okrent in his book *Last Call: The Rise and Fall of Prohibition*, as the entire federal budget that year.

And yet when Prohibition ended, all did not stay the same in American bars. Tastes had changed dramatically. Canadian and Scotch whiskey had filled in the gaps when American distilleries had shut down. Gin, which had been relegated to physicians' cabinets before Prohibition, experienced a boom in the 1920s—easy to make, easy to mix, and pleasant enough to drink, it replaced whiskey as the go-to quaff for speakeasy patrons. At the end of Prohibition, in 1933, *Fortune* noted that gin had gone from a mixer to the main event: "The alcohol industry of the 1920s made it a drink. The younger drinking generation was weaned on it and an entirely new body of drinkers, women, prefer it to whiskey."

Prohibition, ushered in by the Eighteenth Amendment, was brought to a close in 1933 with the Twenty-First. Though state and local prohibitions continued, Americans in countless cities poured out of their homes on December 5, 1933, the official end of national Prohibition, for a drink. But amid the excitement, America's once and future whiskey distillers were left wondering: what would the Americans of the coming decades drink? And what were the chances they'd come back to whiskey?

Ruin to Revival

As it had been after the Civil War, the whiskey industry after Prohibition was weakened considerably. Most distilleries had shut down, consumer preferences had changed, and Canadian whiskey, almost unknown before 1920, was now, along with scotch, a major force on the scene.

Supply of decent whiskey was a real problem. Prohibition had begun with about 64 million gallons in barrels, which, since it had already been produced, could age legally, though it couldn't be sold. Nevertheless, in the next decade about 60 million gallons were consumed by humans and one million by the "angels" of evaporation. And while loose medicinal whiskey licenses allowed 20 million gallons more to go into barrels between 1932 and 1933, that wasn't nearly enough to meet expected demand. Though the industry was now highly regulated, fraud was once again rampant, though more often than not consumers turned to alternatives like rum and gin.

One reason to despair of replenished whiskey stocks was the paucity of distillers. Most had shut down, though a few had disassembled their equipment, trucked it to Canada, and resumed production there. Many of those that remained in mothballs were bought up by the far-sighted owners of National Distilling, which along with Schenley owned the lion's share of distilleries and brands in 1933. National, the descendant of the Whiskey Trust, had accumulated some 200 brands. Of the 20 million gallons of whiskey produced between 1932 and 1933, National was responsible for half, and Schenley a quarter.

Even though by the end of 1933 whiskey distilling was back in top gear, with National's various plants making whiskey at a rate of 32 million gallons a year and Hiram Walker, owned by Canada's Seagram, building a 100,000-gallons-a-day distillery in Peoria, it wasn't enough; quality, straight whiskey wouldn't be readily available until 1937. Prices rose vertiginously, a situation the government tried to remedy in 1934 by allowing unlimited imports from Canada and Scotland. The move helped, but it also pulled more drinkers away from American whiskey in favor of its lighter foreign cousins. Domestic distillers didn't help the situation by mixing much of their remaining aged stocks with unaged whiskey or pure grain alcohol, creating a breed of lighter-bodied blends that further alienated the American palate from the traditional rough-edged bourbon.

By the end of the decade, despite continued economic woes, the American whiskey industry had more or less recovered—only to be hit by World War II. The effect of the war on American whiskey is often underappreciated, but it couldn't have been more drastic: from October 1942 to mid-1944, whiskey distilleries were almost completely diverted to producing industrial-grade alcohol for the war effort, while high taxes on bonded whiskey kept the 117 million gallons of existing stocks off the market.

By the fall of 1943, the country was starting to panic. The *New York Times* called for limited production to resume, if only to counteract bootleggers. Most people turned to Caribbean rum and gin for their Christmas tipple. "We will soon be a rum and gin drinking nation if this keeps up," said one consumer. Hoarding was so widespread that the Senate launched an investigation into whiskey shortages. One witness said "hundreds and hundreds of individuals—many of them persons who never drink a drop—have bought up whiskey as an investment."

In the summer of 1944, with Allied forces on the offensive in Europe and the Pacific, the War Production Board, which controlled, among many other things, the alcohol industry, announced a "distillers holiday" for the month of August. Producers complied eagerly, churning out 54 million gallons in thirty-one days. Another holiday, in January 1944, produced another 20 million gallons, and by summer the ban was lifted completely. But distillers faced another problem: to make bourbon, they needed corn, and almost all the nation's corn was going to feed soldiers and, as peace returned, war-ruined Europe. At best the country was getting blended whiskey, with thirty percent bourbon mixed with seventy percent grain neutral spirits. Even when, in 1946, some corn was made available to distillers, it was "third grade stuff, rotted or moldy as the result of being badly stored or kept longer than necessary and could not be used for human consumption either here or abroad," noted the *Baltimore Sun*. The country, the paper reported, faced a "straight bourbon drought."

If bourbon suffered, rye took a fatal hit. Never as popular as its corn-based sibling—it was a "bastard whiskey," noted a *New York Times* columnist—rye, the favorite distilling grain of America's first president, fell out of favor almost completely during the 1920s. A substantial part of the blame lies with rye itself: more temperamental a crop than corn, it is also less efficient and harder to distill; it can easily turn to a sticky paste that gums up distilling equipment. Plus, rye was never popular with the Ohio Valley distilleries, either the fine brands to the south of the river or the mass producers to its north. Indeed, when Peoria's Hiram Walker, one of the country's largest distillers, bought up a series of Maryland distilleries after the war, it shut them all down and used their stocks for blends.

But the real fault lay in changing consumer taste: as Americans turned to lighter drinks like rum, gin, vodka, and whiskey blends, rye, with its aggressively spicy palate, simply didn't have a place at the bar. In 1972 the Majestic distillery, maker of Pikesville rye, distilled the last barrel of Maryland whiskey and shut its doors (Pikesville continues to be made in small quantities for the Maryland market, but by Heaven Hill, in Kentucky)

By the late 1940s whiskey production was back to normal, but the industry had changed dramatically. The government ban on liquor production and the unlimited demand for industrial grade alcohol had forced scores of small distilleries either to close shop or submit to purchase by the ever-larger "Big Five" distilling companies: National and Schenley were joined by Hiram Walker, Seagram, and Publicker. This last company was based in Pennsylvania and had gained fleeting notoriety in the 1930s by announcing that it had perfected technology to age whiskey overnight (it didn't work).

The dominance of the large distillers and the disappearance of smaller, distinctive brands meant that the once-diverse world of American whiskeys was being slowly replaced by a bland, standardized style. In 1943 Seagram bought the Old Prentice distillery, home of Four Roses, one of the better, more distinctive Kentucky expressions; a few years later, the company made a strategic decision to limit its premium Four Roses offerings to the overseas market, and shift domestic sales to the bottom shelf. What had once been an esteemed name became synonymous with skid row.

In Seagram's defense, however, it was only doing what the market wanted. Flush with rising incomes, consumers faced a dizzying array of new and trendy ways to get snockered. American wine, though still a few decades from stardom, was increasingly acceptable in polite company when European wine wasn't available. Gin and rum were the cornerstones of the new cocktail culture. Beer was everywhere. And for those who did still enjoy an aged brown spirit, there were Canadian and Scotch whiskey, and domestic blends, all of which were lighter without losing too much flavor. If postwar imbibing had a theme, it was session drinking: America drank at lunch, it drank after work, it drank at dinner, and it drank pretty much consistently through the weekend. To do so, though, the country needed smooth, low-alcohol drinks. For the young man in the gray flannel suit, 100-proof bourbon was simply too much.

It is often said that America's love affair with bourbon fell cold in the 1970s; in fact, after a brief postwar bump, it actually began to disintegrate in the 1950s. After the combined experiences of Prohibition and World War II, during which once-standard 100-proof, bottled-in-bond bourbon became as rare as turkey's teeth, there was little interest among postwar consumers in returning to the hard stuff. In 1952 the *Wall Street Journal* noted that bourbon sales were down eight percent over the previous year, while beer and wine sales were up. During the course of the decade Scotch and Canadian whiskey sales doubled. And while in 1959 bourbon finally overtook domestic blends in sales, that was largely because blends were themselves falling into disrepute, as they lacked the complex flavors of imports.

The industry fought aggressively to respond to the trend. In 1958 National was the first major distillery to offer a lower-proof bourbon at 86 proof. By 1964 National's first move had become an industry-wide stampede, the inevitable shift, wrote the *Washington Post*, "by major American distillers to proofs that satisfy the unmistakable public demand for lighter products." Many companies were diversifying out of bourbon completely. Though it kept making its flagship Kentucky Tavern brand, in the 1950s the mid-sized Glenmore Distillery Company began selling gin and vodka. As the company's president, Frank Thompson Jr., said at an annual corporate meeting in 1968, "Rarely do you find a bourbon drinker per se. Now a person is more likely to have a martini before lunch, a beer with the boys after work, a bourbon old fashioned with his wife before dinner and a scotch-based liqueur after dinner."

There was one bright note for bourbon in the 1960s. In 1964 Congress issued a resolution recognizing bourbon as "a distinctive spirit" of the United States, and as such banned the importation of any foreign product labeled with the name. This sounds like a technicality, but it meant that, while the government couldn't prevent a French company from making a whiskey in Toulouse and calling it bourbon, it could block that company from selling its product in the United States—much the same way that France protects the name "champagne." It also gave Congress a bargaining chip at trade negotiations: if France asked the United States to adopt its appellation protections, France would have to do the same for the United States. The move set up bourbon as an internationally recognized, American-made product, a firm base from which to build a strong export market. The resolution, introduced by Senator Thruston Morton and Representative John C. Watts, both of Kentucky, was met with near-unanimous approval; the one significant note of dissent came from

Representative John V. Lindsay of Manhattan, in whose district lived two heiresses. Each had, among their holdings, a distillery in northern Mexico that made and exported bourbon to the American market.

Still, nothing could stop the decline in America's taste for whiskey. Some writers have speculated that a major cause of the problem was the emergence of the drug culture, which gave young people something else to get high with. Others have blamed the economic doldrums of the 1970s, which left people less money to spend on booze. This would be a first in human history, alcohol usually being a salve for personal finance woes. In any case, the shift in drinkers' preferences was a real, undeniable story: between 1960 and 1975 whiskey's share of the liquor market dropped from 74 percent to 54 percent, while the "whites"— vodka, gin, and unaged rum and tequila—climbed from 19 percent to 35 percent. In 1980 whiskey finally lost its absolute majority of the market, tipping to just 48.6 percent of sales.

By the end of the 1970s, then, the whiskey industry had suffered its third cataclysmic hit in sixty years: first Prohibition, then the war, then consumer flight. Between 1969 and 1977 the industry grew at a rate of 2 percent to 3 percent, where it had been 5 percent to 7 percent in the 1960s. The return on investment dropped from 12 percent—already the break-even point for most investors—in 1972 to a mere 7 percent five years later. In 1980 the *Los Angeles Times* wrote that "the sales line on bourbon whiskey over the last decade or so slopes downward as sharply as a ski run in the Alps."

In April 1979 Hiram Walker announced it would close its 1,000-employee distillery in Peoria, the last in a city once defined by its liquor business, where a dozen distilleries had employed tens of thousands of men and women. The city was devastated. As one woman, a bottle-line operator, told the *Baltimore Sun*, "When your sense of security is raped like that, and rape is the word for it, a kind of rush goes through the whole community." Like most employees, she had been a lifer. Now her life, as she knew it, was over. "The day we got the news, there were men crying at their desks."

And yet, as so often happens, in the middle of the worst came the first rays of a better future. The same 1980 *Los Angeles Times* article that noted bourbon's alpine decline was headlined "Bourbon—Ripe for a Revival?" The big distillers were growing confident that they had hit bottom; one spokesman for National told the paper that "bourbon was down only 4 percent last year. It may be leveling off." In response, National was bringing out a 114-proof expression of one of its signature brands, Old Grand Dad. It was, the *Times* noted, "A move that some would equate with General Motors coming out with a 16-passenger Cadillac with fins." But it wasn't without justification. Not only were sales bottoming out, but demand was steady, and even growing, for the remaining higher-proof, aggressive bourbons on the market. Brown-Forman, at the time one of the mid-sized distilling companies, was doing gangbusters with its Old Forester, Early Times, and Jack Daniel's brands, with sales up 14 percent in 1980.

Though overall whiskey sales continued to slump through the 1980s, whiskey makers became more adept at niche marketing, targeting specific consumers with a range of affordable, premium brands like Maker's Mark and Jack Daniel's. In 1984 the predecessor of Buffalo Trace released Blanton's, the first single-barrel whiskey. Critics and consumers took note. In 1992, the year Jim Beam released Baker's, Knob Creek, and Basil Hayden's, Florence Fabricant of the *New York Times* could declare: "Once the raw drink of the frontier, bourbon is now beginning to follow single-malt scotch onto the after-dinner drinks list."

Whiskey Today

American whiskey continued to ebb through the 1990s, and by 2003, just 13.4 million cases were sold according to the Distilled Spirits Council of the United States. Then, in the mid-2000s, American whiskey sales began to steadily rise, both domestically and overseas. This uptick was led by demand for so-called superpremium labels: single barrels, small batches, and vintage-dated bottles. According to Kevin Kosar's *Whiskey: A Global History*, bourbon production has doubled since 1999. True, that's starting from a very low base. But it's solid, sustained growth nonetheless. And individual brands, particularly the biggest and best-known, are hitting records—in 2010 Maker's Mark sold 1 million cases for the first time. "I've witnessed a total transformation of the bourbon industry," Bill Samuels Jr., chairman emeritus of the distillery, told *USA Today*. "It's gone from a disrespected swill to the selection of connoisseurs and young trendsetters the world over."

A big part of the story has been overseas sales. The multinational corporations that now own major brands like Jack Daniel's, Four Roses, and Maker's Mark have easy access to foreign markets and experience at selling liquor to them. Foreign bourbon sales more than doubled during the 2000s, from $303.8 million in 2000 to $768 million in 2010. The Business and Economic Research Institute at Middle Tennessee State University reports that Tennessee had seen whiskey go from being its eleventh-largest export in 1997 to its fourth-largest a decade later, accounting for $478 million worth of sales. (Thanks largely to the export strength of Jack Daniel's—where overseas sales account for fifty percent of sales—Tennessee now exports more whiskey than Kentucky.) Russia, South Africa, and Western Europe are big markets, but Asia is, as in so many things, the focus today. The demand for all things American, the relatively low price of American whiskey versus scotch, and the speed and volume with which American distillers can respond to market expansions makes it a readily present, and readily consumed product worldwide.

That also means, unfortunately, that there are

many American-produced whiskeys that most Americans will never get a chance to try. Four Roses and Wild Turkey both make superpremium bourbons exclusively for the Japanese market, while Buffalo Trace makes export-only, cask-strength Blanton's that outshines the already excellent domestic expression. On the other hand, there are a variety of whiskey products designed for foreign markets that Americans are probably better off never encountering. Jim Beam makes a bourbon-and-port product (not bourbon finished in port barrels, but bourbon actually mixed with port) for the Southeast Asia market that to me suggests grease scrapings spiked with prune juice. Apparently it's a big hit in Singapore.

The reasons for the domestic boom are many. The rise in the popularity of scotch during the previous decade brought many drinkers back to brown liquor, but the high prices for premium single malts may have sent would-be fans into the welcoming, more affordable arms of American whiskeys. It also helped that the cultural turn toward a nostalgic, retro phase—speakeasies, porkpie hats, and obscure cocktails being just a few of the moment's markers—made American whiskeys the drink of the moment. Bourbon and rye, unlike scotch, go well in a wide variety of mixed drinks, so bartenders like them. It helped, too, that the generation consuming those cocktails was too young to remember bourbon as "disrespected swill."

Whatever the cause of the boom, the response from the big distillers has been to go on an expansion binge, spending some $150 million on new facilities in Kentucky alone. Wild Turkey recently doubled production with a new $50 million distillery. Maker's Mark also put $50 million into expansion, and Beam spent $18 million. Veteran master distillers who spent most of their lives living and working within a few miles of home are now global brand ambassadors, jetting off to Moscow or Cape Town to judge cocktail competitions or meet with high-level sales representatives.

At the same time, after decades of brand consolidation, the industry is returning to the diversity of labels that once populated the liquor store shelves. In some cases, they are bringing back old brands. In other cases, they are creating wholly new ones—Heaven Hill's Larceny, Wild Turkey's Russell's Reserve. Even Maker's Mark, long proudly iconoclastic with its single expression, debuted Maker's 46 in 2010. And, of course, the ranks of non-corporate, craft distilleries are rapidly joining the parade.

What follows is a list of some of the most significant trends in the whiskey industry—some for the good, some for the bad.

The Return of Rye

In 2006, Eric Asimov, the New York Times's wine critic, pronounced rye to be the "world's great forgotten spirit." Consider it found. Today rye whiskey is booming, driven almost wholly by the bar trade. Rye's strong pepper and fruit notes makes it an obvious member in any cocktail maven's starting lineup, either as the base for once-again favorites like Sazeracs and Manhattans or as a substitute for bourbon in, say, a mint julep.

Rye is still minuscule compared with bourbon; according to industry numbers reported by the whiskey writer Chuck Cowdery, from May 2009 to April 2010 Jim Beam Rye, the bestseller in the category, sold just 42,356 cases, whereas Jim Beam's white label bourbon sold millions. Still, this is a big step up from rye's near-complete disappearance in the second half of the twentieth century. Moreover, these numbers don't capture the rising popularity of rye among the grassroots craft distillers, many of whom are starting out with rye as a way to differentiate themselves.

Among the more exciting aspects of the return of rye has been the revitalization of regional rye styles. In 2012 Mountain Laurel Spirits debuted Dad's Hat Rye, based on a traditional eastern Pennsylvania style mash bill, which blends about 80 to 85 percent rye with 15 to 20 percent barley malt, giving it a somewhat spicier taste than the corn-heavy rye mash bills found in a typical Maryland rye (or the 100 percent rye mash bills found in popular expressions like Whistlepig).

The Potemkin Distillery

A term coined by Cowdery, a "Potemkin distillery" refers to a company that appears to make its own whiskey, but in reality sources it from someone else in bulk. Legally and ethically, there is nothing wrong with this, as long as distillers are open about it. It's been a long time since anyone believed that the Gap made its own t-shirts, or Apple made every part of an iPad. All major distillers sell whiskey to such brands, either as a side business or to get rid of surplus product. Lawrenceburg Distillers Indiana, located in southern Indiana (and now owned by MGP Ingredients), is famous for only making bulk whiskey. Many whiskeys that originate at a place like Lawrenceburg including Templeton Rye and Redemption—outshine startup whiskeys made from scratch.

Moreover, third party sourcing is, in most cases, a necessity in the short term. The brute facts of whiskey aging mean that a startup distillery has to sink hundreds of thousands of dollars into an operation, then wait a year or more to figure out if it's doing things correctly, let alone move a product to market. As a shortcut, many distillers go to a large distiller and either buy whiskey "off the rack"—that is, already made and ready for sale—or order a specific recipe. A good number of startups say they will eventually start distilling and aging their own products. But many either never intend to or decide against it at some point. Some at least go part of the way, redistilling or blending their sourced whiskeys, aging them, or bottling them themselves. Others are really just marketers, who assemble a supply chain of distillers, aging facilities, bottlers, and shippers to move a product.

Again, as long as these folks explain where their whiskey comes from, there shouldn't be a problem. However, many operations choose to mask their products' provenance, making use of unregulated terms like "made" and "product of" to imply a single hand behind the still. After all, what does it mean to make something? Does it mean assembling the final product from parts produced from elsewhere?

Does it mean overseeing the work of others? And what does it mean to call something a "product of" Iowa? Does that mean the whiskey was distilled, aged, and bottled there, or just some combination of those steps? Because, as anyone involved in the process will retort, unless you grow your own grain and blow your own glass, some part of your product is going to be sourced elsewhere.

There are, fortunately, a few telltale signs of a Potemkin distillery. The first is the fine print. While an operation may be allowed by regulators to use vague words like "made," one thing it can't do is lie. With that fact in mind, combined with the assumption that, authenticity being as valuable as it is, distillers who can boast of making everything in house will do so, examine the many claims made on the bottle. Does it say who did the distilling? Does it say where—and is it in the same state as the folks who own the brand? You won't necessarily find firm answers. But if you don't find concrete evidence that a whiskey was distilled, aged, and bottled by the same people, you can pretty safely assume it wasn't.

Another dead giveaway is the mythmaking. With some exceptions, the more trumped up the origins story told on the side of the bottle, the more likely that the whole thing is fiction. Templeton rye is a great example: its owners have spent wads of cash to convince drinkers that there was once a robust Iowa whiskey industry, that Al Capone was among its biggest patrons, that the ancestor of Templeton Rye was the hit of Chicago speakeasies in the 1920s (if it was, it wasn't anything we'd want to drink today), and that Templeton is the first rye "made in Iowa" since Prohibition. There may have been an Iowa whiskey industry, and it may be technically true that Templeton is made in Iowa, at some stage in the whiskey process. But it is distilled in a sprawling industrial facility in Indiana.

Craft Distilling

According to the American Distilling Institute, which promotes the craft side of the industry, the number of small (that is, producing less than 100,000 proof gallons a year), independent distilleries in the country went from just 24 in 2000 to 234 at the end of 2011. What accounts for the ten-fold increase? Like the popularity of whiskey itself, it is powered by a cultural turn toward nostalgic symbols of the American past, in this case the traditional methods of hands-on distillation. At the same time, like the craft beer movement that got underway in the 1980s, it comes from a recognition that an industry that was once defined by small-scale, local producers is, today, dominated by a few global operations. Therefore, there's an enormous opportunity for artisanal whiskey makers. It also helps that, again like craft beer in the 1990s, craft distilling in the 2000s has benefited from a loosening of local and state laws that previously made small-scale production all but impossible.

The genealogical link to craft brewing becomes even more clear when you consider where craft distilling concentrates: Colorado, California, the Pacific Northwest, Michigan—in other words, the heartlands of American craft beer. It's not a coincidence. While not every craft distillery sprung from a brewery, there is a striking overlap between the two: Anchor Brewing in San Francisco was an early, and very successful, entrant into the rye revival with its Old Potrero line; alongside it stands Rogue, New Holland, and Ranger Creek. Still others, like Corsair or Balcones, are *sui generis* but have owners who cut their chops making beer elsewhere.

Still others are the product of newcomers to the field who, either by luck, perseverance, genius, or a well-timed helping hand—or a combination of all four—have figured out how to turn out a drinkable, if not always laudable, whiskey. A cottage industry of distilling consultants has popped up in recent years, the most famous being Dave Pickerell. The former master distiller at Maker's Mark, Pickerell is the Johnny Appleseed of craft distilling: his efforts have been critical in launching Whistlepig rye in Vermont, Woodinville of Washington State, Green Brier in Tennessee, and George Washington rye in Virginia.

Like any industry, particularly any new industry, not all craft distillers are created equal. There is, unfortunately, an ideology, inherited from the craft-brewing world, that lionizes anything craft and abhors anything big or corporate. But it is not only possible to laud the ethos of craft distilling while criticizing some of the sector's products—it is absolutely necessary to do so. Small may be good, but it is not sufficient to produce good whiskey. Like anything that is hard to do, most people will fail at it, no matter how commendable their intentions.

At the same time, Big Whiskey is not the same as Big Beer. Jim Beam, Brown-Forman, and Heaven Hill do, in fact, make fantastic whiskey. They also make some less-than-mediocre whiskey. But they can hardly be accused of cynically churning out bland, low-quality whiskey.

If anything, craft distilling today is where craft brewing was in the mid-1990s—the first blush of a renaissance, in which hundreds of aspirants enter the market to meet fervent but relatively unsophisticated consumer demand. As drinkers become better informed, however, many if not most of those early entrants will fall out, leaving a few proven winners. Who those will be is, at this point, anyone's guess, but as a general rule it will be those who learn not to confuse initial public demand with approval and then rest on their achievements; it will be those who use the profits from that early demand to pay for continuous improvement, so that in ten or twenty years they will be able to look back and laugh, and shudder a little, at their earliest fumbles at making whiskey.

White Whiskey

Another way that new distillers get around the profit lag is to siphon off some of their distilled product and sell it unaged. This is a very recent phenomenon; I remember touring the Four Roses distillery in 2007, where they let you take a sample of their clear, virginal distillate, and thinking that it would make a great, cheap marketing ploy. Charitably speaking, some of the big players that have started selling their own unaged spirits are doing so as a way of demonstrating the quality of their starting ingredients—as if to say, "Here's how good our whiskey is before it goes into a barrel; just imagine it four years from now." Most, however, are just trying to ride the wave of a fad that, I predict, will crest and break in the next five years.

Flavored Whiskey

Even if whiskey has outlasted its skid row and cowboys image, it can still be intimidating to drinkers raised on unassuming white liquors. It was only a matter of time before someone at one of the big distillers wised up to a trick already perfected by the likes of Absolut and Stolichnaya—flavoring. Recognizing that the once wary are now the guardedly interested, Jim Beam and others want to help the whiskey-curious approach the stuff without fear. And so they sand down the rough edges by adding a healthy dose of cherry, or cinnamon, or honey. Of course, the world already had malt whiskey-based drinks like Drambuie and the whiskey-like Southern Comfort, but the whiskey identity is downplayed. With the new wave of products, like Jim Beam's Red Stag and Evan Williams's Cinnamon Reserve, the whiskey is front and center.

I'm not a fan of these whiskeys, as demonstrated by their absence from the review section of the book. However, I appreciate the possibility that they will bring more people into contact with whiskey, some of whom will transition into fans of whiskey itself. Nevertheless, like flavored vodkas and rums before it, there's also something unoriginally cynical about the genre. It treats consumers like children, unable to approach whiskey on its own terms.

Alt-whiskey

There are really two categories here, experimental expressions and alternative whiskeys. Both challenge the conventional wisdom about what constitutes a good whiskey by tweaking the recipes or the distilling and aging processes.

Experimental whiskeys are limited-edition releases, often from established distillers. Buffalo Trace, for example, has two lines of experimental releases. One is the Single Oak Project, in which whiskey is aged in barrels made from wood selected for differenct qualities, including wood taken from different parts of the same tree. Cornheads can compare, say, the effects of upper-trunk wood versus lower-trunk wood. The other is the Experimental Collection, a semi-regular release of small bottles of whiskey treated in unconventional ways: In 2007 it released four whiskeys, two partly aged in chardonnay barrels, and two in zinfandel barrels, with one of each pair staying in for six years and the other for ten. In 2011 it released an oat and a rice whiskey. Not all the releases are successful, and it's unlikely that any make the distillery money. But the goal is not to invent the next insanely great bourbon—it's to play with formulas and give drinkers a peek at what whiskey can be.

Woodford takes a slightly different approach with its Master's Collection. The releases are emphatically not experimental; according to Chris Morris, the master distiller for Brown-Forman, each release is perfected before hitting the shelves, so that consumers aren't just getting the distillery's blooper reel. Still, the upshot is the same: Woodford's releases have included bourbon finished in wine barrels, bourbon finished in maple barrels, bourbon made with sweet mash (i.e., no setback was used), and rye finished in once-used barrels.

If experimental whiskey is jazz, alt-whiskeys are punk rock. These are not riffs on an established formula; rather, they are free form and emphatically anti-tradition. Much in the same way that craft brewing moved from a focus on replicating fundamentals to tweaking convention and even inventing new styles whole cloth, craft distilling is taking whiskey-making in a variety of new directions, many of them borrowed directly from recent brewing innovations. There are, for example, a variety of whiskeys made with non-traditional mash bills—Town Branch bourbon, from Kentucky, is made from fifty-one percent corn and forty-nine percent malted barley. There is also a willingness to borrow from scotch makers: several recent whiskeys are "finished" in wine barrels; others are "smoked"—in the case of

Balcones's Brimstone, the malted barley is smoked over a scrub grass fire, to give it a campfire note. Alt-whiskey also embraces non-traditional grains: Koval, in Chicago, makes single-grain whiskeys with spelt, millet, wheat, and oat, alongside rye.

Distilling from beer is another alt-whiskey trend. Of course, all whiskey is technically made from beer—a grain mash—but the typical distiller's beer is to real beer as baker's chocolate is to a candy bar. Several new distilleries, however, are taking shelf-ready brews and turning them into whiskey, including Corsair, from Nashville; Charbay, from California; Rogue, from Oregon; and New Holland, from Michigan. Aside from a fertile field for experimentation, it's also a great opportunity for attracting new consumers by pairing up with well-regarded breweries—Charbay, for example, brews with Bear Republic beers, while Berkshire Mountain Distillers has a partnership with Boston Brewing, maker of Sam Adams.

Smaller Barrels

Time may wait for no man, but in the world of craft whiskey, many distillers are unwilling to wait for time. Rather than while away the two to four years that are standard for the big distillers, craft operations- which have likely spent a small fortune on equipment, barrels, and warehouse space before turning a penny of profit—are turning to smaller barrels. Some are as tiny as five gallons (the standard barrel holds fifty-three gallons). The smaller size increases the ratio of volume to the inside surface of the barrel, and thus the rate at which the liquid moves in and out of the wood surface. Supposedly, the liquid picks up the oaky flavors and dark colors of the wood more quickly, and usually within a year a distiller will have something with the vanilla and caramel notes associated with whiskey. It's a controversial strategy; such whiskeys typically taste unfinished, overly grainy, and lacking in the complex floral and fruit notes that come from years spent maturing in a barrel.

Very young whiskeys aren't bad as a category; they're just different. One thing that minimal aging does is let the flavor of the original grains come through, which can be great for cocktails. Some compare young whiskeys with minimally aged *blanco* tequila, which is good for margaritas, whereas *añejo* tequila, which is aged much longer, is better for sipping.

The search for faster aging is nothing new. After Prohibition, when whiskey stocks were practically nonexistent, Dr. Carl Haner of Philadelphia's Publicker Commercial Alcohol Company, at the time one of the country's largest distillery companies, claimed to have a secret technique to produce a whiskey that was indistinguishable from a fifteen-year-old—in just twenty-four hours. Haner's process, which he never revealed, didn't catch on.

The Eclipse of Age Statements

Many premium whiskeys come with age statements, which serve as guarantees that the whiskey in the bottle is at least as old as the number on its label—and some of it may be older, depending on the blend. But in recent years several venerable brands have lost their age statements, including W.L. Weller Special Reserve and Evan Williams Black Label. No-age-statement whiskey is already a hot trend in scotch, where high demand and the rise of innovative, rule-bending distillers have made the flexibility of N.A.S. labels a big plus.

The decline of age statements is controversial among whiskey enthusiasts. Some see them as a guarantee of quality, age being a good, if not perfect, proxy for high standards (if you have the patience and cash to let a whiskey sit for seven years or more, you probably aren't churning out swill). Defenders of N.A.S. labels say it gives distillers more room to play around with blends. It is, they counter, what's in the glass that counts. And all decisions are made by a master distiller—if he or she decides a barrel is ready, it's arbitrary to say the barrel still has to wait a year (which is why some whiskeys, like Four Roses, never used age statements in the first place). And remember that by law, any bourbon under two years old has to come with a precise age statement, as does any bourbon labeled "straight" that's under four years old.

The worry, however, is that for even most

whiskey lovers, taste is slippery. They may not detect changes from year to year, but without the safeguards of age statements, over a long enough period of time, they may end up with a whiskey that not only is younger, but tastes younger too. Eventually, the critics say, given the relentless consumer demand, we could end up with very few bourbons that are a day older than two years, even if they maintain the reputation of being much older, thanks to the vagueness of N.A.S. releases.

That's a fair concern. But given the proliferation of distillers, it's hard to imagine it being an all-consuming trend. Some brands, and some distillers, might slip. But as long as there are consumers who demand older whiskeys, there will be a supply of them.

How to Enjoy Whiskey

The question of how to enjoy whiskey is one that answers itself: enjoyment is subjective, so enjoy it however you want. There can be no right answer. You can enjoy it neat (that is, on its own), with ice, with water, with cola, with deer's blood if that's your thing. Some people go apoplectic at the thought of adding anything at all to their whiskey; others insist on precisely room-temperature water. I have no truck with any of them, and certainly no argument for drinking it any other way. All I can do is offer a few tips to novice drinkers, in the hopes that they eventually find their own preferences.

The first thing to remember is that all whiskey is different, and each will react differently to water. Generally speaking, though, higher-proof whiskeys tend to blossom with a few drops of water, and particularly high-proof whiskeys practically demand it just to be palatable. (Again, that's up to you: legend has it that Booker Noe, a former master distiller at Jim Beam, preferred to sip barrel-proof whiskey, neat, upwards of 130 proof.) The same goes for older whiskeys, which tend to be dense and settled; a few drops of water helps release sleeping aromas and flavors.

A well-crafted whiskey will often undergo

dramatic changes with a little water. The next time you sit down with a glass, take a whiff and a sip of it uncut. Note the aromas and flavor. Then add a few drops of water and swirl it around. Notice a difference?

On the flip side, there's a reason whiskey can't be sold at less than 80 proof: it would be too watery. As it is, I can think of few 80-proof whiskeys that need more than a couple of drops of water, if even that. And I feel that most, though not nearly all, 80-proofers suffer from adding water: instead of opening up, they wilt. In the Whiskey Accounts section of this book, I've tried to indicate which ones hold up under the effects of water, but again, it's totally subjective. The only way to know how much water to add, if any, is to try it yourself.

Whether to add water, or ice, or nothing at all also depends on your mood, the weather, the company, and what you feel like drinking under those circumstances. I tend not to drink a lot of whiskey in the summer, in part because I prefer chewy, fiery whiskeys that light a match in my belly—not the best on a sweltering summer day. But a lighter whiskey, on the rocks, especially one with lots of citrus and floral notes, can be the perfect cooler.

Having made clear my tolerant side, let me turn to the matter of cocktails. Aside from a few basics, like a Manhattan, I tend to avoid them. No matter how good the bartender, it's a rare bar where the best drink in the house isn't already on the shelf behind him. But that's just me. I know there are some genius cocktail artists out there, and they make some delicious drinks, including delicious whiskey drinks. I've enjoyed many, and fallen in love with a few.

Where I part company with the crowd is the increasingly common appearance of premium whiskey in mixed drinks. Well-financed, poorly educated drinkers seem to believe that ordering an old fashioned made with 23-year-old Pappy Van Winkle is a sign of status, when in reality it's a sign of ignorance and disrespect. As with most troubling trends in the liquor world, I tend to blame this one on premium vodka, which, correctly or not, is sold as an ingredient, never to be sipped on its own. I hope most bartenders know that there are whiskeys for mixing and whiskeys for sipping, and that Jim Rutledge doesn't spend hundreds of hours on each new iteration of Four Roses "Mariage" just so it can be infused with bacon. Dolling up a twenty-dollar pour of whiskey in homemade bitters and organic sugar is like putting racing stripes and ground effects (albeit artisanal ones) on a Bentley.

Tasting

There's whiskey drinking, and there's whiskey tasting. You don't always have the inclination or attention span to focus on the nose and mouthfeel and finish; sometimes you just want something that tastes good. But other times, especially when you're encountering a new whiskey, you'll want to approach it with a bit more thought.

There are basically four things you're looking for when it comes to tasting: how it smells, how it feels in your mouth, how it tastes, and how it lingers, if at all, after you've swallowed it. A good whiskey will be pleasant from start to finish; a great whiskey will be complex and at times challenging, but always rewarding. In fact, you might find that the whiskey you consider the most complex and well crafted is not necessarily your favorite: an art lover can recognize Picasso's genius even if, personally, he's partial to Rockwell.

The first thing you need is to procure the right glass. If you're out at a bar, this may not be possible, though a good bar will always have the right equipment, even if you have to ask. The important point is to get something with a wide bowl relative to the mouth: a brandy snifter is great, and a red-wine glass will do in a pinch. There are dozens of whiskey-specific designs on the market, though the dominant one, and my personal choice, is the Glencairn glass. It has a squat stem but a relatively tall bowl and narrow mouth, which allows a lot of aromas to build up within the glass. It's also the perfect size for assessing a whiskey's color, allowing just enough light to push through the liquid without washing it out.

The first thing to do is give the whiskey a good swirl, to release aromas into the glass. Then pass the mouth of the glass under your nose, just briefly. Never stick your nose right in the glass, at least on the first pass. Even a relatively low-proof whiskey can give off heady amounts of alcohol that will singe the nostrils and prevent you from appreciating the finer points of the aroma. Once you've assessed the aromatic potency, take deeper whiffs. While doing so, sort out your first impressions. What are the dominant general notes—floral, fruit, chocolate? Then dig deeper. What kind of floral? Is it more earthy, like geraniums, or sweet, like lilacs? Do the fruit aromas lean toward citrus, or berries?

Then add a few drops of water, which helps to "wake up" some of the flavors trapped inside the whiskey. Take another whiff, to see how the whiskey is developing, especially after the water. Are new aromas coming out? Or does it smell weaker, like the water is breaking down the nose?

Finally, it's time for a taste. A lot happens quickly as the whiskey plays across the tongue. You're looking at a three-step sensation: what it tastes and feels like right as it enters your mouth, how it changes as it sits on your tongue, and what it's like as you're swallowing it. Try to pick out the most notable flavors and dissect them. If there's spice, is it more cinnamon, like an Atomic Fireball, or smoky, like a chili pepper? Or is it more like black or white pepper? Is there a wine-like flavor, and if so is it buttery, like a chardonnay, or dark and chewy, like a Burgundy? At the same time, think about how the whiskey feels in your mouth: is it thin and oily, or thick? Give this some thought, since it's important to keep the senses apart—how a whiskey feels can bias what you think of its taste, and vice versa.

Make sure the whiskey washes over your entire tongue—but don't slosh it. Let it take its time. By now you'll be well aware that whiskey is a volatile substance, given to change at the slightest alteration in its surroundings. So it shouldn't be surprising when it changes rapidly as soon as it enters the wet warmth of your mouth.

After a few seconds, let it slide down your throat. Here you'll find a whole new set of sensations. Does it burn, and in what way? Does the spice linger? Like wine, whiskey can be extremely dry, leaving little behind, or it can stay with you, leaving all sorts of residual sweet and spicy notes; sometimes there's even a sour tone.

In the same way that there's no one way to enjoy whiskey, there's no set list of tasting notes—everyone's body chemistry is slightly different, and it will have a lot of influence over what they taste in the whiskey. So if the fellow next to you finds cherry cola notes and you don't, it doesn't mean your taste buds are deficient. That said, learning to discern the flavors in a whiskey is an acquired skill; and like any skill, some pick it up quickly, while others need practice. But almost everyone can develop a knowl-edgeable palate with enough experience.

While there's a wide range of tastes to be found across the world of whiskeys, and with the caveat that everyone will find something a little different, some flavors are more common than others. Scotch-style malt whiskey, for example, will have lots of peaty, sulphury, and feinty notes, thanks to the peat used to dry the malt, while in bourbon, candy, fruit, and wood notes will dominate.

On pages 70–71 is a table of common whiskey notes that appear on either the nose or the palate. They're organized under broad categories, not all of which make immediate, intuitive sense. But the taxonomy is less about similar flavors than about flavors that tend to occur together.

Organizing a Tasting

Drinking alone is never as fun as drinking in a group, and the same goes for tasting. It's a good way to explore new whiskeys, or to compare well-known whiskeys in different combinations. Depending on how formal you want to make a tasting, there are a few basic things to keep in mind.

EQUIPMENT. Make sure everyone has the same glassware—you can order a half-dozen Glencairn-style glasses online, for practically nothing. If you're going all out, give everyone one glass for each whiskey to be tasted, so they can compare them side by side. You should have at least one large glass or bucket for tasters to dump their whiskey into—not everyone will want to drink more than a few sips. And make sure to have a bottle of filtered, room-temperature water. Eschew ice—this is about tasting, not drinking, and ice will weaken the whiskey's intensity.

FOOD IS A MUST. At the very least, you should provide some unsalted water crackers, which help clear the palate without offending any taste buds. If you're trying new whiskeys, this is probably the best way to go. If you know the whiskeys well, though, you could try pairing them with different foods—chocolates, caramels, nuts, berries, citrus, smoked fish, meats, all depending on what you think complements each expression.

And while it's not necessary, a good tasting host provides each guest with a pad and pen for note taking. Impressions come very quickly and fleetingly, so it's good to have a way to record them. Again, if you're going all out, you could print out sheets with sections for nose, taste, finish, and overall impression. But make sure you know your audience—the worst thing you could do is intimidate people with what is supposed to be an enjoyable undertaking. After all, it's just whiskey.

Typical Tasting Aromas and Flavors

WINEY	WOODY	SULPHURY	FEINTY
Sherried	**New wood**	**Vegetable**	**Sweaty**
Chardonnay	Sandalwood	Brackish	Yeast
Port	Ginger	Cabbage water	
Applejack	Black pepper	Stagnant	**Tobacco**
	Allspice	Marsh gas	Dried tea
Nutty	Nutmeg		Pipe tobacco
Almond	New oak	**Coal-Gas**	Tobacco ash
Marzipan	Chili pepper	Cordite	
Salted nuts	Mint	Ash	**Leathery**
Chesnuts	Cumin	Matches	Leather
Pumpkin seeds	Hickory		upholstery
Toasted almond	Cinnamon bark	**Rubbery**	New cowhide
Caraway seeds	Cedar wood	Pencil eraser	Saddle leather
	Cumin	Oak dust	
Chocolate	Clove		**Honey**
Cream	Buttery oak		Clover honey
Butter	Spicy oak		Beeswax
Milk chocolate	Clove		
Cocoa	Spearmint		
Bitter chocolate			
Chocolate	**Vanilla**		
mousse	Caramel		
Dark chocolate	Toffee		
Fudge	Brown sugar		
	Molasses		
	Maple syrup		
	Nougat		
	Butterscotch		
	Custard		
	Toasted		
	Coffee		
	Coffee grounds		
	Fennel		
	Fennel		
	Aniseed		

PEATY	FLORAL	FRUITY	CEREAL
Medicinal	**Floral**	**Citric**	**Mash**
Iodine	Coconut	Orange	Porridge
	Lavender	Tangerine	Cheerios
Smokey		Orange zest	
Bonfire	**Greenhouse**	Lemon zest	**Cooked**
Hickory smoke	Geranium	Meyer lemon	**Vegetable**
Mesquite	Cut flowers	Orange peel	Sweet corn
Char			Corn chips
	Hay	**Fresh Fruit**	Plump corn
	Mown hay	Apple	
	Dry hay	Pear	**Husky**
	Dried herbs	Peach	Dried hops
	Herbaceous	Apricot	Ale
	Wheatgrass	Banana	Pancakes
		Strawberry	
		Raspberry	**Meaty**
		Cherry	Boiled pork
			Pork sausage
		Cooked Fruit	Grilled pork
		Stewed apple	
		Marmalade	
		Jam	
		Barley sugar	
		Candied fruit	
		Candied fruit	
		Glace cherries	
		Dried Fruit	
		Raisin	
		Fig	
		Dried apricot	
		Prune	
		Fruit cake	
		Solvent	
		Bubblegum	
		Wood varnish	

Jefferson's
Presidential
Select

Years **18** Old

*Elegantly crafted
and subtly muted by
wheat. This offering
is a well matured
bourbon with a medium
but firm body and
complex finish. A true
connoisseur's bourbon.*

94 PROOF · 47% ALC./VOL.

**KENTUCKY
STRAIGHT
BOURBON
WHISKEY**

BATCH No. 30 BOTTLE No. 1235

*Distilled from Wheat
in the Fall of 1991*

AGED IN
Stitzel - Weller Barrels

How to Read a Whiskey Label

Interpreting a whiskey label can be a confounding experience for anyone trying to make an informed choice of what to drink or what to give as a gift. Some bottles will display a lengthy declaration and backstory about the contents, others are terse and/or cryptic, while others plainly state the case. On the opposite page is an example of a whiskey label—and an amazing whiskey at that— with a good deal of information. Below are annotations by me regarding each element on the label.

NAME: Jefferson's is the brand name of this whiskey and Presidential Select is the "expression" or particular offering from the brand. Some brands offer a single expression and others produce multiple types of whiskey. McLain & Kyne, the company that operates the Jefferson's brand, does not distill its own whiskey; it selects excellent stocks from other producers and offers it to the public under its own name. (For more on Jefferson's see pages 164–166.)

AGE STATEMENT: This whiskey is labeled 18 Years Old, which means the distilled spirit was stored in a new charred oak barrel for at least 18 years before it was bottled. Not all whiskey carries an age statement, which does not, in all cases, reflect the quality of the drink. Older whiskey tends to be more expensive for obvious reasons— it was stored for a long time and a good deal of it will have evaporated each year.

ALCOHOL BY VOLUME/PROOF: By law, all whiskey bottles must state the level of alcohol by volume. Often this is abbreviated as Alc/Vol. It is a whiskey tradition to include the proof, which is simply double the alcohol by volume. Whiskey is available from a minimum of 40 percent Alc/Vol (80 proof) and up. The highest proof whiskey in this guide is Col. E.H. Taylor Barrel Proof at 67.25 percent Alc/Vol (134.5 proof). Proof can be a measure of value for money, since most whiskey leaves the barrel at a very high proof and is diluted with water before bottling.

LIQUID MEASURE: By law, liquor bottles for sale in the U.S. must somewhere display the measurement of its contents in metric values. (In the case of Jefferson's 18 Year Old, it is printed on a side label.) Whiskey is most popularly sold in bottles labeled 750ML (milliliters), which converts to a little over 25 U.S. ounces. This measurement equals one-fifth of a gallon and thus, a "fifth" of whiskey. Of course, both larger and smaller bottles of whiskey are also available on the market.

KENTUCKY STRAIGHT BOURBON WHISKEY: Bourbon whiskey can be made anywhere in the U.S., but it has to be made in the Bluegrass State to be labeled "Kentucky" bourbon whiskey. The term straight means the whiskey was aged in oak for at least two years before bottling. In this case, the whiskey was aged for a considerably longer period.

BOTTLE NO./BATCH NO.: The inclusion of the bottle and batch numbers allows drinkers to compare bottles from the same batch or across batches.

DISTILLED FROM WHEAT: Because this is a bourbon, it is not distilled from wheat alone (then it would then be a wheat whiskey), or even mostly wheat. Instead, this means that it is considered a wheated bourbon, which is made from at least 51 percent corn with the inclusion of wheat as some other unspecified percentage of the grains used in distillation. In this case, there may also be a portion of rye, but it is not stated on the label.

AGED IN STIZEL-WELLER BARRELS: This additional information indicates that the new barrels used to store the whiskey came from the famous, but now shuttered, Stitzel-Weller distillery. Was the whiskey itself made by Stitzel-Weller? Jefferson's isn't saying. News is that Stitzel-Weller, now owned by Diageo, may be releasing stored whiskey and distilling new whiskey in the near future.

About the Whiskey Accounts

The "Whiskey Accounts" section of this book is organized by maker and/or brand in alphabetical order. Included for each is background and historical information about the company that offers the whiskey to consumers. Each "expression" (that is, individual offering) has its own tasting notes, separated into text regarding nose, color, body, and palate (including finish), as well as general notes about the whiskey. In the upper right corner of the entry is the proof and, when known, its age. I gleaned the minimum age of the whiskey either from the statement on the bottle or from publicly verified information.

At the bottom center is the price with dollar signs corresponding to the following range of costs to the consumer in U.S. dollars per bottle:

$	=	$20 or less
$$	=	$21–40
$$$	=	$41–60
$$$$	=	$61 or more

I have based the dollar amounts from average prices found in both my local shops and as advertised on the Internet for the bottles pictured in the accounts. Several whiskeys rated in this book are offered only in 375 ml (12.68 ounces) bottles and the dollar amounts in these accounts are based on this size. The vast majority of whiskeys covered in this book are sold in a standard 750ml measure and the prices indicated are for this size of bottle. You may find bottles that cost much more or less than the range of prices I have indicated. These are strictly estimates. And like so many things in life, price is not always commensurate with value

Rating whiskey is a vastly subjective undertaking. I have included ratings as an indication of my own personal taste. My low marks for a whiskey does not make it "bad." I just don't recommend it. So why include them at all? The ratings (and price ranges) are for the neophyte, curious, and adventurous drinkers out there to give them some type of benchmark about making informed choices. When you order at the bar or buy a bottle for yourself or for a special occasion or as a gift, I can say from personal experience that it can help to have an opinion from someone else. I would never urge drinkers not to *try* what many may consider subpar whiskey or a drink that receives a particularly low mark in a book, on a website, or magazine for that matter. Drinking unusual or daring or even unappealing whiskey is a learning moment, too.

My ratings are also driven by my own desire to figure out which whiskeys I value more than others, which to avoid, and why. There are so many whiskeys to try and hopefully, so much time to figure it all out. With this in mind, the ratings in this book follow this scale:

★★★★ = Phenomenal

★★★ = Excellent

★★ = Good

★ = Decent; some flaws, but drinkable.

NR = Not recommended

Here's hoping that *American Whiskey, Bourbon & Rye* will enhance your own exploration of what makes whiskey such a fascinating and enjoyable part of life.

Whiskey
Accounts

Ancient Age

Ancient Age is produced by Buffalo Trace, but since 1992 it has been owned by Age International, a subsidiary of the Japanese sake giant Takara Shuzo Co., Ltd. All of Age International's whiskeys made at Buffalo Trace—including Rock Hill Farms, Blanton's, and Elmer T. Lee—use Mash Bill #2, which is higher in rye content than the rest of Buffalo Trace's offerings (the exact proportions are a company secret).

Ancient Age is what you might call "bargain plus" bourbon. Priced in the low teens, it's better than many of its bottom-shelf mates. That's faint praise, though: upper-bottom shelf is a tough place to be. For a few dollars more, you could get a much better whiskey, like Evan Williams (see page 131). Ancient Ancient Age, on the other hand, is a steal, if you can find it—the whiskey is rarely distributed outside Kentucky and its neighboring states.

One thing Ancient Age has going for it is nostalgia: this is one of the whiskey brands that appeared in wonderfully odd mid-century print advertisements. An Ancient Age magazine ad in 1943 featured a buxom Native American woman holding a platter, on which rested two heavily serifed capital "A"s sporting—what else—cartoon knights heads. The ad copy read: "A is for ancient... A is for age... AA is for the whiskey of the flavor years." Of course, AA stands for other things liquor related, but, at the time, the coincidence must not have occurred to the brand's copywriters.

AGE INTERNATIONAL, INC.
229 WEST MAIN STREET, SUITE 202
FRANKFORT, KY 40601
TEL: 502-223-9874
E-MAIL: nknox@ageintl.com

PRODUCER
BUFFALO TRACE DISTILLERY
113 GREAT BUFFALO TRACE
FRANKFORT, KENTUCKY 40601
TEL: 800-654-8471
E-MAIL: info@buffalotrace.com
www.buffalotrace.com

BRANDS
ANCIENT AGE KENTUCKY STRAIGHT BOURBON WHISKEY
ANCIENT ANCIENT AGE KENTUCKY STRAIGHT BOURBON WHISKEY

Ancient Age Kentucky Straight Bourbon Whiskey

AGE
3 years old

PROOF
80

NOSE
Dark fruits, marzipan and some loamy, vegetal notes

COLOR
Russet

BODY
Thin

GENERAL
Ancient Age is Sahara-dry; it makes the mouth pucker long after it's gone. A solid bargain whiskey, but it's far outshown by Ancient Ancient Age.

PALATE
A pop of rye and a quick, smooth finish.

PRICE
$

RATING

Ancient Ancient Age Kentucky Straight Bourbon Whiskey

AGE
10 years old

PROOF
86

NOSE
A classic bourbon nose, with tons of oak and cedar notes, some leather, corn, and cinnamon toast

COLOR
Russet

BODY
Light

GENERAL
One of the best value whiskeys on the shelf. Well-balanced and flavorful, it has enough depth to sip on its own or to use as a mellow mixer. Despite its high-rye mash bill, there's very little rye on the nose.

PALATE
Full of lingering wood and black pepper

PRICE

$

RATING

Angel's Envy

Like a growing number of American craft whiskeys, including New York's Hillrock, the four-year-old Angel's Envy sits for four to six months in barrels that once held fortified wine (in this case, ruby port). Its curvaceous bottle, with wings emblazoned on the back, led Frank Bruni of the *New York Times* to call it "Scarlett Johansson to Old Grand-Dad's Abe Vigoda." Fans of the *Godfather*'s Sal Tessio will hopefully understand this as more of a compliment to Angel's Envy than a knock on Old Grand-Dad.

Angel's Envy's name comes from the term "angel's share," or the fraction of whiskey lost to evaporation during the aging process. This whiskey is the creation of Lincoln Henderson, who put in decades of work as Brown-Forman's master distiller before retiring, then coming back to help start this new line. The company behind it, Louisville Distilling, is still relying on whiskey it "sources" from other makers, but plans to make its own product once it finishes construction of its distillery. While the basic idea of a port-finished bourbon will remain constant, Henderson reportedly plans to tweak the expression each year.

LOUISVILLE DISTILLING
COMPANY, LLC
7202 HIGHWAY 329
CRESTWOOD, KY 40014
TEL: 502-241-6064
E-MAIL: info@angelsenvy.com
www.angelsenvy.com

Angel's Envy Kentucky Straight Bourbon Whiskey

AGE
4–6 years old

PROOF
86.6

NOSE
Subtle, with chocolate milk, roses, and stewed fruit

COLOR
Deep gold

BODY
Light

GENERAL
A decent whiskey, but the port finish doesn't add as much nuance as one might expect (or hope for). Not a first choice at the bar, but it's nothing to turn away.

PALATE
Just the slightest spice on the tongue. It finishes quickly, with a lingering cinnamon ping.

PRICE
$$$

RATING
★★

Baker's

BEAM INC.

510 LAKE COOK ROAD

DEERFIELD, IL 60015

TEL: 847-948-8888

www.beamglobal.com

info@jimbeam.com

Baker's is one of the four bourbons in the Jim Beam Small Batch Collection of premium whiskeys, which also include Knob Creek, Basil Hayden, and Booker's. To be fair, in this case "small batch" is a relative term, since Beam makes more Baker's in a few weeks than most craft distillers make in a year. Named for Baker Beam, the grand-nephew of the distillery's namesake, the whiskey is based on a recipe derived from the standard Jim Beam mash bill—it reportedly contains about fifteen percent rye (the precise mash bill is a closely held company secret) and is aged for seven years.

Baker's Kentucky Straight Bourbon Whiskey

AGE	**7** years old
PROOF	**107**

NOSE	COLOR	BODY
Vaporous, with caramel apples, strawberries, and corn chips; a little water brings out pear and sandalwood.	Mahogany	Medium to full

GENERAL	PALATE
A solid but hardly stunning high-proof bourbon, Baker's is well-balanced between grain and flower, wood and sweetness. A good strong everyday, after-work pour.	Lots of sweet flavors and almost no spice. There's plenty of bite at the end, with a sweet spiciness.

PRICE	RATING
$$$	

Balcones

Chip Tate, the mastermind behind Balcones, opened his Waco, Texas distillery in 2009. Three years later, his single-malt whiskey, made with peated malt imported from Scotland, won Britain's "Best in Glass" competition against such storied names as Balvenie and Macallan. Not bad for a few years' work.

Tate infuses all his whiskey with a Southwestern flair; his first, Baby Blue, is a young whiskey made with "Hopi" blue corn. He does everything by hand, usually by himself—he even made his own copper stills. Like many young distillers, Tate is a constant tinkerer, employing multiple techniques and styles: to make his Brimstone whiskey, he smokes his whiskey using a proprietary (i.e., secret) process. And he's not content to stick with whiskey: along with a forthcoming rum, he makes Rumble, a whiskey liqueur made with Texas honey, sugar, and figs.

BALCONES DISTILLING, LLC
212 SOUTH 17TH STREET
WACO, TX 76701
TEL: 512-294-6735
E-MAIL: info@balconesdistilling.com
www.balconesdistilling.com

BRANDS

BABY BLUE CORN WHISKY

TRUE BLUE CASK STRENGTH CORN
    WHISKY

BRIMSTONE TEXAS SCRUB OAK
    SMOKED CORN WHISKEY

TEXAS SINGLE MALT WHISKY

Balcones Baby Blue Corn Whisky

AGE	**4** months
PROOF	**92**

NOSE	COLOR	BODY
Corn flakes, yeast, and peanuts, mostly, but also a feinty, vegetal odor	Chestnut	Thin

GENERAL	PALATE	
This has all the immature notes one would expect from a young whiskey. While it shows promise, Balcones has a ways to go before it makes this a winning expression.	Reminiscent of a dry white wine with a lot of cereal and candy notes	

PRICE	RATING
$$$	**NR**

Balcones True Blue Cask Strength Corn Whisky

AGE
No age statement

PROOF
123

NOSE
Peanuts, sweet tea, and butterscotch (with some iodine and boiled veggies after adding a little water).

COLOR
Mahogany/ burnt umber

BODY
Full

GENERAL
The finish is long and a little sour. The feinty notes on the nose and palate reveal Balcones's scotch influences.

PALATE
Iced tea, rubber, and salted nut flavors

PRICE
$$$

RATING
NR

Balcones Brimstone Texas Scrub Oak Smoked Corn Whisky

AGE
Less than **2** years old

PROOF
106

NOSE
Barbecue, corn mash

COLOR
Mahogany

BODY
Thin to medium

GENERAL
If you like the flavor of mesquite, this might be your thing. Possibly an interesting pairing (or ingredient) for barbeque.

PALATE
Like a BBQ-flavored corn chip

PRICE
$$$

RATING
NR

Balcones Texas Single Malt Whisky

AGE
No age statement

PROOF
105

NOSE
Brash, aggressive, but with sweet, fruity notes.

COLOR
Mahogany

BODY
Thin to medium

GENERAL
Here's where Balcones really comes into its own. It has all the smoke, slight sweetness, and fruit of a single malt, but enough fire to remind you it's from Texas.

PALATE
Lots of spice up front, but with a strong fruity and smoky undertone

PRICE
$$$$

RATING
★ ★

Basil Hayden's

BEAM INC.

510 LAKE COOK ROAD

DEERFIELD, IL 60015

TEL: 847-948-8888

www.beamglobal.com

info@jimbeam.com

Basil Hayden was a Marylander who moved to Kentucky in the late eighteenth century. Like most settlers, he distilled his own whiskey, and like many Maryland transplants, he reportedly used more rye in his recipe than his neighbors. Though his exact formula is lost to the ages, this whiskey, made by Jim Beam as part of its Small Batch Collection, pays tribute to Hayden by veering from its normal high-corn recipe with a refreshingly high-rye mash bill. The whiskey is aged for eight years and bottled at 80 proof, making it the lightest of the Small Batch Collection whiskeys (the others being Knob Creek, Booker's, and Baker's).

If Basil Hayden's reminds you of Old Grand Dad, it's no coincidence: it's the same whiskey, aged for a longer time. Basil Hayden is, in fact, the eponymous "Old Grand-Dad."

Basil Hayden's Kentucky Straight Bourbon Whiskey

AGE **8** years old		
PROOF **80**		

NOSE	COLOR	BODY
Full of dark fruit—plums and cherries, mostly—as well as cinnamon, candy corn and a touch of vanilla	Tawny/ auburn	Light

GENERAL	PALATE	
A nice sipping whiskey, and certainly the odd duck in the Beam Small Batch collection. Since most bars will have most of them, try Basil Hayden's against Baker's to experience the difference in the two mash bills.	Very spice forward, much less sweet than it smells, with a medium-length, white-pepper finish.	
	PRICE **$$**	RATING

Belle Meade

Belle Meade is the first spirit from Nelson's Green Brier Distillery, located alongside fellow whiskey makers Corsair and Collier & McKeel in Nashville, Tennessee's burgeoning Distillers' Row. The distillery is a reincarnation of sorts: the founders, brothers Charles and Andy Nelson, are great-great-great-grandchildren of a Tennessee distiller, also named Charles Nelson, who ran one of the state's most prolific post-Civil War whiskey companies.

Like many early distillers, Charles Nelson was an immigrant grocer and wholesaler (in this case from Germany). He found a lucrative side job in procuring and selling whiskey, which led him to set up his own still operation outside Nashville. According to the Nelson brothers, their ancestor sold nearly 380,000 gallons of whiskey in 1885, compared with Jack Daniel's output of less than 23,000 gallons that same year. Nelson died in 1891, and statewide prohibition in 1909 forced the distillery to close. Just over 100 years later, Nelson's descendants have revived the Green Brier name with a bourbon sourced from MGP Ingredients Indiana distillery; they plan to offer their own distilled whiskey by 2015.

NELSON'S GREEN BRIER DISTILLERY

1200 CLINTON STREET

NASHVILLE, TN 37203

E-MAIL: andy@greenbrierdistillery.com

E-MAIL: charlie@greenbrierdistillery.com

PRODUCER

MGP INGREDIENTS, INC.

CRAY BUSINESS PLAZA

100 COMMERCIAL STREET

P.O. BOX 130

ATCHISON, KS 66002

TEL: 800-255-0302

www.mgpingredients.com

Belle Meade Bourbon

AGE

5½– 7½ years old

PROOF

90.4

NOSE

Rye, apple, pickles, cherry, and vanilla

COLOR

Chestnut

BODY

Light

GENERAL

Minus the alcohol, you might think you were sniffing cherry cola. But it's not cloying; it has a nice balance on the nose, palate, and finish. It will be interesting to see whether Green Brier can maintain the quality level when it debuts its own, in-house whiskey.

PALATE

Dried fruit and leather, like port. It ends in a nice, throaty spiciness, with leather, tobacco, and cinnamon.

PRICE

$$

RATING

★★

Bellows

LUXCO

5050 KEMPER AVENUE

ST. LOUIS, MO 63139

TEL: 314-772-2626

E-MAIL: contactus@luxco.com

www.luxco.com

....

PRODUCER

BEAM INC.

510 LAKE COOK ROAD

DEERFIELD, IL 60015

TEL: 847-948-8888

www.beamglobal.com

info@jimbeam.com

Bellows & Co. opened its doors in 1830 as a wine and spirits importer, specializing in blended scotch whisky. The company was bought in 1941 by National Distillers, which in turn was acquired by Beam in 1987. In January 2013, Beam sold Bellows to Luxco, along with a raft of other low-end liquors.

Bellows long ago ceased being anything but a brand name, which today is applied to a range of bargain liquor products, including a blended scotch, a light rum, a London dry gin, and a straight bourbon. They're all that's left of the "Bellows Instant Bar," a fifteen-bottle "home entertainment system" sold in the 1960s and '70s that also included calvados, Madeira, and vermouth. None of the Bellows products rise above the bottom shelf, though Bellows bourbon makes a solid base for a whiskey cocktail.

Bellows Kentucky Straight Bourbon Whiskey

AGE	No age statement
PROOF	**80**

NOSE	COLOR	BODY
Light on the nose, some candy apples, orange zest, and light oak	Deep copper	Thin

GENERAL	PALATE
Bellows is purely a commodity bourbon—adequate for making quick cocktails, but nothing to drink straight.	A bit of cough-syrup hints with a vague spiciness woven in. There's a hint of habanero and metal at the very end.

PRICE	RATING
$	**NR**

Berkshire

Founded in 2007 outside Great Barrington, Massachusetts, Berkshire is a pioneer in the "dirt to glass" school of distilling. Virtually everything that goes into its whiskey, gin, and rum is sourced locally; its supply of corn comes from a farmer just two miles away. The company's co-distillers, Chris Weld and Colin Coan, use a small 1960s test still originally made for Brown-Forman. It's nowhere near big enough for industrial whiskey production, but it's perfect for a startup distillery. In 2012 Berkshire announced a partnership with Boston Brewing Co., maker of Sam Adams, to begin producing a whiskey using distilled beer.

BERKSHIRE MOUNTAIN
DISTILLERS, INC.
P.O. BOX 922
GREAT BARRINGTON, MA 01230
TEL: 413-229-0219
EMAIL:
chris@berkshiremountaindistillers.com
www.berkshiremountaindistillers.com

BRANDS
BERKSHIRE BOURBON WHISKEY
BERKSHIRE NEW ENGLAND
CORN WHISKEY

Berkshire Bourbon Whiskey

AGE	No age statement
PROOF	**86**

NOSE	COLOR	BODY
Lots of corn, white pepper, leather, sesame, and strong wood notes. Some feinty funkiness sliding into a dark tea scent.	Deep gold	Light

GENERAL	PALATE	
This bourbon has an odd profile: the grain, spice, and wood components combine but don't quite meld. For a relatively new craft offering, Berkshire is better than most; it will be interesting to try future expressions.	Cream and Christmas spices	
	PRICE	RATING
	$$	★

Berkshire New England Corn Whiskey

AGE
No age statement

PROOF
86

NOSE
Rubber tires, dried hay, chlorine, and malt balls; a steaming pile of cornbread.

COLOR
Deep copper

BODY
Thin

GENERAL
It's a fine example of only slightly aged corn whiskey. Perhaps more time in wood might improve this drink.

PALATE
Attic timbers along with lentils, corn pudding, and some mid-palate spice; odd lingering fishiness.

PRICE
$$

RATING
NR

Bernheim

Bernheim is one of the only wheat whiskies on the market, a species not to be confused with wheated bourbon: wheat whiskey has all or mostly wheat in its grain bill, while wheated bourbon is mostly corn, with the addition of a measure of wheat.

Bernheim five-year-old whiskey was developed by the legendary Heaven Hill distillers Parker Beam and his son Craig after the company bought the Old Fitzgerald brand in 1992. Old Fitz was a wheated bourbon, which meant that Heaven Hill, heretofore not known for wheat-heavy whiskies, suddenly had a lot of the grain on hand. Staring at a pile of wheat one day, Craig Beam wondered what would happen if you reversed the wheated-bourbon style and created a "corned" wheat whiskey?

The resulting Bernheim wheat whiskey is named after a pair of nineteenth-century German immigrant brothers, Isaac W. and Bernard Bernheim, who established a distillery in Louisville. Isaac is also the partial namesake of I.W. Harper, a storied bourbon brand that's now only sold in foreign markets (the I.W. in the name comes from Isaac W., who appended the name "Harper" to make it sound more authentically frontier).

HEAVEN HILL DISTILLERIES

P.O. BOX 729

BARDSTOWN, KY 40004

TEL: 502-348-3921

www.heavenhill.com

Bernheim Original Kentucky Straight Wheat Whiskey

AGE
No age statement

PROOF
90

NOSE
Caramel, marzipan, powdered sugar, and bright fruits, especially apricot, bananas, and melons. Add a touch of water and you get vanilla notes and a little blackberry jelly.

COLOR
Deep copper

BODY
Medium to light

GENERAL
This is a fun, unique whiskey. It's smooth and slightly sweet without being cloying; nice and light without sacrificing depth. The spicy finish is just right.

PALATE
Cashews, tangerine, and raw sugar. The finish trails off, with a lingering peppery goodness.

PRICE
$$

RATING

Black Dirt

Along with Hillrock, Finger Lake Distilling, and
Tuthilltown, the Warwick Valley Winery and Distillery
is part of the flowering of liquor producers in upstate
New York. It has been making brandies and *eaux de
vie* since 2003. Its first whiskey release, Black Dirt,
is a three- year-old bourbon, introduced in 2012.

WARWICK VALLEY WINERY AND
DISTILLERY
114 LITTLE YORK ROAD
WARWICK, NY 10990
TEL: 845-258-4858
www.wvwinery.com

Black Dirt Bourbon

AGE
3
years old

PROOF
90

NOSE
Feinty, yeasty, corn, hay

COLOR
Burnished

BODY
Thin

GENERAL
Black Dirt has a very strong
barley nose and just a slight hint
of wood and maple sweetness on
the palate. It's very hot for a 90
proof whiskey and could pair well
with citrus in a cocktail to compliment its vegetal notes.

PALATE
Cereal, hot porridge,
maple sugar, lots of heat

PRICE
$$

RATING

Black Maple Hill

CALIFORNIA VINEYARDS, INC.

1025 TANKLAGE ROAD, SUITE F

SAN CARLOS, CA 94070

TEL: 650-595-1768

E-MAIL: info@cvibrands.com

www.cvibrands.com

PRODUCER: UNKNOWN

Black Maple Hill is proof of a whiskey verity: you don't have to know who made it to know it's good. Few top-shelf whiskeys are as shrouded in mystery. It is owned and distributed by California Vineyards, Inc. of San Carlos, California, near San Francisco, but they don't make it. Kentucky Bourbon Distillers reportedly blends and bottles it, but until recently, KBD didn't make a drop of whiskey—which means the stuff inside the Black Maple Hill bottle comes from somewhere else. Many people believe it comes from Heaven Hill, which has warehouses down the street from KBD in Bardstown. Paul Joseph, the owner of California Vineyards, attests that his whiskey comes from two sources, and always has, but he's not telling from whom. Until rooontly, one could find other Black Maple Hill expressions, including a rye and an older bourbon, but these days the standard eight-year-old bottling is all that is available.

Black Maple Hill Small Batch Bourbon

AGE	**8** years old
PROOF	**95**

NOSE	COLOR	BODY
Lots of bright fruits, notably lemon and pears, along with some well-behaved wood notes, leather, menthol, vanilla, and potato chips	Mahogany	Full and rich

GENERAL	PALATE
If you can find it, buy it. Black Maple Hill is a dangerously drinkable whiskey, with enough big bright fruits to make it nice on ice in the summer and enough rich buttery spice to make it a neat winter warmer.	A boatload of spice, Bit-O-Honey candy, oak, and corn. The finish is buttery and just a touch medicinal.

PRICE	RATING
$$	

Blanton's

In a way, the bourbon renaissance began with Blanton's. Introduced in 1984, it was the world's first single-barrel bourbon expression. Blanton's is produced by Buffalo Trace and named after one of the distillery's former presidents, Albert B. Blanton. The whiskey is aged in Buffalo Trace's famous Warehouse H, reportedly the only steam-heated whiskey warehouse in the world.

Blanton's uses Buffalo Trace's rye-heavy Mash Bill #2, which is also used in Ancient Age, Elmer T. Lee, Hancock's Reserve, and Rock Hill Farms—all of which are owned by Age International, a subsidiary of Takara Shuzo Co, Ltd. in Japan. Ownership questions are usually trivia, but in Blanton's case the international backstory is important: while regular Blanton's is a very, very good whiskey, there are three even better, ultra-premium expressions—Straight from the Barrel, Special Reserve, and Gold Edition—that are only available overseas.

More trivia: bourbon fans recognize Blanton's by its stopper, topped by a racing horse and jockey. But did you know there are eight different stoppers, each in a different pose? And that each pose has a different letter near the horse's feet? When placed in order, they spell the whiskey's name.

AGE INTERNATIONAL, INC.
229 WEST MAIN STREET, SUITE 202
FRANKFORT, KY 40601
TEL: 502-223-9874
E-MAIL: nknox@ageintl.com

PRODUCER
BUFFALO TRACE DISTILLERY
113 GREAT BUFFALO TRACE
FRANKFORT, KENTUCKY 40601
TEL: 800-654-8471
E-MAIL: info@buffalotrace.com
www.buffalotrace.com

Blanton's Original Single Barrel Bourbon <small>BBL 255, RICK 9; W'HOUSE B1</small>

AGE
No age statement

PROOF
93

NOSE
Figs, apple, cereal, toffee, and stewed fruit

COLOR
Mahogany

BODY
Full and rich

GENERAL
For me, this is the whiskey that started it all. My grandfather drank it, and through him, and Blanton's, I got to know what quality brown liquor was all about. And what a great choice. It's the archetypal bourbon: stewed fruit, toffee, butter, and just enough wood

PALATE
Buttery, oaky, with a winey tartness set against pancake batter and almonds. The finish is sweet, reminiscent of a grape Jolly Rancher, with enough spice to balance.

PRICE
$$$

RATING

Booker's

Booker Noe was a grandson of Jim Beam and the
company's master distiller from 1965 to 1992. Noe
wasn't shy about playing favorites among the
barrels, and he would select a few to bottle uncut
and unfiltered as gifts. To mark his retirement, the
company began selling his selection to the public
under his name. The whiskey is based on the
standard Jim Beam mash bill, aged between six and
eight years and bottled at around 120 to 130 proof.
Jim Beam keeps its mash bills secret, but it's widely
reported that the standard is 70 percent corn, 15
percent rye, and 15 percent barley. Despite the high
alcohol content, Noe preferred to drink it neat, save
for a few drops of water to help it open up.

BEAM INC.

510 LAKE COOK ROAD

DEERFIELD, IL 60015

TEL: 847-948-8888

www.beamglobal.com

info@jimbeam.com

Booker's Bourbon

BATCH #C04-A-28

AGE

6–8
years old

PROOF

121–130

NOSE	COLOR	BODY
Cola, floral notes, cumin, butter, and leather	Auburn/ mahogany	Full and chewy

GENERAL	PALATE
Heavenly complex bourbon and for its proof, a surprisingly smooth drink. Add good water or a few ice cubes, let it sit for a minute, and sip.	Lots of spice, chili peppers, oak, and sweet tea; medium finish, and dry, with a little spice at the very end.

PRICE	RATING
$$$	★★★⯪

Breaking and Entering (B&E)

ST. GEORGE SPIRITS

2601 MONARCH ST.

ALAMEDA, CA 94501

TEL: 510-769-1601

EMAIL: info@stgeorgespirits.com

www.stgeorgespirits.com

PRODUCER: UNKNOWN

St. George Spirits, the makers of Breaking and Entering and St. George Single Malt (see separate entry page 253), is among the oldest craft distilleries in the country. Founded in 1982 with a focus on *eau de vie*, it makes its home in Alameda, California, just south of Oakland.

St. George's best-known product is Hangar One Vodka, but it has been making a push into the whiskey field. While the company's single malt is entirely homegrown, Breaking and Entering is a portfolio of some eighty different Kentucky bourbon barrels, which St. George blends at its distillery. According to St. George, the whiskeys are all five to eight years old. Unlike many companies that quietly source their whiskey, St. George is upfront about it—its website calls the process "barrel thieving." It also trumpets the work that goes into blending so many whiskeys, a skill widely appreciated in Scotland, but less so in America.

Breaking & Entering Bourbon Whiskey

AGE	5–8 years old
PROOF	86

NOSE	COLOR	BODY
Raisins, sandalwood, fennel, and some banana	Russet	Thin

GENERAL	PALATE
The nose on Breaking & Entering is a lot of fun, but it promises more than the palate delivers. Despite the tea and bread, it's thin and muted, with a slightly medicinal aftertaste.	Black tea and dark bread, along with a little cherry candy; lengthy finish.

PRICE	RATING
$$	★

Breakout

At first glance, there are questionable aspects to this eight-year-old whiskey: the name and bottle suggest marketing ploy, and the obscure sourcing leaves one wondering whose whiskey one is drinking. What the bottle doesn't tell you is that, while Breakout is, indeed, sourced, it's overseen by veteran distiller Dave Scheurich. The founding master distiller at Woodford Reserve, Scheurich came out of retirement to run the operations at Breakout's owner, the Tennessee Spirits Company (which in turn is a division of Capital Brands).

According to the company, it is working on a distillery of its own, near Pulaski, Tennessee. There is obviously some serious money behind the operation, both because it was able to lure Scheurich out of retirement and because Breakout, despite being on the market for just a few years, is available in most national markets. Tennessee Spirits also sells Jailer, a Tennessee-style whiskey, though it has a much more limited distribution.

TENNESSEE SPIRITS CO.

PO BOX 71

ONE WHISKEY WAY

PULASKI, TN 38478

TEL: 888-784-2946

www.tennesseespiritscompany.com

PRODUCER: UNKNOWN

Breakout Rye

AGE	PROOF
8 years old	**86**

NOSE	COLOR	BODY
Cola, geranium, pepper, white grapes, and wet grass	Tawny	Light

GENERAL	PALATE
There's not a lot of depth to this whiskey, but it's a fun, easy drink. It has a great nose and a light body, perfect for a simple, fresh cocktail.	Pepper, caramel, and port; quick, neat finish, with a little cinnamon Red Hots.

PRICE	RATING
$$	

Breckenridge

BRECKENRIDGE DISTILLERY

1925 AIRPORT RD

BRECKENRIDGE, CO 80424

TEL: 970-547-9759

EMAIL: bryan@breckenridgedistillery.com

www.breckenridgedistillery.com

PRODUCER: UNKNOWN

Breckenridge makes a wide variety of tippling products, including rum, vodka, bitters, and liqueurs. For its branded whiskey, it sources unaged spirits from elsewhere, then ages it in its own facility. The whiskey is a high-rye mash bill, with 56 percent corn, 38 percent rye, and 6 percent malted barley. The company owns a 4,000 square-foot facility where it also makes vodka (at 9,600 feet above sea level, Breckenridge claims it is the world's highest distillery). Thanks to a recent expansion, Breckenridge is now distilling its own whiskey, and expects to have the aged product on shelves by 2014. It also has a single-barrel bourbon and a scotch-style whiskey in the works.

Breckenridge Distillery Colorado Bourbon

AGE	PROOF
2–3 years old	**86**

NOSE	COLOR	BODY
Rye-forward nose packed with corn, marzipan, pine, and dark fruits; vanilla and a touch of citrus.	Tawny	Light

GENERAL	PALATE		
It may say Colorado on the label, but this is Kentucky-sourced whiskey, and it shows on the nose and palate. Breckenridge is a solid expression, but anyone looking for something new and daring will be disappointed.	Apple juice, mint, and cayenne pepper running from start to finish.		
	PRICE	RATING	
	$$$	★ ★	

Buck

Buck is a sourced whiskey distributed by Frank-Lin
Distillers Products, a California-based liquor
company. Frank-Lin puts a lot of effort into selling
Buck as a "wild west" whiskey, complete with a
rodeo rider on the front label.

FRANK-LIN DISTILLERS PRODUCTS

2455 HUNTINGTON DR.

FAIRFIELD, CA 94533

TEL: 800-922-9363

www.www.frank-lin.com

PRODUCER: UNKNOWN

Buck Kentucky Straight Bourbon Whiskey

AGE **8** years old		
PROOF **90**		

NOSE	COLOR	BODY
Oak-heavy, with vanilla, orange, and caramel	Russet	Thin

GENERAL	PALATE	
There's not much depth or complexity here, despite the age. Buck is a good choice as a light cocktail component or with ice and soda on a warm day.	Some nuts, and a bit of feintiness, with a lot of corn on the finish	
	PRICE **$$**	RATING

Buffalo Trace

BUFFALO TRACE DISTILLERY
113 GREAT BUFFALO TRACE
FRANKFORT, KENTUCKY 40601
TEL: 800-654-8471
E-MAIL: info@buffalotrace.com
www.buffalotrace.com

Buffalo Trace is both the current name for one of the country's most storied distilleries and the name of its signature brand. Its name comes from a local story that migrating buffalo forded a narrow portion of the Kentucky River near the distillery site. The distillery has quite a lineage: the location was originally home to the Rock Hill Farms estate, owned by Albert B. Blanton, whose family built a small distillery on site in 1812. In 1870, Col. E.H. Taylor bought the land and opened his O.F.C. Distillery (standing for either Old Fire Copper or Old Fashioned Copper; no one can quite agree). Eight years later, George T. Stagg bought the distillery and Taylor was out; in 1904, after Stagg retired, it was renamed in his honor. In 1929 it passed into the hands of Schenley, a large spirits company. In 1992 the distillery was bought by Sazerac Co., which in 1999 renamed it Buffalo Trace. It is now is listed on the National Register of Historic Places.

Along with the Buffalo Trace buy, Sazerac purchased the Weller and Old Charter brands, and has continued to expand its portfolio through acquisition and development. The company makes a variety of whiskeys for itself, as well as several for Pappy van Winkle and several more for Age International, a Japanese company, whose products include Blanton's, Ancient Age, and Hancock's Reserve.

Sazerac Co. is not nearly as large as Jim Beam or Brown-Forman in terms of market share or volume of whiskey produced, but it retains a level of acclaim far above either of its competitors, thanks to the generally high quality of its products and its willingness to innovate. It makes two lines of experimental whiskeys: one is simply called the Experimental Collection, in which different releases are subject to different unique variables, like wine-barrel finishes or differences in wood grain. The other is called the Single Oak Project, in which different releases bear the marks of different cuts of wood, but always from the same tree—thereby singling out the qualities of the wood for comparison.

The distillery introduced its eponymous bourbon whiskey in 1999. It is crisp and ice-sheet smooth, making it a fantastic beginner's quaff. It's what one might call a "session whiskey," for those of us who like to spend an entire session drinking good bourbon.

Buffalo Trace Kentucky Straight Bourbon Whiskey

AGE
No age statement

PROOF
90

NOSE
Corn meal, rye spice and a ton of wheat, along with oak, raspberries and a little feintiness; brightens a bit with a splash of water.

COLOR
Russet

BODY
Medium and smooth

GENERAL
Buffalo Trace is a perfect example of a "dry" American bourbon. It is considerably less sweet than most whiskeys in its class. It's also one of the best "value-premium" whiskeys on the market. For everyday drinking, it doesn't get much better.

PALATE
Buttery, corny, camp-smoky goodness; closes with a slightly minty, anesthetic tap.

PRICE

RATING
★ ★
★

Bulleit

DIAGEO NORTH AMERICA

801 MAIN AVENUE

NORWALK, CT 06851

TEL: 646-223-2000

www.diageo.com

PRODUCER: BULLEIT BOURBON

FOUR ROSES DISTILLERY

1224 HICKORY GROVE ROAD

LAWRENCEBURG, KY

TEL: 502-839-3436

www.fourrosesbourbon.com

PRODUCER: BULLEIT RYE

MGP INGREDIENTS, INC.

CRAY BUSINESS PLAZA

100 COMMERCIAL STREET

P.O. BOX 130

AICHISON, KS 66002

TEL: 800-255-0302

www.mgpingredients.com

BRANDS

BULLEIT BOURBON FRONTIER
    WHISKEY

BULLEIT RYE AMERICAN WHISKEY

Bulleit is a brand of whiskey owned by the global spirits giant Diageo, plc. The brand is quite old, according to Tom Bulleit, the present-day force behind it. First made by Augustus Bulleit between 1830 and 1860, it was brought back in 1987 and relaunched in 1999 as a sourced whiskey.

Bulleit Bourbon and its newer companion, Bulleit Rye, may share the same brand name, but they are in fact made for Diageo by different distilleries. Bulleit Bourbon is made by Four Roses in Lawrenceburg, Kentucky, with a high-rye mash bill. Bulleit Rye is also made in a town called Lawrenceburg, this time in Indiana at the former Lawrenceburg Distillers Indiana, now owned by MGP, Inc. Don't let the imposing corporate name fool you: MGP makes some good whiskey, especially rye. For a long time the distillery provided the rye whiskey for Seagram's 7; today it makes many of the leading sourced ryes on the market. The mash bill is 95 percent rye and 5 percent malted barley. Bulleit Rye is aged for four years, Bulleit Bourbon for six years.

Bulleit Bourbon Frontier Whiskey

AGE
6–8
years old

PROOF
90

NOSE

Cola, hibiscus, and marigold, along with caramel and oak; water brings out sandalwood and peanuts.

COLOR

Auburn

BODY

Medium

GENERAL

Bulleit strikes all the right notes, but no more. It's a perfect candidate for a robust cocktail—enough strength to stand up among company, but nothing unique to make it stand out in a mint julep.

PALATE

Grapes and red wine notes on the palate, finishing with a slight sweetness.

PRICE

$$

RATING

Bulleit Rye American Whiskey

AGE
4–7
years old

PROOF
90

NOSE

Cherry cola, vanilla, nail polish remover, and a hint of iodine

COLOR

Mahogany

BODY

Light to medium

GENERAL

Like all MGP-sourced ryes, Bulleit is to rye as a vintage Volvo is to cars: solid and safe. It's a fine choice for a Manhattan cocktail.

PALATE

Cloves, cinnamon, menthol, and orange zest, as well as some sweet flowery undertones. Finishes with a long, numbing bite.

PRICE

$$

RATING

Burnside

EASTSIDE DISTILLING

1512 SOUTHEAST 7TH AVENUE

PORTLAND, OR 97214

TEL: 503-926-7060

EMAIL: bill@eastsidedistilling.com

www.eastsidedistilling.com

....

PRODUCER

UNKNOWN

Burnside is a four-year-old bourbon from Eastside Distilling in Portland, Oregon (the label redundantly calls it a "barrel-aged" bourbon, suggesting that bourbon might usually be aged in containers other than barrels). The distillery is located on Portland's Distillery Row, alongside House Spirits, the New Deal Distillery, the Stone Barn Brandyworks, and the Vinn Distillery. The company also makes vodka, flavored whiskeys, and a range of rums.

Eastside calls its whiskey "procured," rather than the usual term "sourced," though the distinction is larger than the two synonyms suggest. Burnside buys most of its fermented mash, but then does the distilling and aging on site, whereas most sourced whiskeys arrive already distilled and aged.

Burnside Bourbon

AGE	
4 years old	

PROOF
96

NOSE	COLOR	BODY
Vanilla, bananas, butterscotch, and a touch of barley	Chestnut	Light to medium

GENERAL	PALATE
The vanilla/banana combination on the nose and palate is prominent and pleasantly surprising. With the cinnamon kick at the end, this is a confectionery dream of a whiskey.	Bananas and barley, with a cinnamon bomb halfway through, which lingers into the finish.

PRICE	RATING
$$	★ ★

Cabin Still

Cabin Still was originally a bottom-shelf offering from the now-defunct Stitzel-Weller distillery, the sort of bourbon that gave the entire genre a bad image in the latter part of the twentieth century. One decanter, from 1969, is shaped like a hillbilly sitting on a barrel with a jug of Cabin Still in one hand and a shotgun in the other. The proprietor of Stitzel-Weller, Julian Van Winkle, Jr., sold off the brand along with W.L. Weller, Old Fitzgerald, and Rebel Yell in 1972. (He retained Old Rip Van Winkle.)

Today Cabin Still is made by Heaven Hill, which ages it for three years (though it carries no age statement) and bottles it at 80 proof; it is no longer sold in hillbilly decanters, but it still sits on the bottom shelf.

HEAVEN HILL DISTILLERIES

P.O. BOX 729

BARDSTOWN, KY 40004

TEL: 502-348-3921

www.heavenhill.com

Cabin Still Kentucky Straight Bourbon Whiskey

AGE	No age statement
PROOF	**80**

NOSE	COLOR	BODY
Funky corn and gingko leaves	Russet	Silk-thin

GENERAL	PALATE
Cabin Still is not a fine whiskey, but it's not boring. The funk and gingko on the nose are a welcome oddity, and the multiple spices on the finish are well pronounced. Worth trying straight, for curiosity's sake.	Apple juice, pepper and white wine, with a finish of cinnamon, black pepper, and garam masala.

PRICE	RATING
$	★

Catoctin Creek

CATOCTIN CREEK DISTILLING

37251 E RICHARDSON LANE

PURCELLVILLE, VA 20132

TEL: 540-751-8404

EMAIL: info@catoctincreek.com

www.catoctincreekdistilling.com

Located in the heart of Virginia wine country, Catoctin Creek is one of a growing number of "dirt to glass" distilleries emphasizing organic ingredients and low-impact production methods. The distillery was founded by Becky and Scott Harris in 2009, and along with its Roundstone Rye it makes a gin, pear brandy, and white dog (unaged whiskey). Roundstone is 100 percent Kansas rye aged in white oak.

Roundstone Rye

AGE	
5	
months old	

PROOF	
80	

NOSE	COLOR	BODY
White wine, iodine, and rubbery funk	Russet	Light

GENERAL	PALATE
Fans of classic rye will be disappointed, but those looking for a unique expression of the grain will enjoy Roundstone Rye's deeep funkiness.	Buttery and little spicy, though it reminds one mostly of cheap Valentine's Day candies.

PRICE	RATING
$$	★

Charbay

Founded in St. Helena, California in 1983, Charbay was one of the country's first artisanal distilleries. Today it is best known for its vodkas and European-style brandies and *eaux de vie*, but it also makes a series of whiskies that has become something of a cult item among West Coast connoisseurs.

Each expression in the series, created and overseen by Marko Karakesevic, the son of the distillery's founder, begins with a different beer from a local brewery. A favorite is Bear Republic, a brewery in nearby Healdsburg. The first release, aged for two years in French oak, was distilled from a pilsner; the second, aged for a single day, came from a double IPA (India Pale Ale). The latest, labeled a "hop-flavored whiskey," is distilled from Bear Republic's flagship Racer 5 IPA in copper cognac stills, then aged in French oak for twenty-two months.

CHARBAY WINERY AND DISTILLERY

4001 SPRING MOUNTAIN ROAD

SAINT HELENA, CA 94574

TEL: 707-963-9327

EMAIL: marko@charbay.com

www.charbay.com

Charbay "S" Hop-Flavored Whiskey

AGE	PROOF
22 months old	**99**

NOSE	COLOR	BODY
Hops, clover, beeswax, and iodine	Russet	Thin

GENERAL	PALATE
This is one the most unique whiskeys on the market; not for everyone, but not to be missed by the adventurous. Cast over the whole experience is a dessert-wine overtone, similar to a *vin santo*. Intriguing stuff.	Bitterness and malty sweetness, plus some cinnamon heat; toward the end, the beer notes come forward.

PRICE	RATING
$$$$	★ ★

Collier & McKeel

COLLIER & MCKEEL DISTILLERY

1200 CLINTON STREET

NASHVILLE, TN 37212

www.collierandmckeel.com

info@collierandmckeel.com

Tennessee whiskey, thanks to Jack Daniel's, may be among the most famous styles of liquor on the planet, but there are surprisingly few distilleries in the state. That's starting to change, with Nashville's Collier & McKeel in the lead. Located in an area near downtown that is fast becoming a distillers' row—both Corsair and Green Brier are located nearby—Collier & McKeel has been making and selling whiskey since 2011. The mash bill is fairly standard, at 70 percent corn, 15 percent rye and 15 percent malted barley. Like Jack Daniel's and George Dickel, it then passes through maple charcoal to round out the edges.

Collier & McKeel Tennessee Whiskey

AGE		
No age statement		

PROOF		
86		

NOSE	COLOR	BODY
Leather, sourdough, and wood	Tawny	Thin

GENERAL	PALATE	
Strong feintiness and barley mash dominate this pour. There's enough funk here to make Bootsy Collins smile, but it lacks depth and balance of flavor.	A lot of sweetness up front, followed by sweet and sour notes.	

	PRICE	RATING
	$$$	**NR**

Colonel E.H. Taylor

BUFFALO TRACE DISTILLERY

113 GREAT BUFFALO TRACE

FRANKFORT, KENTUCKY 40601

TEL: 800-654-8471

E-MAIL: info@buffalotrace.com

www.buffalotrace.com

....

BRANDS

E.H. TAYLOR BARREL PROOF

E.H. TAYLOR SINGLE BARREL

"Colonel" Edmund Haynes Taylor Jr., though not an actual a colonel, commanded an outsize influence on the state of Kentucky and its late nineteenth-century whiskey business. A great-nephew of President Zachary Taylor, he was, at different times, the mayor of Frankfort, a state representative, and a senator, even as he built the O.F.C. Distillery (now Buffalo Trace) into a regional whiskey powerhouse. It was Taylor who, in 1897, convinced Congress to pass the Bottled-in-Bond Act, which gave the Kentucky bourbon industry a federally approved means to distinguish its products from the lower-grade whiskeys being made by the "high-wines" industry north of the Ohio River.

In Taylor's honor, Buffalo Trace began to release the E.H. Taylor series in early 2011, each of which represents a unique spin on the distillery's conventional expressions.

Colonel E.H. Taylor Barrel Proof Straight Kentucky Bourbon Whiskey

AGE	PROOF
No age statement	**134.5**

NOSE	COLOR	BODY
Oak, maple syrup, rosewater, unsweetened chocolate, hay barn, and almonds; a little water brings out cigar box, dried tea, and even a little Now & Later candies.	Auburn/ mahogany	Full and robust

GENERAL	PALATE
This is a big, bold, well-rounded and super high-proof drink, but it's surprisingly manageable with just a few drops of water. Delicious and intriguingly complex.	Cough syrup, cherry candy, ginger, and port; finishes with jalapeno peppers, Atomic Fireball, and menthol.

PRICE	RATING
$$$$	★★★

Colonel E.H. Taylor Single Barrel Straight Kentucky Bourbon Whiskey

AGE
7
years old

PROOF
100

NOSE
Black tea, clover honey, sherry, banana, barley, and butter

COLOR
Tawny

BODY
Medium to full

GENERAL
This is a complex, rich, and mature whiskey with a whole cereal and spice rack in the nose, palate, and finish. The colonel would be proud,

PALATE
Cinnamon, maple, and cherry cola, finishing with spearmint and wood.

PRICE
$$$$

RATING

Copper Fox

Copper Fox is the brainchild of Rick Wasmund, a
former financial planner and insurance salesman
from upstate New York, who began making whiskey
after an internship at the Bowmore Distillery in
Scotland. Introduced in 2006, Wasmund's Single
Malt Whisky was among the first American single
malts. But you'd never confuse it for a Highland
dram: instead of peat, Wasmund's is all about
apple. Wasmund uses apple wood to smoke his
malt and ages the whiskey in apple wood barrels.
To speed up the infusion of wood flavors, he
tosses into the barrel what amounts to a giant
tea bag full of toasted apple wood chips.

   Wasmund was one of the first of the new generation of craft distillers and a pioneer in the use of
local, organic ingredients. His apple wood is
harvested from old trees from nearby orchards
and his barley and rye grain come from a nearby
organic farm.

   Copper Fox sells unaged versions of both
expressions, which you can buy in a kit along with a
two- or five-liter oak barrel so you can make your
own aged whiskey. It may be a gimmick, but
Wasmund says it's been overwhelmingly successful,
and anything that exposes people to the difficulty of
getting the aging process right can't be all bad.

COPPER FOX DISTILLERY
9 RIVER LANE
SPERRYVILLE, VA 22740
TEL: 540-987-8554
E-MAIL: RW@copperfox.biz
www.copperfox.biz

BRANDS
COPPER FOX RYE WHISKY
WASMUND'S SINGLE MALT WHISKY

Copper Fox
Rye Whisky

AGE	
1	
year old	

PROOF	
90	

NOSE	COLOR	BODY
Smoke, seaweed, fish, pepper, cocoa	Tawny	Light to medium

GENERAL	PALATE
Copper Fox tastes much better than it smells. The tea and anchovy notes make it an odd duck (or fish) on the American whiskey shelf.	Salty, almost anchovy-like, along with lapsang souchong; the tea continues on the finish, but with a little sweetness.

PRICE	RATING
$$	★

Wasmund's
Single Malt Whisky

AGE	
No age	
statement	

PROOF	
96	

NOSE	COLOR	BODY
Apples everywhere, plus burnt rubber, fenugreek, sweat, campfire, and bubblegum	Tawny	Thinnish

GENERAL	PALATE
No one else makes whiskey like Wasmund's, for better or worse. This is all apples, all the time, from the first whiff to the last echo of the finish. It's interesting, but the feintiness here is not for the faint of heart.	Apple, alongside smoked salmon skin, salt, and fennel; quick finishing.

PRICE	RATING
$$	★

Corner Creek

Corner Creek is a private-label, eight-year-old whiskey produced by Kentucky Bourbon Distillers—and since KBD has not, until very recently, distilled its own whiskey, that means Corner Creek comes from some other, unspecified source. In the whiskey world, that's not all that rare, and KBD does the same for several noted brands. Otherwise, not a whole lot is known about this whiskey.

KENTUCKY BOURBON DISTILLERS
1869 LORETTO ROAD
BARDSTOWN, KY, 40004
TEL: 502-348-0081
E-MAIL: kentuckybourbon@bardstown.com
www.kentuckybourbonwhiskey.com

PRODUCER: UNKNOWN

Corner Creek Reserve Bourbon Whiskey

AGE
8
years old

PROOF
88

NOSE
Marzipan, leather, cumin, and candy corn

COLOR
Chestnut

BODY
Full and chewy

GENERAL
Not a great whiskey, but it's so down-the-line typical and easy to drink that it makes a fine everyday pour.

PALATE
Juicy, with a palate redolent of sour apple, cherries, and pine sap; the finish is harsh but refreshing.

PRICE
$$

RATING

Corsair

CORSAIR DISTILLERY

1200 CLINTON STREET #110

NASHVILLE, TN 37203

615-200-0320

E-MAIL: darek@corsairartisan.com

www.corsairartisan.com

For a startup distillery, Corsair has one of the broadest portfolios on the market—and aside from a standard gin offering, one of the strangest. Its regular-production lines include a pumpkin-spiced white dog (unaged whiskey), a "red" absinthe, and "Triple Smoke," which blends barley smoked over cherry wood, peat, and beech wood. Then there are the experimentals: whiskey made with everything from obscure grains (triticale, quinoa) to hop and elderflower infusions.

Corsair has two facilities, one in Bowling Green, Kentucky, and one in Nashville's Marathon Village. The Village is an old industrial quarter near downtown that is also home to the Green Brier and Collier and McKeel distilleries (as well as Antique Archaeology, a brick and mortar outlet for the reality television show *American Pickers*).

Though Corsair has won critical acclaim with its experimentals, most of them are one-off productions, and very hard to find outside Tennessee and Kentucky; if you want to try them, it's best to stop by the Corsair tasting room the next time you're in Music City. However, Triple Smoke, its only regular-production whiskey, is available across most of the country.

Corsair
Triple Smoke
American Malt
Whiskey

AGE
No age statement

PROOF
80

NOSE
Tar, mint, smoke, tobacco, grain, caramel, licorice, and oak with a little yeasty funk underneath

COLOR
Deep copper

BODY
Full and oily

GENERAL
Triple Smoke shouldn't work. It sounds too gimmicky, too complex. But it does, somehow. Its layers of spice and smoky depth are a nice change of pace in the American whiskey scene.

PALATE
Spice up front that resolves itself into turbinado sugar, Band-Aid, pine, and iodine. It finishes in a lingering spearmint.

PRICE
$$$

RATING
★ ★

Cyrus Noble

HAAS BROS.

1808 WEDEMEYER ST, SUITE 160

SAN FRANCISCO, CA 94129

TEL: 415-282-8585

EMAIL: info@haas-brothers.com

www.haas-brothers.com

....

PRODUCER

HEAVEN HILL DISTILLERIES

P.O. BOX 729

BARDSTOWN, KY 40004

TEL: 502-348-3921

www.heavenhill.com

Cyrus Noble is named after a San Francisco distiller active in the 1860s and '70s. Owned by Haas Brothers, a California wholesaler, this whiskey is sourced from Heaven Hill in Kentucky and aged for five years in oak in San Francisco. The mash bill is 75 percent corn, 20 percent rye, and 5 percent malted barley.

Cyrus Noble Bourbon Whiskey

AGE	**5** years old
PROOF	**90**

NOSE	COLOR	BODY
Menthol cigarette ash, black pepper, cinnamon bread, geraniums, and strawberries; a little water brings out antique furniture and oranges.	Auburn	Thinnish

GENERAL	PALATE	
A decent whiskey; the ashy notes on the nose and menthol on the palate are interesting.	Sweet corn, menthol, and black pepper	

PRICE	RATING
$$	★

Dad's Hat

Pennsylvania was once the heartland of
American rye whiskey, and its products were
well-regarded and well-consumed across
the country. "Pennsylvania rye," often called
"Old Monongahela," was spicy and robust,
in sharp contrast to the whiskey from the East
Coast's other great rye-producing state, Maryland,
which tended to be sweeter and softer (and
more often than not blended with other spirits
and fruit juices). But the precipitous decline
of rye during the early twentieth century, and
the consolidation of brands and rye production
in Kentucky, washed out many of those
regional qualities. No one has made whiskey
in Pennsylvania for decades.

Herman Mihalich, the founder of Mountain
Laurel Spirits, would like to change that. Mihalich
grew up in western Pennsylvania, near the
Monongahela River. His dive into whiskey was
inspired by the old-school ryes he remembers his
father and grandfather drinking when he was a
child. After years spent researching Pennsylvania's
whiskey-making past, Mihalich launched Dad's Hat
Rye in 2012, the first new take on "Old
Monongahela" in almost a century.

Made from a mash bill of 80 percent rye,
15 percent malted barley, and 5 percent malted rye,
Dad's Hat is offered in an unaged version and a
seven- to nine-month-old aged expression. Mihalich
says that the company will release older whiskeys
in the future.

MOUNTAIN LAUREL SPIRITS

925 CANAL STREET

BRISTOL, PA 19007

TEL: 215-781-8300

EMAIL: hmihalich@dadshatrye.com

www.dadshatrye.com

Dad's Hat Pennsylvania Rye Whiskey

AGE
6
months old

PROOF
90

NOSE
Licorice, cherries, and a bit vegetal

COLOR
Russet

BODY
Light

GENERAL
This is a great turnout for such a young whiskey and from such a new distillery. Rye fans will love it—the vegetal notes on the nose and palate underline that this is not another average, anonymous rye.

PALATE
Peppery on the tongue, with mint, oak, and okra. The finish is pleasantly abrupt.

PRICE
$$$

RATING

Dead Guy

In 2006 Rogue Ales, best known as a pioneer Oregon brewery, sauntered into the distilling world with Dead Guy Whiskey, a companion to its flagship Dead Guy Ale. Like the beer, Dead Guy Whiskey is made from four different types of malt (Northwest Harrington, Maier Munich, Klages, and Carastan). It's then fermented with distiller's yeast, double-distilled in a Vendome pot still, and, according to the distillery, "ocean aged" (presumably for its proximity to the Pacific) for one month in American white oak barrels.

Rogue entered the craft distilling market at the right time, just as the shelves were beginning to blossom with strange new expressions from strange new distilleries. But even in the accommodating world of craft whiskey, the reception was uncharacteristically harsh: "It may very well be the worst whiskey ever made," wrote Geoffrey Kleinman of DrinkSpirits.com. Rogue went back to the still and a few years later produced what most now consider a workable, if still subpar, drink.

ROGUE SPIRITS

2320 SOUTHEAST OSU DRIVE

NEWPORT, OR 97365

TEL: 541-867-3660

EMAIL: johnc@rogue.com

www.rogue.com

Dead Guy Whiskey

AGE
1
month old

PROOF
80

NOSE
Corn nuts, Nehi grape soda, and apricots

COLOR
Pale straw

BODY
Thin

GENERAL
Dead Guy Whiskey has improved significantly over the last several years, but comes up short. This is hardly a whiskey at all, it's more like a grappa or *eau de vie* on the nose and palate.

PALATE
Barley, lavender candy, some soap, and hardly any bite. Yet, it has a long, grappa-like burn.

PRICE
$$

RATING
NR

Dry Fly

DRY FLY DISTILLING

1003 EAST TRENT AVENUE

SPOKANE, WA 99202

TEL: 509-489-2112

EMAIL: don@dryflydistilling.com

www.dryflydistilling.com

For a crop as diverse as wheat, it rarely shows up as the dominant part of a whiskey mash bill, let alone the majority grain. In fact, Dry Fly Distilling makes one of the only wheat whiskeys in wide circulation; the two others are Bernheim, from Heaven Hill, and Lion's Pride Wheat, from Koval.

Dry Fly, operating in Spokane, Washington, since 2007, also makes a vodka, gin, and bourbon, but the wheat whiskey is what it's known for outside the state. It's made from locally sourced grains and aged for eighteen months.

Wheat tends to make for a sweeter and smoother whiskey, with less heft, than corn. It's a common enough ingredient in so-called "wheated" bourbons like Weller and Maker's Mark, which famously lean toward the oilly side. But it's rare on its own, perhaps because most distillers are wary that they'll end up with something cloying and one-dimensional.

Expect to see more offerings from Dry Fly in the coming years. Plans are afoot for a port-barrel-finished wheat whiskey, a triticale (a wheat-rye hybrid grain) whiskey, and a cask-strength wheat whiskey, bottled at 120 proof.

Dry Fly Washington Wheat Whiskey

AGE
2 years old

PROOF
80

NOSE
Gingersnaps, bright fruits (lemons and apricots), beech, and oak

COLOR
Chestnut

BODY
Light

GENERAL
This pour has an intriguing nose and palate and is much sweeter than other wheat whiskeys on the market. It's light and spicy and all together quite a different style.

PALATE
Ginger, resolving into a melon and cantaloupe funk; the finish is almost non-existent.

PRICE
$$

RATING

Eagle Rare

The 1970s saw an ornithological trend in the whiskey world. In 1974 Austin Nichols introduced its 80 proof Wild Turkey, which took flight more like a peregrine falcon than its somewhat lumbering namesake. Heaven Hill's Fighting Cock came out around the same time, and in 1975 Seagram brought out the 101 proof Eagle Rare. When Seagram divested itself of most of its bourbon portfolio in 1989, it sold the Eagle Rare brand, along with the McAfee's Benchmark brand, to Sazerac. Eagle Rare is now made at the Buffalo Trace Distillery in Frankfort, Kentucky.

Today there are two expressions of Eagle Rare. Both are 90 proof and low-rye, though one is aged for ten years and the other, a part of the Buffalo Trace Antique Collection, for seventeen years. Like all Antique Collection whiskeys, the seventeen-year-old is as rare as, well, eagle's teeth. Even harder to find is the Eagle Rare 101 expression: it was discontinued in 2005 and, to many connoisseurs, it represented the pinnacle of no-fuss, high-quality bourbon making.

The Eagle Rare seventeen-year-old is a limited-release bourbon that varies significantly from year to year, and for those reasons it's not covered here. The Eagle Rare 101 is not covered either, since it's out of production and out of sight, though it should go without saying that if you find a bottle, buy it.

Eagle Rare
Single Barrel
Kentucky Straight
Bourbon Whiskey

AGE
10
years old

PROOF
90

NOSE

Rose hips, honey, caramel, green apples, almonds, and dried fruit

COLOR

Mahogany

BODY

Full and chewy

GENERAL

A good whiskey, but Eagle Rare is a lesser version of its higher-proof forebearer. Still, it's a fine straight-drinking bourbon or mixer.

PALATE

Bubblegum, cherries, and oranges on the palate; ends with a nice, lingering spice.

PRICE

$$

RATING

★ ★

Early Times

Though not a particular distinguished offering, Early Times is famous as the official mint julep whiskey of the Kentucky Derby. Several thousand Early Times mint juleps are consumed in the few minutes it takes the horses to round the track.

The brand dates back to 1860, but it didn't take off until it passed into the hands of Brown-Forman in 1923. Lucky for the Early Times legacy, Brown-Forman had a license to make whiskey for "medicinal" purposes, which meant it could distill during Prohibition. Over the following decades Early Times was one of the country's best-selling brands. Production was moved from the village of Early Times Station, Kentucky, to Louisville, then to Brown-Forman's Shively Distillery, just outside town. For a while, the Shively location was even renamed the Early Times Distillery to reflect the brand's dominant position within the company's portfolio.

In 1983, Brown-Forman decided to divide the Early Times brand into two expressions: it would remain a quality bourbon for the export market, but domestic consumers would have to settle for a bottom-shelf whiskey. Since this new lower-tier Early Times is aged in both new and used barrels, it can't be called bourbon; that's why the label refers to it as "Kentucky whisky." Almost overnight, the brand's domestic reputation sank, while it soared overseas; today it is one of the best-selling foreign whiskeys in Japan.

Eventually Brown-Forman saw the error of its ways, and in 2011 it began producing an Early Times bourbon for stateside drinkers, called Early Times 354 (named for the distillery's permit number). Whether it will ever recover its domestic market share, let alone prestige, remains to be seen.

BROWN-FORMAN

850 DIXIE HIGHWAY

LOUISVILLE, KY 40210

TEL: 502-585-1100

www.brown-forman.com

BRANDS

EARLY TIMES 354 BOURBON

EARLY TIMES KENTUCKY WHISKY

Early Times 354 Bourbon

AGE
No age statement

PROOF
80

NOSE
Lots of pleasant, if artificial, fruits and creamy notes, port, and nuts

COLOR
Russet

BODY
Light

GENERAL
This is a somewhat rough drink, but with a lot of nice spice at the end. The wood along with the fruity nose and palate strike a good balance.

PALATE
Wood, with heat, floral notes, and a certain astringency; the finish is shockingly harsh.

PRICE
$

RATING

Early Times Kentucky Whisky

AGE
No age statement

PROOF
80

NOSE
Fish, marzipan, butter, and apricot

COLOR
Amber

BODY
Thin

GENERAL
Early Times is a smooth straightforward whiskey and is best for mixing with a light cocktail.

PALATE
Oak and butterscotch; the finish is abrupt and total.

PRICE
$

RATING

Elijah Craig

Named for the eighteenth-century Kentucky Baptist preacher who is often, and incorrectly, honored as the "inventor" of bourbon, Elijah Craig is one of the mainstay brands of the Heaven Hill Distillery. (For more on the real story of bourbon, see pages 29–30).

Of course, the rightness or wrongness of the Elijah Craig story has no bearing on the quality of the whiskey. From its standard twelve-year-old expression through its refined eighteen- and twenty-year-old versions, Elijah Craig is superb. All three are made from the same low-rye mash bill, which is the same bill used in another Heaven Hill mainstay brand, Evan Williams. (To see how different two whiskeys made from the same mash bill can taste, compare the excellent Elijah Craig twelve-year-old with the very good Evan Williams Single Barrel (covered on page 133).

The twenty-year-old debuted in 2011 as a one-time bottling for the twentieth anniversary of the Kentucky Bourbon Festival, available only at the Heaven Hill gift shop in Bardstown. In 2012 Heaven Hill put the whiskey back into production, this time with a much wider, though still limited, distribution.

As of this writing, Heaven Hill has suspended production of the eighteen-year-old to make sure it has enough whiskey for the twenty-year-old—after sitting that long in the warm Kentucky hills, there's hardly any whiskey left in the barrels. It is unclear whether Heaven Hill will make the twenty a regular-production expression, or whether it will leave well enough alone and stick with the eighteen. Not that it matters too much either way—they're both out-standing bourbons, though the eighteen is a more balanced drink.

HEAVEN HILL DISTILLERIES
P.O. BOX 729
BARDSTOWN, KY 40004
TEL: 502-348-3921
www.heavenhill.com

BRANDS

ELIJAH CRAIG KENTUCKY STRAIGHT
     BOURBON WHISKEY 12 YEAR
ELIJAH CRAIG KENTUCKY STRAIGHT
     BOURBON WHISKEY 18 YEAR
ELIJAH CRAIG KENTUCKY STRAIGHT
     BOURBON WHISKEY 20 YEAR

Elijah Craig Kentucky Straight Bourbon Whiskey 12 Years Old

AGE
12
years old

PROOF
94

NOSE
Toasted almonds, tangerines, sour apples, and barley, with a little yeasty funk

COLOR
Auburn

BODY
Full and chewy

GENERAL
This is fantastic whiskey, especially for the price. It has a brisk, toasted character reminiscent of a chilly October day.

PALATE
Cherry cola, spearmint, and cardamom. The finish is dry, with a hint of curry.

PRICE
$$$

RATING

Elijah Craig Kentucky Straight Bourbon Whiskey 18 Years Old

AGE
18
years old

PROOF
90

NOSE
Corn, oak, butter, sourdough, leather, and red wine

COLOR
Russet

BODY
Medium to full

GENERAL
An excellent whiskey by all measures: smooth and richly flavorful it lives gloriously in the place where the perfect bourbon nose and taste converge. Though it's out of production for the moment, chances are that demand will make Heaven Hill bring it back. Hurry up, please.

PALATE
Corn, oak, fresh bread, and dried fruit, lingering spice on finish

PRICE
$$$

RATING

Elijah Craig Kentucky Straight Bourbon Whiskey 20 Years Old

AGE
20
years old

PROOF
90

NOSE
Wood, vanilla cola, lots of oak, marzipan, spearmint, and stewed fruit

COLOR
Tawny

BODY
Medium to full

GENERAL
What a difference two years can make. Though this is hardly a mistake, the Elijah Craig 20 is a clear step down from the 18; it is slightly too oaky and unbalanced in comparison. However, an outstanding pour of whiskey by any measure.

PALATE
Tons of spice and citrus, but almost no sweetness, ending in an abrupt, mouth-puckeringly dry finish.

PRICE
$$$$

RATING
★★★⯨

Elmer T. Lee

AGE INTERNATIONAL, INC.

229 WEST MAIN STREET, SUITE 202

FRANKFORT, KY 40601

TEL: 502-223-9874

E-MAIL: nknox@ageintl.com

PRODUCER

BUFFALO TRACE DISTILLERY

113 GREAT BUFFALO TRACE

FRANKFORT, KENTUCKY 40601

TEL: 800-654-8471

E-MAIL: info@buffalotrace.com

www.buffalotrace.com

Over the last decade or so, established distilleries looking to create new brands have turned to their own past and present master distillers as namesakes—hence, Parker's, Blanton's, E.H. Taylor, Booker's, and Elmer T. Lee. A radar bombardier in the Pacific during World War II, Lee joined the George T. Stagg Distillery (now Buffalo Trace) in 1949. He became plant manager in 1969; after retiring in 1985, he became distiller "emeritus." One of his last actions as master distiller was to introduce Blanton's in 1984, the first single-barrel bourbon and the release many people mark as the beginning of the whiskey renaissance.

In honor of Lee's service to the distillery, Buffalo Trace developed the Elmer T. Lee brand, a single-barrel whiskey that, for a time, was selected by distiller emeritus Lee himself. It carries no age statement; Buffalo Trace claims that Lee wanted to pick the barrels when he knew they were ready, not by the number of years spent aging in the rickhouse.

Today the brand is owned by Age International, a Japanese company, which also owns Ancient Age, Blanton's, Rock Hill Farms, and Hancock's Reserve. All are made by Buffalo Trace, and all use their high-rye Mash Bill #2.

Elmer T. Lee Kentucky Straight Bourbon Whiskey

AGE

PROOF **90**

NOSE
Flowery (redolent of lilies), alongside citrus and spearmint; some water brings out the grain.

COLOR
Russet

BODY
Light to medium

GENERAL
Elmer T. Lee has a classic bourbon profile, but it is a little too far on the shallow end of the whiskey pool for greatness. That said, the floral notes are magnificent. It would make a great Manhattan component.

PALATE
Raisins and apple; the finish is long, ending in a prolonged grainy note with a not all-together pleasing metallic of brass.

PRICE **$$**

RATING

Evan Williams

Made by Heaven Hill, the Evan Williams range of expressions is the complete package: starting with the bargain everydayness of the four-year-old Green Label, it rises through the midrange Black Label (aged seven years, though see below), 1783 (aged ten years), and White Label Bottled in Bond (scarce outside the mid-South), to peak at the wonderful, and scandalously inexpensive Single Barrel (also aged about ten years).

Evan Williams not only uses the same low-rye mash bill as one of Heaven Hill's other primary lines, Elijah Craig, but their namesakes also share similar histories. Evan Williams was a Welsh immigrant who, like Craig, settled in Kentucky in the late eighteenth century and began distilling local grains.

Evan Williams Black Label recently caused a stink when it dropped its seven-year age statement. Heaven Hill and other distilleries that have recently followed suit say getting rid of age statements is about flexibility: a precocious six-year-old barrel may be just as ready as the average seven-year-old. But some whiskey drinkers fear that dropping age statements is a sly way to justify selling younger whiskey, thereby getting more product out the door faster.

The real star of the series is Evan Williams Single Barrel. At a common price point of under thirty dollars, it may be the best deal on the shelf. It was one of the first regular-production whiskeys to be vintage dated, so you know precisely how old it is; true fans will be able to read the rickhouse information (i.e., where the barrel sat in the warehouse) and tell you what to expect given its relative exposure to heat, humidity, and cold drafts.

The Evan Williams label also appears on three flavored whiskeys—a cinnamon, a cherry, and a honey—as well as three seasonal liqueurs. As I've explained elsewhere, we're not touching that stuff.

HEAVEN HILL DISTILLERIES
P.O. BOX 729
BARDSTOWN, KY 40004
TEL: 502-348-3921

....

BRANDS

EVAN WILLIAMS 1783 KENTUCKY
    STRAIGHT BOURBON WHISKEY

EVAN WILLIAMS KENTUCKY STRAIGHT
    BOURBON WHISKEY (BLACK
    LABEL)

EVAN WILLIAMS KENTUCKY STRAIGHT
    BOURBON WHISKEY (GREEN
    LABEL)

EVAN WILLIAMS SINGLE BARREL
    VINTAGE BOURBON

Evan Williams 1783 Kentucky Straight Bourbon Whiskey

AGE
No age statement

PROOF
86

NOSE
Apricots, oak, maple candy, and cinnamon

COLOR
Tawny

BODY
Medium and oily

GENERAL
Finely balanced, but the nose promises more than the palate can deliver.

PALATE
Port, cloying sweetness, lingering cinnamon

PRICE
$$

RATING

Evan Williams Kentucky Straight Bourbon Whiskey BLACK LABEL

AGE
No age statement

PROOF
86

NOSE
Flowers, corn, and intense barley, with a little sweetness and Cajun spiciness

COLOR
Tawny

BODY
Light

GENERAL
Solid and unassuming—Evan Williams is your friend, but not your best bud. It's best as a mixer, where its solid, unassuming character will hold up well.

PALATE
Vague spiciness, with a flat, mellow finish

PRICE
$

RATING

Evan Williams Kentucky Straight Bourbon Whiskey GREEN LABEL

AGE
No age statement

PROOF
86

NOSE
Acrid, with a touch of smoke, chocolate, and orange slices

COLOR
Tawny to auburn

BODY
Light

GENERAL
A solid session whiskey. Like the Black Label, it has a strong backbone and would make a great base for a cocktail.

PALATE
Indefinable spice note up front, though with a creaminess in taste and texture. It finishes with cinnamon.

PRICE
$

RATING

Evan Williams Single Barrel Vintage BATCH: 2002

AGE
9+ years old

PROOF
86.6

NOSE
Pear, candy apple, and cherries, along with light oak, cinnamon and a touch of sweet iced tea

COLOR
Russet

BODY
Chewy

GENERAL
This is the real stand out of the Evan Williams line. For the money, there is no better bourbon than Evan Williams Single Barrel. Every step, from nose through the finish, is wonderfully, pleasingly complex and satisfying.

PALATE
Bright and fruity palate of lemon and orange, with oak, corn chips, and sherry; the finish is quick, with lingering tangerine and orange zest.

PRICE
$$

RATING

Ezra Brooks

LUXCO

5050 KEMPER AVENUE

ST. LOUIS, MO 63139

TEL: 314-772-2626

E-MAIL: contactus@luxco.com

www.luxco.com

Ezra Brooks is not particularly distinguished bourbon; if you were to play chess with whiskey bottles, Ezra Brooks would be a pawn. But like pawns, it's a utility player: it has enough heft for mixing, but nothing unique that would disturb the harmony of a cocktail. Old Ezra 101 is a bit stronger, obviously, but surprisingly smooth at that proof, and still a decent candidate for an Old Fashioned.

PRODUCER	BRANDS
HEAVEN HILL DISTILLERIES	EZRA B. SINGLE BARREL
P.O. BOX 729	KENTUCKY STRAIGHT
BARDSTOWN, KY 40004	BOURBON WHISKEY
TEL: 502-348-3921	OLD EZRA KENTUCKY
www.heavenhill.com	STRAIGHT BOURBON
	WHISKEY

Ezra B. Single Barrel Kentucky Straight Bourbon Whiskey
BARREL NUMBER 365/HAND BOTTLED 7-09

AGE
12
years old

PROOF
99

NOSE

Rubber, leather, corn, wood, musk, and barley, with some very subtle floral and citrus notes

COLOR

Tawny

BODY

Medium and juicy

GENERAL

Dark and brooding, Ezra B. is a bit like drinking a cigar box. The balance is skewed toward wood and leather and nuts without much fruit or flower. It's an interesting profile and an excellent value for a twelve year old.

PALATE

Leather, nuts, and cigar box; finish is brief and ashy, like drinking a cigar.

PRICE

$$

RATING

Old Ezra
Kentucky Straight
Bourbon Whiskey

AGE

7

years old

PROOF

101

NOSE

Dark fruit notes, with oregano, pencil shavings, old leather, and dirty flowers, but there's also perfume, toffee, and a little oak

COLOR

Chestnut

BODY

Full

GENERAL

A fun mint julep base and interesting for its darker, scotch-like notes, but otherwise, Old Ezra is nothing to write home about.

PALATE

Cough syrup, alongside chocolate and tobacco; finish is long and minty.

PRICE

$

RATING

F.E.W.

FEW SPIRITS

918 CHICAGO AVENUE

EVANSTON, IL 60202

TEL: 847-920-8628

E-MAIL: info@fewspirits.com

www.fewspirits.com

Along with Koval, F.E.W. Spirits has brought Chicago distilling back into action after nearly a century of privation. But while Koval is pursuing the organic, exotic trend (it's home to America's only spelt whiskey), F.E.W. is taking the retro path, both in its packaging design and its liquor. Technically, F.E.W. isn't a Chicago spirit at all, but a resident of Evanston, just north of the city limits. That's significant, because Evanston was a focal point of prohibitionist activity and was officially dry from 1858 to 1972; retail liquor stores couldn't operate there until 1984. In fact, F.E.W. cheekily takes its name from the initials of one of the city's leading anti-liquor activists, Frances Elizabeth Willard.

F.E.W. makes a gin, white whiskey, rye and bourbon. The bourbon is a standard mash bill, with 70 percent corn, 20 percent rye, 10 percent malted barley.

F.E.W. Bourbon

AGE		
No age statement		
PROOF		
93		

NOSE	COLOR	BODY
Pine, sloe berry, turpentine, and wood	Tawny	Thin

GENERAL	PALATE	
This bourbon has a mushy cereal note on the nose and the front of the palate, which clashes with the sharp pine and turpentine acridity. Despite this effort, I expect that F.E.W. will one day be making good whiskey.	Quite hot, with varnish and apple juice; quick finish.	
	PRICE	**RATING**
	$$$	**NR**

Fighting Cock

Fighting Cock is part of the bird-watcher's trio of bourbons to appear in the 1970s, alongside Eagle Rare and Wild Turkey 80 proof. It's a rye-heavy expression, aged for six years by Heaven Hill and marketed with a strong emphasis on the "cock," perhaps in hopes of capturing the macho frat-boy sector. The sad thing is, this whiskey deserves better. Like Rebel Yell, it's a surprisingly decent whiskey burdened by a marketer-driven name.

HEAVEN HILL DISTILLERIES
P.O. BOX 729
BARDSTOWN, KY 40004
TEL: 502-348-3921
www.heavenhill.com

Fighting Cock Kentucky Straight Bourbon Whiskey

AGE	**6** years old
PROOF	**103**

NOSE	COLOR	BODY
Honeysuckle and a basket of fruit: orange, apples, bananas, and apricots	Mahogany	Thin

GENERAL	PALATE	
Fighting Cock is vaporous and boozy. It does open up nicely with water, releasing some apricot notes, but overall it's a little too oily and sweet.	Cinnamon, pepper, oak, and other spices; sweet finish.	
	PRICE	RATING
	$	

Four Roses

FOUR ROSES DISTILLERY

1224 HICKORY GROVE ROAD

LAWRENCEBURG, KY

TEL: 502-839-3436

www.fourrosesbourbon.com

BRANDS

FOUR ROSES BOURBON

FOUR ROSES LIMITED EDITION

    SMALL BATCH KENTUCKY

    STRAIGHT BOURBON WHISKEY

FOUR ROSES SINGLE BARREL

    KENTUCKY STRAIGHT BOURBON

    WHISKEY

Until recently, one of America's best and highest-volume bourbon distillers was also one of its least respected. For decades, Four Roses, located in Lawrenceburg, Kentucky, and then owned by Seagram, sold quality whiskey overseas, and bottom-shelf whiskey at home.

Things weren't always so: during the mid-twentieth century, Four Roses was the highest-selling bourbon in the United States. But in the 1950s its owner, Seagram, decided to curtail Four Roses' domestic sales and focus on the European and Asian markets. Seagram continued to produce a blended whiskey for the U.S. called Four Roses American, which made the brand name synonymous with Skid Row boozin'. It wasn't even made at its beautiful, Spanish Mission Style Four Roses Distillery in Kentucky, but at the Seagram plant in Lawrenceburg, Indiana (now owned by MGP Ingredients).

The bourbon was so popular in Japan that when Seagram went to sell the brand and its distillery in 2002, Kirin Holdings Company, best known for its beer, snatched it up. It immediately canceled Four Roses American and began creating new, high-quality bourbons for both American and overseas consumers.

Like Buffalo Trace, Four Roses uses two different mash bills:

Mash Bill B:

    60 percent corn

    35 percent rye

    5 percent barley

Mash Bill E:

    75 percent corn

    20 percent rye

    5 percent barley

But unique among big distillers, it also has five yeast strains, each of which imparts a different set of flavor notes:

Yeast Strain F: Herbal notes

Yeast Strain K: Powerful, spice

Yeast Strain O: Dark, rich fruits

Yeast Strain Q: Floral

Yeast Strain V: Light fruitiness

By combining these two mash bills and five strains, the distillery produces ten different recipes. Such variety allows Four Roses to quickly mix and match flavors, which explains how, in just a few years, it has managed to produce an impressive range of expressions. They include the flagship Yellow Label and a single barrel bourbon, begun in 2004, which according to Four Roses master distiller Jim Rutledge is the best-selling single-barrel bourbon in Kentucky. There's also a small batch bourbon, which debuted in 2006; two Japan-only expressions, Super Premium "Platinum" and Fine Old Bourbon "Black"; two barrel-strength anniversary editions (one marking the 120th birthday of the distillery, the other marking Rutledge's forty years in the bourbon business); and "Mariage," a perennially changing blend of some or all of its recipes.

Four Roses Bourbon

AGE
No age statement

PROOF
80

NOSE
All high notes, particularly banana and sweet tea, though a little water brings out some tobacco funk.

COLOR
Tawny

BODY
Light

GENERAL
A great starter whiskey. It's low proof and easy to drink, sweet, but well balanced, and not overly hot. Lighter cocktails pair quite well with Four Roses 80 proof.

PALATE
Very sweet, though not cloyingly so; there's a sourness, almost like a Lemonhead candy.

PRICE
$

RATING
★ ★

Four Roses
Small Batch Kentucky
Straight Bourbon
Whiskey ^{2012 RELEASE}

AGE		
No age statement		

PROOF
90

NOSE	COLOR	BODY
Hibiscus, grape jam, eucalyptus, honey, roasted nuts, and Now & Later candy	Russet/ tawny	Medium

GENERAL	PALATE
A truly great session bourbon; not too heavy and full of captivating notes. For those tracking these things, the 2012 expression is a marriage of five recipes.	Roasted almonds, honey, butter, and leather. The effect is like a spicy mead, especially on the finish.

PRICE	RATING
$$	

Four Roses
Single Barrel Kentucky
Straight Bourbon
Whiskey ^{WAREHOUSE QN; BARREL 60-1B}

AGE		
No age statement		

PROOF
100

NOSE	COLOR	BODY
Musty closet, strawberries, fruitcake, and cedar, with some menthol coming out with water.	Tawny/ auburn	Medium

GENERAL	PALATE
Wonderfully aromatic, it promises a bit more than it delivers on the palate. (Though bear in mind that Four Roses' single barrel releases vary significantly). In absolute terms, this is a solid whiskey with good depth that deserves experiencing.	Honey, vanilla, peach, and antiseptic. There's a long, black-pepper finish.

PRICE	RATING
$$	

Garrison Brothers

Garrison Brothers claim that their whiskey is the first "real, authentic straight bourbon whiskey made outside of Kentucky or Tennessee." What's more interesting, though, are their claims that the abundant Texas heat allows the whiskey, already sitting in fifteen-gallon barrels, to mature more quickly than the equivalent whiskey in fifty-three-gallon barrels sitting in a Bardstown rickhouse.

Its white corn and winter wheat, the latter grown on the distillers' farm, are combined with barley from the Pacific Northwest (the only non-local ingredient) and water from Garrison's own well. The whiskey is non-chill-filtered, which gives it an occasional cloudiness in the glass.

GARRISON BROTHERS

1827 HYE-ALBERT ROAD

HYE, TX 78635

TEL: 830-392-0246

EMAIL: dan@garrisonbros.com

www.garrisonbros.com

Garrison Brothers Texas Straight Bourbon Whiskey ^{BOTTLE 1216}

AGE	PROOF
2 years old	**94**

NOSE	COLOR	BODY
Spent mash, Play-Doh, and porridge	Mahogany	Thin to medium

GENERAL	PALATE
Garrison Brothers whiskey has been improving over the years, but it's not quite there yet. Like many of the new generation of craft whiskeys, this one tastes unfinished, with lots of cereal and wet grain notes and not enough of the complex qualities it might acquire from a few more years in the barrel.	Mid-palate spiciness, accompanied by rosemary and cereal; the finish is long, leaving a slight bitterness.

PRICE	RATING
$$$$	**NR**

George Dickel

GEORGE A. DICKEL & CO.

1950 CASCADE HOLLOW ROAD

TULLAHOMA, TN 37380

TEL: 931-857-4110

www.dickel.com

BRANDS

GEORGE DICKEL TENNESSEE SOUR
    MASH WHISKY BARREL SELECT

GEORGE DICKEL TENNESSEE SOUR
    MASH WHISKY

CASCADE HOLLOW

GEORGE DICKEL TENNESSEE SOUR
    MASH WHISKY NO. 8

GEORGE DICKEL TENNESSEE SOUR
    MASH WHISKY NO. 12

The perennial Tennessee also-ran to Jack Daniel's, George Dickel has, in fact, much older roots in the state. George Dickel was a German immigrant who came to America in 1844 and set up a merchant shop in Nashville, Tennessee. Like many nineteenth-century purveyors, Dickel bought whiskey from area distillers and bottled it under his own label, often re-distilling it before offering it for sale.

Dickel took the logical next step in 1884 and bought a controlling interest in one of his preferred sources, the Cascade Hollow Distillery, located in nearby Tullahoma. (The Dickel's website says George founded the distillery himself in 1870, but that story, according to whiskey expert Charles K. Cowdery, has been debunked). Four years later in 1088, Dickel fell from a horse and suffered career-ending injuries.

Dickel was among the first to chill-filter his whiskey, a process that removes certain oils and fatty acids that can make bourbon cloudy when poured over ice. This was once a big selling point, though today, many distillers proudly choose not to chill-filter, claiming that the oils and acids are important to a whiskey's taste.

Dickel was also a pioneer in the Lincoln County Process, by which sugar maple charcoal is used to filter out some of the whiskey's rough edges. Each distiller does it differently: Jack Daniel's drips whiskey through a charcoal-filled column, while Dickel puts its whiskey in a charcoal-filled vat and lets the two mingle for about a week. Use of the Lincoln County Process is, primarily, what separates a Tennessee whiskey from a bourbon whiskey.

After Dickel's death in 1894, his wife and in-laws continued to run the distillery and renamed it after the patriarch. In 1910 Tennessee went dry, and production of the brand moved first to Louisville, then to Frankfort, Kentucky, where it was made at the Stagg Distillery, today called Buffalo Trace. The Cascade brand survived Prohibition but was sold to whiskey giant Schenley Industries in 1937. By then the brand used an entirely different recipe, and it didn't go through the Lincoln County Process; indeed, advertisements from as late as the early 1950s trumpet "Geo. A. Dickel's 'Cascade' Kentucky Straight Bourbon Whiskey."

Schenley Industries reopened the Dickel Distillery in 1958, thanks to the labor of an employee named Ralph Dupps. Assuming the role of master distiller, Dupps concentrated on recreating Dickel's original recipes. Since Cascade was still being made in Kentucky, the new whiskey was called "George Dickel." The distillery originally released two expressions, Dickel No. 8 and Dickel No. 12, the primary difference being proof and age: 80 and 4 to 6 years, and 90 and 8 to 10 years, respectively. The ages are unofficial, and, thus, the bottles carry no age statement. The two share a very corn-heavy mash bill: 84 percent corn, 8 percent rye and 8 percent malted barley. Now owned by Diageo, Dickel has recently come out with two extensions on the brand: Dickel Barrel Select, a "small-batch" version of its standard product, and Cascade Hollow, a younger (three year old) derivation. Cascade Hollow carries an age statement because it's required of any "straight" whiskey aged under four years. Dickel created it after the distillery stopped making Dickel No. 8 in the early 2000s following years of overproduction and low consumer demand; though production restarted after demand for Dickel's products increased, the long lead time needed to bring a mature whiskey to market necessitated a younger, interim product. Hence Cascade Hollow.

George Dickel Tennessee Whisky Barrel Select

AGE
No age statement

PROOF
86

NOSE
High notes, with citrus, maraschino cherries, and apricot, along with acetone and salted peanuts

COLOR
Russet

BODY
Light

GENERAL
Decent wood and cereal notes combine nicely here with tangerine and vegetals. It's light and slightly sweet and certainly a good choice for a sour cocktail.

PALATE
Forward spice punch, woody and very sweet, with a soft thin mouthfeel. It finishes fast, but with a slight lingering bite.

PRICE
$$

RATING

George Dickel Tennessee Whisky Cascade Hollow

AGE
3 years old

PROOF
80

NOSE
Artificial candy notes, including bubblegum, cherry, and Flintstones' vitamins, along with some barley and Cheerios.

COLOR
Russet/tawny

BODY
Light

GENERAL
For an expression introduced as a stopgap measure during a drop in production, it's a surprisingly good whiskey: smooth, not overly sweet, and with some nice cherry and sour notes popping here and there.

PALATE
Pepper, cinnamon, and cherries, resolving in a sweet, slightly spicy finish.

PRICE
$

RATING
★↗

George Dickel Tennessee Whisky No. 8

AGE	No age statement
PROOF	**80**

NOSE	COLOR	BODY
Oatmeal and cherry	Auburn	Thin

GENERAL

Drinking George Dickel No. 8, I can't get away from the thought of Robitussin poured over corn-flakes. It's cloyingly medicinal with heaps of grain notes.

PALATE

Vanilla, mash/cereal, and a slight hint of watermelon water; long spicy finish.

PRICE	RATING
$	

George Dickel Tennessee Whisky No. 12

AGE	No age statement
PROOF	**90**

NOSE	COLOR	BODY
Caramel, geraniums, yeast, bananas, orange, and candy apple	Auburn	Light

GENERAL

No. 12 is a significant step up from No. 8. It's a fantastic iteration of the smooth Tennessee character, though, if that's not your thing, it will strike you as overly sweet.

PALATE

Muted spice and very sweet, with almond, cherry, and banana, resolving into a lingering, soft burn.

PRICE	RATING
$	

Hancock's President's Reserve

AGE INTERNATIONAL, INC.

229 WEST MAIN STREET, SUITE 202

FRANKFORT, KY 40601

TEL: 502-223-9874

E-MAIL: nknox@ageintl.com

PRODUCER

BUFFALO TRACE DISTILLERY

113 GREAT BUFFALO TRACE

FRANKFORT, KENTUCKY 40601

TEL: 800-654-8471

E-MAIL: info@buffalotrace.com

www.buffalotrace.com

Made by Buffalo Trace in Frankfort, Kentucky, and one of the brands owned by the Japanese company Age International, Hancock's Reserve is named after one of the earliest settler families that once occupied the site of the present-day distillery. Like the rest of the Age International whiskeys made at Buffalo Trace—including Blanton's, Elmer T. Lee, and Ancient Age—Hancock's is made with the distillery's Mash Bill #2, which has a higher rye content than most bourbons.

Hancock's President's Reserve Single Barrel Bourbon Whiskey

AGE
No age statement

PROOF
88.9

NOSE
Buttery, with wood, vanilla, apple cinnamon, bubble gum, and cloves

COLOR
Tawny

BODY
Medium and oily

GENERAL
Often lost amid the rush of great expressions on offer from Buffalo Trace, Hancock's is worth seeking out. It's well balanced and delivers a good load of spice. A fine after-dinner bourbon.

PALATE
A spice bomb on the palate, along with port, and grape-flavored chewing gum; finishes with a lingering mintiness.

PRICE
$$

RATING

Heaven Hill

Heaven Hill is the namesake bourbon of the Heaven Hill Distilleries, the largest independent spirits producer in the United States. Founded in 1934 by a group of investors along with the five Shapira brothers—David, Ed, Gary, George, and Mose—the company offers a wide range of products, including Christian Brothers Brandy and Two Fingers Tequila. But it is best known for its whiskeys. Its many well-regarded brands include Evan Wiliams, Elijah Craig, Bernheim, Rittenhouse, Larceny, and Old Fitzgerald. Heaven Hill also offers several less-estimable bottles, such as Cabin Still and Henry McKenna. In 2012 Heaven Hill released "Red State" and "Blue State" bourbon to mark the presidential election. Savvy consumers weren't fooled: they were both more or less repackaged Evan Williams. Whatever your political leanings, that's not a bad thing—Evan Williams is good whiskey.

Heaven Hill also produces whiskey for many private-label or "sourced" whiskeys; though its client list is a well-kept secret, whiskey aficionados suspect that some of the whiskey sold by Kentucky Bourbon Distillers (KBD) and Black Maple Hill originates at Heaven Hill.

For most of Heaven Hill's history, its master distiller has come from a member of the Beam family, starting with Joseph Beam, Jim Beam's first cousin and an original investor in the company. He was succeeded by his son, Harry, who in turn was succeeded by Earl Beam, a nephew of Jim Beam. He was followed by the current father-and-son team of Parker and Craig Beam. This lineage is completely separate from the Beam company, where a different line of the family dominates.

In 1996 a fire consumed the Heaven Hill Distillery in Bardstown, Kentucky. It was a scorcher; wrought-iron gas lamps were reduced to metallic puddles. The fire left the company bereft of both aging stock and production equipment. In a display of industry solidarity, Beam and Brown-Forman, two of Heaven Hill's biggest competitors, donated whiskey and space on their production lines until the ailing company could recover.

HEAVEN HILL DISTILLERIES
P.O. BOX 729
BARDSTOWN, KY 40004
TEL: 502-348-3921
www.heavenhill.com

In 1999, Heaven Hill bought the Bernheim Distillery near Louisville from Diageo and began production in the fall of 2000. Today all of Heaven Hill's whiskey is distilled at the Louisville plant, but it is aged and bottled in Bardstown at their old distillery site.

Below is a review of Heaven Hill's eponymous brand; other Heaven Hill products, such as Bernheim, Elijah Craig, and Evan Williams, are reviewed under their own names.

Heaven Hill Kentucky Straight Bourbon Whiskey

AGE
No age statement

PROOF
80

NOSE	COLOR	BODY
Herbaceous funk, with saltwater taffy	Russet	Light

	PALATE
Heaven Hill has a classic sour mash bourbon whiskey nose and it's a fine choice as a low-price mixer.	A pop of pepper and it's done; slightly medicinal finish.

PRICE	RATING
$	

Henry McKenna

This bourbon's label claims it is "Kentucky's Finest Table Whiskey." What makes a whiskey "table" ready is unclear; no other whiskey sports the term on its bottle (and really, all whiskey is fit for the table, unless you're under it). However, that's the motto adopted by the bourbon's eponymous creator, an Irish immigrant who opened his distillery in Fairfield, Kentucky in 1855. It folded, but the brand was later resurrected by Heaven Hill. Today it's aged for ten years and bottled at 100 proof.

HEAVEN HILL DISTILLERIES

P.O. BOX 729

BARDSTOWN, KY 40004

TEL: 502-348-3921

www.heavenhill.com

Henry McKenna Straight Bourbon Whiskey

AGE	PROOF
10 years old	**80**

NOSE	COLOR	BODY
Funky corn mash, toffee, salted peanuts, and banana bread	Chestnut	Thin

GENERAL	PALATE
This is a no-nonsense light whiskey with a healthy dollop of sweetness and wood.	Sugary candy, chardonnay, and a little tartness. The finish brings out a certain feinty edge.

PRICE	RATING
$	

High West

HIGH WEST DISTILLERY & SALOON

703 PARK AVENUE

PARK CITY, UT 84060

TEL: 435-649-8300

E-MAIL: david@highwest.com

www.highwest.com

....

PRODUCER

VARIOUS

....

BRANDS

BOURYE

DOUBLE RYE!

RENDEZVOUS

SON OF BOURYE

It's a shame that the word "blend" still carries such negative connotations in American whiskey circles. Blending is precisely what Park City, Utah's High West does, and does pretty well. The company, started in 2007 by a former biochemist named David Perkins, distills some of its own product, and has plans to expand its capacity significantly over the next few years. But its best whiskeys, like its Rendezvous Rye, are blends of expressions sourced from other distilleries. The value comes in High West's skill in mixing young and old whiskeys to produce something totally new (among others, Bourye, a combination of bourbon and rye).

Blending whiskeys from different distilleries is a mainstay in Scotland, but in the United States it's still frowned upon, perhaps because "blenders" used to be people who would combine very small amounts of decent whiskey with lesser stuff, neutral grain spirits, or water. Now a growing number of American distilleries are trying to import the blending art and give it a good name on these shores, with High West in the lead.

High West Whiskey Bourye
BOTTLE 128, BATCH 11613

AGE		
No age statement		

PROOF

92

NOSE	COLOR	BODY
Pepper, oak, lilacs, and bright fruits	Tawny	Medium and slightly chewy

GENERAL	PALATE
As the name implies, this is a blend of bourbon and rye whiskeys. But it's more rye than bourbon. A bit underwhelming, despite the evocative description—it simply doesn't come together like it should.	Cloves, cherry syrup, pecans, and sweet tea, tumbling into a rich, warm finish.

PRICE	RATING
$$	

High West Whiskey Double Rye! BATCH 12025, BOTTLE 1482

AGE		
No age statement		
PROOF		
92		

NOSE	COLOR	BODY
Funky, oaty, and herbaceous, with tobacco, geraniums, and barley	Deep gold	Light

GENERAL	PALATE	
Not the best High West release, but Double Rye! is solidly assembled, though its curious blend of herbal and oat notes will have fans and detractors in equal numbers.	Nutmeg, clove, cinnamon candy, and Juicy Fruit gum	
	PRICE	**RATING**
	$$	★ ★

High West Whiskey Rendezvous 12D04/20-47

AGE		
6 years old		
PROOF		
92		

NOSE	COLOR	BODY
Tennis shoe, barley, yeast, and smoker's breath, along with raisins and cereal	Deep copper	Light to medium

GENERAL	PALATE	
There's tons of funk in this whiskey. It's not for everyone, but adventurous scotch lovers should take note.	Rye and potato chips; it finishes with a little tobacco and white pepper	
	PRICE	**RATING**
	$$$	★ ★

High West Whiskey
Son of Bourye

AGE
No age
statement

PROOF
92

NOSE

Wood and jammy sweetness on the nose, as well as light pepper and dill

COLOR

Deep copper

BODY

Medium

GENERAL

Much more successful than its father, with more pronounced bourbon notes and a better balance between the bourbon and rye components,

PALATE

A little red and sweet pepper, mint, and green grass. There's a touch of cinnamon on the finish.

PRICE

$$$

RATING

Hillrock Estate

Located a few hours north of New York City in the Hudson River Valley, the Hillrock Estate Distillery is part of a trend toward "field to glass" production. The grains are all grown on site, the water comes from a nearby stream, and the malting is done on a purpose-built floor. Hillrock's first expression is its Solera-Aged Bourbon, with a high-rye (37 percent) mash bill. In the solera process, a barrel of aged whiskey is partially emptied and topped off with unaged spirit. After a few years, the process is repeated. Doing so not only speeds aging, but also produces a more consistent product. Solera aging is usually associated with sherry and Hillrock is one of the first American companies to use it for bourbon. After a period of aging, the bourbon is "finished" in twenty-year-old Oloroso sherry casks. This is a twist: many Oloroso sherries are matured in bourbon barrels.

HILLROCK ESTATE DISTILLERY
408 POOLES HILL ROAD
ANCRAM, NY 12502
TEL: 518-329-1023
E-MAIL: info@hillrockdistillery.com
www.hillrockdistillery.com

Hillrock Solera-Aged Bourbon

AGE	No age statement
PROOF	**92**

NOSE	COLOR	BODY
Meaty, with barley, maple, vanilla, perfume, and candied fruits	Auburn	Medium

GENERAL	PALATE
A beautiful whiskey, especially from such a young distillery. The dried fig notes come through clearly on the palate, and I could sniff the perfumed nose all day.	Clove, dried figs, toffee, spun sugar, resolving into curry and butterscotch.

PRICE	RATING
$$$$	★★★

Hirsch

PREISS IMPORTS/ANCHOR BREWERS
AND DISTILLERS
1705 MARIPOSA STREET
SAN FRANCISCO, CA 94107
TEL: 415-863-8350
E-MAIL: info@AnchorSF.com
www.anchordistilling.com

....

PRODUCER
UNKNOWN

....

BRANDS
HIRSCH SELECTION
HIRSCH 20 YEAR OLD

When you talk about the Hirsch label, you're really talking about two very different sets of expressions. The first is a legendary bourbon, a sixteen-year-old, pot-stilled whiskey made at the likewise legendary and completely extinct Michter's Distillery in Schaefferstown, Pennsylvania. Distilling at the Michter's plant went back to the eighteenth century, but reached its heyday between the Civil War and Prohibition, when it was called Bomberger. After World War II it opened again under new management, who brought in Charles Everett Beam, a descendant of Jacob Beam, the 1800s patriarch of the Beam family, as his master distiller. Beam started producing whiskey under the Michter's label, though the plant itself was called Ponnco.

In 1974 Adolf H. Hirsch, a retired executive at the liquor giant Schenley Industries, bought 400 barrels of whiskey from the distillery, aged it for sixteen- and twenty-year-old expressions, and bottled it under his name. The Pennco plant (renamed Michter's in 1975) shut down in 1988, making Mr. Hirsch's supply a dwindling treasure. The twenty year old is long since gone from this earth, save for the possibility of a few bottles lurking in a collector's basement, but the sixteen year old can still be found at high-end whiskey bars and bespoke auction houses.

Needless to say, these two whiskeys are not covered in this book. If you find them, you don't need a guidebook to tell you what to do.

The second set of Hirsch expressions have almost nothing to do with the first. After the success of the initial batch, the Hirsch brand was bought by Henry Preiss of Preiss Imports, a wine and spirits importer. In 2010, Preiss was incorporated into Anchor Brewers and Distillers, the same folks who make Anchor Steam beers and Old Potrero (see pages 217–218). Also brought into the fold was Berry Bros. and Rudd, a royally chartered wine merchant in London. Preiss put the Hirsch label on a still-expanding portfolio of whiskeys, ranging from an inexpensive small-batch bourbon to a twenty-five-year-old rye, a Canadian rye, and a four-year-old corn whiskey. In contrast to the original Hirsch, the new generation of offerings is sourced from an unnamed distillery. Of these, only the twenty year old and the small-batch bourbon are relatively easy to find.

Hirsch Selection Small Batch Reserve Kentucky Straight Bourbon Whiskey

AGE
No age statement

PROOF
92

NOSE
Cake batter, almond, butter, white pepper, and vanilla

COLOR
Auburn/ mahogany

BODY
Light

GENERAL
Oh so quick, this is an *amuse-bouche* of a whiskey. Taken together, it's like drinking a spicy birthday cake.

PALATE
Like sugary cereal, finishing in a flash of mint and pepper.

PRICE
$$

RATING
★ ★

Hirsch Selection Special Reserve American Whiskey

AGE
20
years old

PROOF
86

NOSE

Butterscotch, custard, and marzipan

COLOR

Tawny

BODY

Medium

GENERAL

The nose overwhelms with butterscotch notes, but the palate is surprisingly balanced. Still, for a superannuated bourbon, it has a strange profile, with none of the vanilla or stewed fruit one might hope for.

PALATE

Meat, spice, wood, and polish; finishes dry with almost no spice.

PRICE

$$$$

RATING

Hudson

A pioneer in East Coast craft distilling, Tuthilltown Spirits opened in 2001 just outside New Paltz, New York, under the guidance of Ralph Erenzo and Brian Lee. It was the first distillery to open in the state for decades, an event made possible in part by Erenzo's ceaseless lobbying in Albany to allow distilling in New York.

The whiskey, sold under the Hudson label and packaged in distinctive, squat 375 ml (12.68 oz) bottles, began appearing on shelves in the New York City region in 2006. Since then, it has more or less dominated its corner of the local whiskey market. The first expression released was Hudson's Baby Bourbon, a young, 100 percent corn whiskey; it was followed by a four-grain bourbon, a single malt, and the company's Manhattan Rye. They also offer an unaged Hudson Corn Whiskey, gin, vodka, and the occasional *eau de vie*.

In 2010 the Scottish whiskey company William Grant and Sons bought the Hudson label, but left production in the hands of Tuthilltown. Grant provides Tuthilltown with always-welcome financial resources, but more important, it brings the knowledge assets of a 140-year-old spirits company to bear on what is still essentially a startup outfit. Hudson has all the makings of a great future distillery, and hopefully Grant will help it get there.

TUTHILLTOWN SPIRITS

14 GRISTMILL LANE

GARDINER, NY 12525

TEL: 845-633-8734

E-MAIL: gable@tuthilltown.com

www.tuthilltown.com

BRANDS

HUDSON BABY BOURBON

HUDSON FOUR-GRAIN BOURBON

HUDSON MANHATTAN RYE

HUDSON SINGLE MALT

Hudson Baby Bourbon Whiskey BATCH 22, BOTTLE 2990

AGE
Less than **4** years old

PROOF
92

NOSE
Cereal, Nutter Butter cookies, a hint of marzipan, and oak

COLOR
Auburn/ mahogany

BODY
Thin

GENERAL
It's a young'un, and obviously so—aggressively grainy and herbaceous. The corn "make" on the palate is too strong, but the grassy finish is interesting.

PALATE
Vegetal, pencil eraser; finishes quickly, with cut grass.

PRICE
$$

RATING
NR

Hudson Four Grain Bourbon Whiskey BATCH 20, BOTTLE 2897

AGE
Less than **4** years old

PROOF
92

NOSE
Funk, sweet molasses, paint thinner, tumeric, and corn mash

COLOR
Tawny/ auburn

BODY
Thinnish

GENERAL
Much like the Baby Bourbon, the Four Grain is, well, grainy, full of breakfast cereal notes. It's also very sweet on the tongue and finish, with the addition of extreme feintiness.

PALATE
Sugar, grain, coffee, iodine and hay; the finish is quick, with a lingering spice and coffee-candy sweetness.

PRICE
$$$

RATING
NR

Hudson Manhattan Rye Whiskey

AGE
Less than
4
years old

PROOF
92

NOSE
Cereal, metal, very little floral or fruit

COLOR
Tawny

BODY
Medium

GENERAL
Heavy cereal dominates this drink with brassy and woody undertones. There is a slight hint of sherry in the finish that is appealing.

PALATE
Baseball glove, new shoe-rubber

PRICE
$$$

RATING
NR

Hudson Single Malt Whiskey

AGE
4
years old

PROOF
92

NOSE
Cereal, orange pekoe tea, salmon skin, oregano, and fermented fruits

COLOR
Tawny

BODY
Thin and oily

GENERAL
The American single-malt category is a difficult one for domestic distillers to master. Like the rest of the Hudson expressions, there is too much cereal on the nose and palate and in this case, a lingering sourness.

PALATE
Christmas spices, sour fruits, and cereal. It has a long, bitter finish.

PRICE
$$$

RATING
NR

Jack Daniel's

BROWN-FORMAN

850 DIXIE HIGHWAY

LOUISVILLE, KY 40210

TEL: 502-585-1100

E-MAIL: Brown-Forman@b-f.com

www.brown-forman.com

PRODUCER

JACK DANIEL DISTILLERY

182 LYNCHBURG HIGHWAY

LYNCHBURG, TN 37352

TEL: 931-759-6357

www.jackdaniels.com

BRANDS

JACK DANIEL'S OLD NO. 7 (BLACK
    LABEL)

JACK DANIEL'S (GREEN LABEL)

GENTLEMAN JACK

JACK DANIEL'S SINGLE BARREL
    SELECT

Jack Daniel's is easily the most iconic U.S. whiskey around the world and far and away the best-selling whiskey in America. Not bad for a spirit that until the 1950s was hardly known outside Tennessee and a certain rarified set of Hollywood high-rollers.

Jasper Newton Daniel, known as "Jack" for as long as anyone could remember, was born in the late 1840s; where and precisely when is unknown, since his birth records were reportedly destroyed in a courthouse fire. He registered his eponymous distillery in 1875 in Lynchburg, Tennessee.

Charcoal-filtering spirits was popular at the time, and to set his whiskey apart, Daniel dripped his unaged whiskey through ten feet of sugar maple charcoal, a process that took inordinately long, but produced an exceptionally smooth drink.

Daniel died from sepsis in 1911, supposedly from an infected toe that he injured after kicking his safe one morning. Ownership of the distillery passed to his nephew, Lem Motlow (Daniel had no children). When Tennessee went dry in 1909, production moved to nearby states, and didn't return until 1938, when Motlow, by then a state senator, had the ban on distilling overturned. The distillery spent no money on advertising, but it developed a cult following among the likes of Frank Sinatra, William Faulkner, and Winston Churchill.

The company and its flagship whiskey, Old No. 7, were well positioned when they were bought by the liquor giant Brown-Forman in 1956. With sudden access to what must have seemed like an inexhaustible advertising budget, Jack Daniel's took off. Over the next two decades it sales grew by ten percent annually, even as American whiskey sales dropped. From 1973 to 1986 sales nearly tripled.

Jack Daniel's, still located in the "dry" Moore County, is one of the few distilleries that doesn't double distill its whiskey, a long-held tradition in the South. It does, however, sell more than one expression these days: along with the traditional, black-labeled Old No. 7, there's Gentleman Jack, which is charcoal filtered twice, once before and once after it's aged; there is also a Single Barrel expression and the younger, Green Label.

Jack Daniel's has twice lowered the proof on its flagship Old No. 7, from 90 to 86 in 1987 and again to 80 in 2002, putting it in line with most other whiskeys in its class.

Jack Daniel's Old No. 7 Tennessee Whiskey BLACK LABEL

AGE No age statement		
PROOF **80**		
NOSE Floral with orange peel and salted peanuts	**COLOR** Tawny/ auburn	**BODY** Light
GENERAL Jack Daniel's is ice-rink smooth and consistently hits its classic Tennessee whiskey mark. Muted spice and chocolate notes combine with serious sweetness to make this one of the most popular whiskeys in the world.	**PALATE** Spice and some chocolate; quick finish.	
	PRICE $	**RATING**

Jack Daniel's No. 7 Tennessee Whiskey GREEN LABEL

AGE
No age statement

PROOF
80

NOSE	COLOR	BODY
Pineapple, melons, honeysuckle, and powdered sugar	Russet/tawny	Light to medium

GENERAL	PALATE
Not much going on: it's very light and sugar-pack sweet. It's a weaker, lighter-bodied version of the standard Jack Daniel's No. 7.	Blandly sweet, with a hit of corn

PRICE	RATING
$	

Gentleman Jack Rare Tennessee Whiskey

AGE
No age statement

PROOF
80

NOSE	COLOR	BODY
Maple syrup, candy corn, banana, and a hint of melon	Tawny	Thin

GENERAL	PALATE
This thick-bodied drink is almost liqueur-like with strong maple syrup overtones.	Maple syrup and white pepper

PRICE	RATING
$$	

Jack Daniel's Single Barrel Select Tennessee Whiskey L-07, 11-4835/BOTTLED 9/20/11

AGE	PROOF
No age statement	**94**

NOSE
Melons and marzipan, ground nuts, grilling spices, stewed fruit, and a touch of wood.

COLOR
Auburn

BODY
Medium to thick

GENERAL
The best of what Jack Daniel's has to offer, Barrel Select is complex, fiery, and full of interesting flavor. The balance tips toward sweetness, but in a satisfying after-dinner drink sort of way, despite the curiously bitter finish.

PALATE
Peppery heat, port, macadamia nuts, and cloves; finish is sour, surprisingly bitter and numbing.

PRICE
$$

RATING
★ ★

Jefferson's

CASTLE BRANDS

122 EAST 42ND STREET, SUITE 4700

NEW YORK, NY 10168

TEL: 646-356-0200

E-MAIL: info@castlebrandsinc.com

www.castlebrandsinc.com

PRODUCER: UNKNOWN

BRANDS

JEFFERSON'S KENTUCKY STRAIGHT
BOURBON WHISKEY VERY SMALL
BATCH

JEFFERSON'S RESERVE VERY OLD
KENTUCKY STRAIGHT BOURBON
WHISKY VERY SMALL BATCH

JEFFERSON'S STRAIGHT RYE
WHISKEY

JEFFERSON'S PRESIDENTIAL SELECT
18 YEAR BOURBON

How's this for confusing: Jefferson's is a brand of whiskeys owned by McLain & Kyne, which in turn is owned by Castle Brands—none of which actually makes the underlying whiskey. It is, instead, "sourced" from unnamed producers. Like the High West Distillery in Park City, Utah, Jefferson's claims its competitive edge as a blender, not a distiller.

The exception is the current expression of Jefferson's Presidential Select, which is made from stock produced by the long-defunct Stitzel-Weller Distillery. (McLain & Kyne used to own the Sam Houston brand, but sold it a few years ago to Western Spirits.)

In 2012 the company released an extremely limited expression of "ocean-aged" bourbon, which spent four years in barrels about a seagoing research ship. McLain & Kyne claims that the rocking motion of the ocean, the fluctuating temperatures at sea and the salty air made the whiskey age almost five times as fast as it would under normal conditions. Only 600 bottles were released, though the company says to expect more to come in what it's calling its "ridiculously small batch" series soon.

Jefferson's is one of the most consistently great brands on the shelf. Like Michter's or Elijah Craig, there are no misses in this portfolio. Every bottle is a winner.

Jefferson's Kentucky Straight Bourbon Whiskey _{BATCH NO. 182/BOTTLE NO. 1895}

AGE		
No age statement		

PROOF
82.3

NOSE	COLOR	BODY
Apricot jam, vanilla, oranges, and flaky pie crust	Chestnut/oloroso	Light to medium

GENERAL	PALATE
This is Jefferson's basic offering, but it could stand up against many superpremium whiskeys. It wavers beautifully between floral and fruit notes. I'd recommend it for an after-dinner pour.	Lemon and butter, sliding into an abrupt, slightly bitter finish.

PRICE	RATING
$$	

Jefferson's Reserve Very Old Kentucky Straight Bourbon Whiskey _{BATCH NO. 96/BOTTLE NO. 1299}

AGE		
No age statement		

PROOF
90.2

NOSE	COLOR	BODY
Pine, almond, caramel, and cereal	Auburn	Medium

GENERAL	PALATE
The nose is redolent of pine, almond, caramel, and cereal; the palate and finish are like an Atomic Fireball, spicy as all get out with a sweet candy edge.	Cinnamon candy

PRICE	RATING
$$	

Jefferson's Straight Rye Whiskey BATCH NO 17/BOTTLE NO. 2150

AGE	**10** years old
PROOF	**94**

NOSE	COLOR	BODY
Bright fruit and floral notes, mixed with some peat, smoky wood, and moss.	Russet	Medium

GENERAL

One of the best ryes on the market. All the requisite notes are here, mixed with some interesting, almost scotch-like dark fruit tones, particularly on the nose. Produced in Canada, Jefferson's rye is a model dual-citizenship whiskey.

PALATE

Raspberries and fruit juice, finishing with pepper, mint, and campfire smoke.

PRICE	RATING
$$	

Jefferson's Presidential Select Kentucky Straight Bourbon Whiskey BATCH NO. 30/BOTTLE NO. 1235

AGE	**18** years old
PROOF	**94**

NOSE	COLOR	BODY
Cherries and other dark fruit, oak, vanilla, mint, maple sugar, and cereal	Mahogany	Full and chewy

GENERAL

Drinking this is like spinning a greatest hits of bourbon album—dark stone fruits, wood, vanilla, cloves, sherry, and a faint touch of bitterness on the finish to counter the sweetness. It should be a federal crime to mix it with anything save a few drops of water.

PALATE

Cake batter, plum sauce, cloves, and sherry; the end is a bit bitter, and full of spice.

PRICE	RATING
$$$$	

Jim Beam

Easily one of the world's most recognized whiskeys, Beam is also the fourth-largest spirits company in the world. It produces a wide range of products, but its bourbons and rye are its signature products, and its roots.

Though the company's namesake was born in 1864, the Beam family's background in distilling goes back at least to Jacob Beam, who moved from Maryland to Kentucky in the late 1780s. By the 1790s, Beam was well known for his whiskey, which was called Old Jake Beam. Beam died sometime in the early 1830s—recordkeeping on what was then the frontier was pretty spotty—but his distillery stayed in the family.

Just before the Civil War, the distillery moved to Nelson County, Kentucky, to take advantage of nearby rail lines. Between Jacob Beam's death and the end of Prohibition, it went through a variety of names, from the original Old Tub to David M. Beam and Co. to Beam and Hart to Clear Springs to eventually, the James B. Beam Co., later shortened to simply Beam. After spending time as a subsidiary of the conglomerate Fortune Brands, Beam is now publicly owned and listed on the New York Stock Exchange.

But who was Jim Beam? Born at the end of the Civil War, young Jim took over the company at just twenty-four years old. He drove the company for nearly sixty years, through Prohibition and two world wars. He not only defined the Jim Beam brand, but along with men like E.H. Taylor, he played a seminal role in defining the standards and characteristics of modern bourbon. Perhaps even more impressive is the legacy of the Beam family offspring: from 1995 to 2003, at least thirty descendants of Jacob Beam have worked as master distillers at various southern whiskey makers.

Beam died in 1947, and so didn't live to see his company's explosive growth during the 1950s. In a single year, between 1952 and 1953, its sales rose thirty percent. The company, now based in Clermont, Kentucky, expanded rapidly, and pushed into export markets in Europe and Asia.

BEAM INC.

510 LAKE COOK ROAD

DEERFIELD, IL 60015

TEL: 847-948-8888

www.beamglobal.com

BRANDS

JIM BEAM KENTUCKY STRAIGHT
    BOURBON WHISKEY

JIM BEAM BLACK DOUBLE AGED

JIM BEAM STRAIGHT RYE WHISKEY

JIM BEAM DEVIL'S CUT
    BOURBON WHISKEY

Though often portrayed as a second-tier product, Jim Beam's basic white label is a fine standby in any liquor cabinet, and its small-batch and specialty offerings stand up well against much more expensive expressions.

Jim Beam Brands isn't known for taking risks with edgy new products, so the 2011 introduction of Devil's Cut caught many by surprise. The name is a play on the term "angels' share," or the amount of whiskey that a barrel loses to evaporation. The Devil's Cut, according to Jim Beam, is the corollary loss absorbed by the wood. This whiskey, then, is an effort to reclaim those precious fluids.

The distillery starts with barrels of six-year-old bourbon, which it empties and refills with about two gallons of water. The barrels are agitated for thirty minutes, during which time the water purportedly pulls out some of the residual alcohol in the wood. The resulting combination is used in place of spring water to bring the barrel-proof whiskey down to its bottled 90 proof.

Jim Beam Kentucky Straight Bourbon Whiskey

AGE	**4** years old
PROOF	**80**

NOSE	COLOR	BODY
Cherry candy, oak, roses, barley and tobacco	Russet	Light

GENERAL	PALATE
Jim Beam has a distinctive set of notes—cherry, high floral, and black pepper—thanks to the relatively high rye content in the mash bill. It's a classic mixer.	Peppery and balanced, with a long, plummy finish

PRICE	RATING
$	

Jim Beam Kentucky Straight Rye Whiskey

AGE	
4	
years old	

PROOF	
80	

NOSE	COLOR	BODY
Cola, cedar, menthol, pepper, and spun sugar	Auburn	Thin

GENERAL	PALATE
For a well-known rye, this isn't especially heavy on the rye notes. It finds a welcome home in mixed drinks.	Spicy but one-dimensional

PRICE	RATING
$	★⯨

Jim Beam Black Double Aged Kentucky Straight Bourbon Whiskey

AGE	
8	
years old	

PROOF	
86	

NOSE	COLOR	BODY
Orange, honey, barley, and Willy Wonka grape	Russet/ tawny	Light to medium

GENERAL	PALATE
Overall, it's surprisingly sparkling—not effervescent, but nearly so. It's sweet but not cloying. If you're going to go Beam for neat sipping, go with the Double Aged.	Cinnamon and apple juice

PRICE	RATING
$	★★

Jim Beam Devil's Cut Kentucky Straight Bourbon Whiskey

AGE
No age statement

PROOF
90

NOSE
Flowers, pencil shavings, butter, and citrus fruits

COLOR
Deep copper

BODY
Light to medium

GENERAL
Aside from the novelty (which is mostly in the story, not the tasting experience), there's no reason to choose it over the standard Jim Beam White Label.

PALATE
Candied fruit, jam, wood, vanilla, and apple

PRICE
$$

RATING

John B. Stetson

For a whiskey born to support a marketing campaign, this isn't bad stuff. The John B. Stetson in the name is, indeed, the famous hat company, the same one that hit it big a few decades back with cologne and, thanks to some hilarious but apparently effective ads, Lady Stetson perfume, as well.

The John B. Stetson brand is overseen by Vision Wine and Spirits, a New Jersey company that sources the actual production to an unnamed Kentucky distillery. It's a four-year-old, four-grain bourbon, bottled at 84 proof.

VISION WINE AND SPIRITS
700 PLAZA DRIVE, 2ND FLOOR
SECAUCUS, NJ 07094
TEL: 201 210 0400
E-MAIL: info@visionwineandspirits.com
www.visionwineandspirits.com

PRODUCER: UNKNOWN

John B. Stetson Kentucky Straight Bourbon Whiskey

AGE
No age statement

PROOF
84

NOSE
Maple, banana cream, cherry, and stewed fruit

COLOR
Deep copper

BODY
Thinnish

GENERAL
If the bourbon's corporate, millinery provenance disturbs you, it's unlikely you're alone. But if you can cut through the mists of marketing, this is a good drink. Not great, but good, which is infinitely better than you would expect.

PALATE
Vague spice, finishes quickly.

PRICE
$$

RATING
★ ★

John J. Bowman

A. SMITH BOWMAN DISTILLERY

1 BOWMAN DRIVE

FREDERICKSBURG, VA 22408

TEL: 540-373-4555

E-MAIL: info@asmithbowman.com

www.asmithbowman.com

BRANDS

BOWMAN BROTHERS VIRGINIA
    STRAIGHT BOURBON WHISKEY

JOHN J. BOWMAN VIRGINIA STRAIGHT
    BOURBON WHISKEY

Until recently, Bowman was Virginia's only commercial distillery. After making a fortune running a bus company in Indiana, Abram Smith Bowman retired in 1934 to a plot of farmland in Reston, Virginia, just outside Washington, D.C. and founded his distillery. When the elder Bowman passed, management was taken over by his sons, Smith and DeLong Bowman. Smith was known for giving out specially made bottles of the company's Virginia Gentleman Bourbon at his annual Princeton class reunions—the label featured a dapper Princeton man being served his drink by a lowly Yalie waiter. The company moved from Reston to Fredericksburg, Virginia in 1988.

For years the company's sole product was Virginia Gentleman, a decent if not stellar lower-shelf whiskey. In 2003 the Sazerac Company of New Orleans bought the distillery and moved primary production to its Buffalo Trace facility.

Today the whiskey is double distilled in Kentucky, then shipped to Bowman where it is distilled a third time and then aged. Bowman also makes rum, vodka, and gin.

Bowman Brothers Small Batch Virginia Straight Bourbon Whiskey

AGE
No age statement

PROOF
90

NOSE
Gardenias, rose hips, and orange blossom, along with cumin and pepper

COLOR
Tawny

BODY
Medium and chewy

GENERAL
A medium-bodied, strong-backed bourbon. Yet it has a gentle side, too, with floral notes on the nose and palate.

PALATE
Hot, black tea, banana, high floral notes, with a medium, spicy finish

PRICE
$$

RATING

John J. Bowman Single Barrel Virginia Straight Bourbon Whiskey

AGE
No age statement

PROOF
100

NOSE
Cola, caramel, sherry, marzipan, stewed fruits, and nuts

COLOR
Tawny

BODY
Light

GENERAL
Delicious! This spirit evokes the wood and honeyed elegance of a rare-books room.

PALATE
Cherry and sherry, lingering peppercorn spice

PRICE
$$$

RATING

Johnny Drum

KENTUCKY BOURBON DISTILLERS

1869 LORETTO ROAD

BARDSTOWN, KY, 40004

TEL 502-348-0081

E-MAIL: kentuckybourbon@bardstown.com

www.kentuckybourbonwhiskey.com

....

PRODUCER: UNKNOWN

....

BRANDS

JOHNNY DRUM KENTUCKY

    STRAIGHT BOURBON WHISKEY

    (GREEN LABEL)

JOHNNY DRUM KENTUCKY

    STRAIGHT BOURBON WHISKEY

    (BLACK LABEL)

JOHNNY DRUM KENTUCKY

    STRAIGHT BOURBON WHISKEY

    PRIVATE STOCK

Like all of the whiskeys from Kentucky Bourbon Distillers (KBD), Johnny Drum is a crowd-pleasing mystery. Because KBD gets all its whiskey from elsewhere, then bottles it at its Bardstown facility, the original source is unknown (that will change in a few years, as KBD now has a distillery up and running). All KBD whiskeys are above average yet broadly accessible; people who don't like whiskey tend to like their stuff (people who like whiskey do, too).

Johnny Drum bourbons, particularly the Green Label, fill two roles in a bar: they are gentle and accessible enough to offer the newbie or the non-whiskey drinker, but they also have enough backbone to serve as a good standby cocktail mixer.

Johnny Drum Kentucky Straight Bourbon Whiskey GREEN LABEL

NOSE Grassy, with cereal and bright fruit notes	**COLOR** Deep copper	**BODY** Light

AGE **4** years old	
PROOF **86**	

GENERAL A great starter whiskey, not overly complex or particularly harsh, but not boring, either. It mixes well, but it's also built for several rounds of straight drinking.	**PALATE** Woody, caramel, and stone fruits	
	PRICE $	**RATING**

Johnny Drum Kentucky Straight Bourbon Whiskey BLACK LABEL

AGE 4 years old		
PROOF 80		

NOSE	COLOR	BODY
Vanilla, butterscotch, and halva	Russet	Thin

GENERAL	PALATE
Not as well-balanced as the Johnny Drum Green Label; it's sweeter and funkier and not quite as smooth.	Hit of spice and cereal before finishing abruptly

PRICE $ **RATING** ★★

Johnny Drum Private Stock Kentucky Bourbon

AGE No age statement
PROOF 101

NOSE	COLOR	BODY
Apple, rose, freshly cut oak, and geranium	Russet	Light to medium

GENERAL	PALATE
Strong and hot, there's some wood and fruit depth in this drink. A goodly amount of water is recommended.	Oak and cherry, hidden under a lot of fire.

PRICE $$ **RATING** ★★

Kentucky Gentleman

BARTON 1792 DISTILLERY

300 BARTON ROAD

BARDSTOWN, KY 40004

TEL: 502-348-3991

www.1792bourbon.com

Kentucky Gentleman, made by Sazerac at its Barton 1792 Distillery, only barely counts as a bourbon: it is made from a blend of 51 percent straight bourbon and 49 percent grain alcohol ("spirits from the finest grains," according to the label); under federal law, this means it can still call itself a bourbon with a straight face. How it sleeps at night is a different question.

Kentucky Gentleman Kentucky Bourbon Whiskey

AGE
No age statement

PROOF
80

NOSE
Nougat and caramel, with a slight feint and polish

COLOR
Deep gold

BODY
Thin

GENERAL
There's not much here. Kentucky Gentleman is a ghost of a bourbon. It offers a vague sweetness and then absolutely nothing—zero impression on the palate.

PALATE
Hit of spice, some lingering mint

PRICE
$

RATING
NR

Kentucky Tavern

Kentucky Tavern was the flagship whiskey of the late, great Glenmore Distilling Company, run for nearly a century by the Thompson family of Louisville. While Kentucky Tavern remained at the center of the business, the company created or acquired numerous other brands, including Yellowstone, Ezra Brooks, and Fleischmann's, a low-end bourbon sold mostly in the northern Midwest. In 1991 the Thompsons finally sold their controlling stake in Glenmore to Guinness, which then merged into the spirit giant Diageo and sold Kentucky Tavern to Barton Brands. Along the way, Barton moved production of Kentucky Tavern to the Tom Moore Distillery in Bardstown. The brand eventually fell under Sazerac's control when the New Orleans company bought most of Barton's brands, and the distillery, where Kentucky Tavern and other whiskey is still made. Oh, and Sazerac renamed the Tom Moore plant the Barton 1792 Distillery.

And yet, for all that, Kentucky Tavern today is a bottom-shelf whiskey; note the similarity in packaging to Kentucky Gentleman, another bargain-basement bourbon. Unlike Kentucky Gentleman, Kentucky Tavern is pure bourbon, not a blend of bourbon and grain alcohol. Kentucky Tavern used to be sold as a bottled-in-bond, 100 proof expression, but today is a mere 80 proof.

BARTON 1792 DISTILLERY
300 BARTON ROAD
BARDSTOWN, KY 40004
TEL: 502-348-3991
www.1792bourbon.com

Kentucky Tavern Straight Bourbon Whiskey

AGE	No age statement
PROOF	**80**

NOSE	COLOR	BODY
Candy apples, mown grass, and a whiff of almond	Deep gold	Thin

GENERAL	PALATE	
Like the similarly named Kentucky Gentleman, Kentucky Tavern is a standard bar bourbon that makes a decent mixer.	Honey and pepper	
	PRICE	RATING
	$	**NR**

Kentucky Vintage

KENTUCKY BOURBON DISTILLERS

1869 LORETTO ROAD

BARDSTOWN, KY, 40004

TEL 502-348-0081

E-MAIL: kentuckybourbon@bardstown.com

www.kentuckybourbonwhiskey.com

PRODUCER: UNKNOWN

Kentucky Vintage is the hardest to find of the four "small batch" bourbons from Kentucky Bourbon Distillers (KBD), the others being Noah's Mill, Rowan's Creek, and Pure Kentucky XO. The company makes several other brands, such as the Johnny Drum expressions and Willett, but the four small batch bourbons form a fine tetrarchy—similar in taste profiles and, probably, age (though the company doesn't reveal just how old they are). As with all KBD products, at least for now, Kentucky Vintage is sourced, i.e., it is bought from another distiller and bottled at the KBD facility in Bardstown.

Kentucky Vintage Bourbon

AGE	PROOF
No age statement	**90**

NOSE	COLOR	BODY
Cherries, caramel, and vanilla	Amber	Light

GENERAL	PALATE
Is there a rule that whiskeys with Kentucky in the name must be underwhelming? Kentucky Vintage is better than the others with a classic bourbon nose and mild spice in the finish. Don't confuse this brand with Kentucky Bourbon Distillers' Vintage Rye and Vintage Bourbon (see pages 260–261).	Hit of spice, some lingering mint

PRICE	RATING
$$	

Kings County

Among the first of the new wave of Brooklyn distilleries, Kings County opened in the northeast corner of the borough in 2010, then moved a few years later to the Brooklyn Navy Yard. The new site features a small garden where the distillers raise some of the grain that goes into their liquors, as well as a "boozeum" that documents Brooklyn's alcohol-soaked past.

KINGS COUNTY DISTILLERY

BROOKLYN NAVY YARD, BLDG 121

63 FLUSHING AVENUE, BOX 379

BROOKLYN, NY 11205

E-MAIL: info@kingscountydistillery.com

www.kingscountydistillery.com

Kings County Bourbon Whiskey

AGE	PROOF
No age statement	**90**

NOSE
Oak, corn mash, sherry, candy sugar, almond; water brings out acetone and baker's chocolate.

COLOR
Deep copper

BODY
Medium to full

GENERAL
Kings County has an odd, though not unpleasant, profile for a young bourbon. It has none of the usual floral, fruit or spice notes; instead, it's all candy and grain. It's a good whiskey for such a young distillery, but not nearly good enough to justify costing more than $25 for just 200 ml (6.76 oz). Price-per-ounce, it's about twice the cost of Blanton's.

PALATE
Barley, mushrooms, sherry, vegetal; finishes quickly, with a slight bitterness.

PRICE
$$$

RATING

Knob Creek

BEAM INC.

510 LAKE COOK ROAD

DEERFIELD, IL 60015

TEL: 847-948-8888

www.beamglobal.com

....

BRANDS

KNOB CREEK SMALL BATCH
    BOURBON

KNOB CREEK SINGLE BARREL
    BOURBON

KNOW CREEK RYE WHISKEY

Illinois may be the Land of Lincoln, but as we all learned in middle-school history class, Honest Abe was born in Kentucky. In honor of the sixteenth president's Bluegrass heritage, Jim Beam named one of its first small-batch whiskeys after the farm where he recalled his earliest memories: Knob Creek. Though today it is officially one of the four whiskeys in the company's Small Batch Bourbon Collection (the others are Baker's, Booker's, and Basil Hayden), Knob Creek is really a portfolio unto itself. Along with the standard, 100-proof small batch, Beam recently released a single barrel and a rye expression.

Before that, though, Knob Creek disappeared for a little while. In early 2009, Beam announced it was facing a shortage of the whiskey, thanks to an underestimation of demand nine years previously, when the whiskey went into its barrels. Beam turned the shortage to its advantage by making it the center of an advertising campaign: "Thanks for Nothing," with ads showing an empty bottle of Knob Creek. The bottles returned to the shelves later that year.

Knob Creek Small Batch Kentucky Straight Bourbon Whiskey

AGE **9** years old		
PROOF **100**		

NOSE	COLOR	BODY
Apricot, apples, and toast	Tawny/ auburn	Full and chewy

GENERAL	PALATE
Haters can hate on this mass-produced "small batch" whiskey, but Knob Creek is high-quality stuff. There's nothing particularly surprising in its overall qualities; it's just a well-executed bourbon. And that's really saying something.	Grilled meat and chili pepper, with a long, cinnamon finish

PRICE	RATING
$$	

Knob Creek Single Barrel Reserve Kentucky Straight Bourbon Whiskey

AGE	**9** years old
PROOF	**120**

NOSE	COLOR	BODY
Caramel, hot wings, geraniums, and fruit cake	Tawny/ auburn	Full and smooth

GENERAL	PALATE
A little too aggressive to be called a classic, like its "small batch" *confrere*, but this is still a top-notch whiskey. Look for the leather notes on the palate—a nice, unique touch.	Oak, leather, and chilis, resolving in a long, burning finish

PRICE	RATING
$$	

Knob Creek Rye Whiskey Small Batch

AGE	**9** years old
PROOF	**100**

NOSE	COLOR	BODY
High floral, cola, vegetal	Russet	Medium

GENERAL	PALATE
A standard and not particularly interesting rye, though Knob Creek is a step up from Beam's basic rye offering.	Spice, medicinal

PRICE	RATING
$$	

Koval

KOVAL DISTILLERY

4241 NORTH RAVENSWOOD AVENUE

CHICAGO, IL 60613

TEL: 312-878-7988

E-MAIL: info@koval-distillery.com

www.kovaldistillery.com

....

BRANDS

KOVAL SINGLE BARREL

RYE WHISKEY

KOVAL SINGLE BARREL

WHEAT WHISKEY

KOVAL SINGLE BARREL

OAT WHISKEY

KOVAL SINGLE BARREL

SPELT WHISKEY

KOVAL SINGLE BARREL

MILLET WHISKEY

Founded in 2008 by Robert and Sonat Birnecker, two former academics, Koval is the first licensed distillery in Chicago since Prohibition—which is amazing, given how large the Chicago distilling industry was before 1920. Like Charbay and Clear Creek on the West Coast, Koval leans heavily on European distilling traditions, focused on making small batches of high-quality grain and fruit liquors. One of the company's hallmarks is the use of exotic (to Americans) grains in its whiskeys, such as, millet and spelt. Until 2013, Koval bottled several whiskeys under the Lion's Pride brand, but has since consolidated both the brand and range—its spelt and wheat whiskeys, once part of its regular portfolio, are now restricted to limited-edition runs.

Koval Single Barrel Rye Whiskey

AGE		
Less than **2** years old		

PROOF		
80		

NOSE	COLOR	BODY
Floral; dark: funky	Pale straw	Light

GENERAL	PALATE	
A good display of the rye spirit. Overall, a very well-made rye whiskey.	Fruit and floral	

PRICE	RATING
$$$	★ ★

Koval Wheat Whiskey

AGE		
Less than **2** years old		

PROOF		
80		

NOSE	COLOR	BODY
High fruit notes	Pale straw	Thin

GENERAL	PALATE	
A delicate, subtle whiskey, and a fine expression of wheat's potential.	Fruity; crème brulee	

PRICE	RATING
$$$	★

Koval Single Barrel Oat Whiskey

AGE
Less than
2
years old

PROOF
80

NOSE	COLOR	BODY
Butter and flowers	Pale straw	Light

GENERAL	PALATE	
Unique and very pleasant. Oat will never be a significant lead actor in the play that is American whiskey, but Koval has shown that it can perform an important supporting role.	Fruit, cream, and spice	

PRICE
$$$

RATING
★

Koval Spelt Whiskey

AGE
Less than
2
years old

PROOF
80

NOSE	COLOR	BODY
Wet mammal, industrial solvent, and fenugreek	Pale straw	Thin

GENERAL	PALATE
If you like spelt bread, you'll love this. If not, avoid it. The pasty chemical edge will turn off ninety-nine percent of drinkers, while the fractional percent will be reminded of grandma's house and cry for more.	Chemical and flour paste

PRICE
$$$

RATING
NR

Koval Single Barrel Millet Whiskey

AGE
Less than
2
years old

PROOF
80

NOSE
Overwhelming funk

COLOR
Amber

BODY
Light

GENERAL
Truly bizarre—it smells and tastes like a piece of wheat toast soaked in grain alcohol. This is an interesting experiment using alternative grains, and, perhaps worth trying by the stout of heart. All others, stay away.

PALATE
Stone fruits

PRICE
$$$

RATING
★

Larceny

HEAVEN HILL DISTILLERIES

P.O. BOX 729

BARDSTOWN, KY 40004

TEL: 502-348-3921

www.heavenhill.com

Until recently, Heaven Hill produced two whiskeys built around wheat: Bernheim and Old Fitzgerald. Then in 2012, to much acclaim, came Larceny, a robust "wheater," aged from six to twelve years and bottled at 92 proof.

The story behind Larceny, and the keyhole symbol on its label, goes like this: back in the day at the Old Judge Distillery in Frankfort, there was a U.S. Treasury agent named Fitzgerald who reportedly had a preternatural sense for the best barrels of whiskey—and a key to the rickhouses. Whiskey would disappear, bit by bit, and for a while no one knew where it was going. True story? Maybe. But it's the genesis of Larceny and Old Fitzgerald (see page 208) whiskey brands.

Larceny Kentucky Straight Bourbon Whiskey

AGE		
6 years old		
PROOF		
92		

NOSE	COLOR	BODY
Salted caramel, lavender, geranium, and barbeque potato chips	Russet	Light

GENERAL	PALATE	
Larceny is a decent wheated bourbon whiskey with a very light touch. Try it straight without ice or water; it doesn't hold up to well to dilution.	Peppery, juicy, soap; finishes long, with cinnamon and spearmint	
	PRICE	**RATING**
	$$	★★

Leopold Bros.

Todd and Scott Leopold, founders and owners of the eponymous distillery in Denver, Colorado, are among the most successful of the latest generation of small distillers. Since opening their doors in 2008, they have: a) created a robust line of vodka, gin, whiskey, and liqueur, b) achieved nationwide distribution and won a trove of national awards, and c) played a leading role in making Colorado a focal point for craft distilling.

Leopold Bros. does a few things differently from the average craft distillery. For one, they run their fermentation at a much lower temperature, which takes longer but theoretically draws out more flavors. And unlike most modern distillers, large and small, Leopold Bros. puts its distillate in the barrel at a low 98 proof, rather than the typical 125 proof. This means less alcohol and more flavoring elements go into the aging process. Doing so is less efficient, but Leopold Bros. claims it produces a more flavorful whiskey (whether it actually does is a separate question).

Along with their American Small Batch Whiskey, Leopold Bros. also makes an apple whiskey, a blackberry whiskey, and two types of peach whiskey.

LEOPOLD BROTHERS

4950 NOME STREET

DENVER, CO 80239

TEL: 303-307-1515

E-MAIL: scott@leopoldbros.com

www.leopoldbros.com

Leopold Brothers American Small Batch Whiskey BARREL 26

AGE	PROOF
No age statement	**86**

NOSE	COLOR	BODY
Lilies, yeast, corn pudding, Listerine mouthwash	Burnished	Light

GENERAL	PALATE	
A little water transforms the floral and corn nose to honey. It's full of strong cereal notes and finishes abruptly.	Honey, flat bread, fish; hot, white pepper finish.	

	PRICE	RATING
	$$	★

Maker's Mark

Bill Samuels, Sr., the founder of Maker's Mark—named for the stamps pewter makers use to identify their wares—sold the first bottle of his whiskey in 1959. Samuels spent most of the 1950s developing a wheated bourbon, the recipe and yeast for which he got from his friend Julian Van Winkle II. (The Samuels family had already been in whiskey making for over a century; T.W. Samuels was a popular antebellum brand.) As a wheated bourbon, this new whiskey was sweeter and smoother than, say, Jim Beam, but not as sweet as Jack Daniel's.

The company, then independent, developed an in-state following, but it wasn't until the 1980s that whiskey fans in New York and San Francisco began opening up to this strange new liquor. Maker's was helped along by its purchase in 1981 by Hiram Walker, which then sold it Allied Lyons, who sold it to Jim Beam in 2005; all three companies promoted the brand heavily, and it worked. Maker's sales shot up, and by the 1990s it was a household name. In 2012, it even won a trademark infringement lawsuit against another spirits company that was hand-dipping its bottles in red wax; Maker's was able to prove that such a step was an integral part of the brand's well-recognized identity.

Until a few years ago, unlike virtually every other establishment distillery, Maker's Mark made a single domestic product, with no variations, no limited editions, no barrel-proof releases, nothing. (Maker's once made a few limited edition whiskeys for export.) All their commemorative Kentucky Derby and University of Kentucky Wildcat bottles? Nice looking, but the stuff inside is always the same.

That all changed in 2010, though, when the distillery brought out Maker's 46, a regular-line product and a tribute to the company patriarch Bill Samuels Jr., who retired that year. Rather than turning off purists, the new expression was so popular that there were immediate shortages and Maker's had to ramp up emergency production.

Though there are significant differences in nose and taste between Maker's Mark and Maker's 46, it's telling how similar their production processes are—telling in that it demonstrates how small changes along the way can make a big difference at the end. Both expressions are aged for the same unspecified number of years. Neither is chill-filtered, a process that removes particulates that can make the whiskey look cloudy but also give it a little extra flavor. At the end, though, while the regular Maker's is dumped and bottled, Maker's 46 goes through another six weeks in a barrel along with seared French oak staves, which gives the whiskey a distinctly woodier palate.

Maker's Mark Kentucky Straight Bourbon Whisky

AGE No age statement		
PROOF **90**		
NOSE Corn, vanilla, apple, butter, and some cherry	**COLOR** Russet/ tawny	**BODY** Medium to full and chewy
GENERAL As a wheated bourbon, this new whiskey was sweeter and smoother than, say, Jim Beam, but not as sweet as Jack Daniel's.	**PALATE** Black pepper, creamed corn, vanilla, and menthol; finishes with a warming, pleasant burn.	
	PRICE	**RATING** ★★★

Maker's 46 Kentucky Bourbon Whisky

AGE
No age statement

PROOF
94

NOSE
Greenhouse floral, dark wood, marzipan, black tea, hickory smoke

COLOR
Tawny/ auburn

BODY
Medium to full

GENERAL
Maker's Mark isn't perfect, but it's very good, so why did they mess with it? Maker's 46 is slightly richer, but also a bit too agressively woody.

PALATE
Maple sugar, black pepper

PRICE
$$

RATING

Masterson's

Why do some of the better whiskeys have the worst names? And why do some of the best recent American ryes come from Canada? Like Whistlepig, its *confrère* across the continent, Masterson's, from California, is a 100 percent Canadian rye purchased, bottled, and sold by an American firm. Unlike Whistlepig, which is building a distillery operation of its own, Masterson's, owned by 35 Maple Street Spirits of Sonoma, California, seems content to keep it Canadian.

About that name: since the whiskey is sourced from Canada but passed off as an American product, it makes sense that its branding would be similarly artificial. But why name a very good whiskey after a man—Bat Masterson—who may have helped tame the Wild West, but probably never tasted a decent whiskey in his life? The Wild West may have been a lot of things, but a place to find great—or even non-toxic—whiskey it was decidedly not.

35 MAPLE STREET SPIRITS

35 MAPLE STREET

SONOMA, CA 95476

TEL: 707-996-8463

E-MAIL: info@togwines.com

www.mastersonsrye.com

PRODUCER: UNKNOWN

Masterson's Straight Rye Whiskey

AGE **10** years old

PROOF **90**

NOSE Honey, lilacs, candy store, and freshly sawed wood

COLOR Russet/tawny

BODY Full and chewy

GENERAL A delicious, woody rye, with a nose like a sunny afternoon. It tastes a lot like Jefferson's rye and Whistlepig, which isn't surprising—all three are sourced from Canada, perhaps from the same producer. If so, they aren't saying.

PALATE Apple, cinnamon

PRICE $$$$

RATING

McAfee's Benchmark

BUFFALO TRACE DISTILLERY

113 GREAT BUFFALO TRACE

FRANKFORT, KENTUCKY 40601

TEL: 800-654-8471

E-MAIL: info@buffalotrace.com

www.buffalotrace.com

Back in the bad old days of the 1970s, distilleries were looking for any edge to save their market share against gin, vodka, and wine. One path was the expensive premium spirit route. But because few makers wanted to take the risk on an expensive, untested high-end product line, several took the cheaper path of creating knock-off versions of established premium brands. Among the prime knock-off targets was Maker's Mark, one of the few successful premium bourbons at the time. Hence McAfee's Benchmark, from Seagram, a not-so-subtle attempt to imitate Maker's marketing. Seagram sold the brand to Sazerac in 1989; it is now made at the Buffalo Trace Distillery, using its proprietary, high-corn Mash Bill #1.

McAfee's Benchmark Kentucky Straight Bourbon Whiskey

AGE	PROOF
No age statement	**80**

NOSE	COLOR	BODY
Bit-O-Honey candy and halva, along with salted nuts and a feinty note of rubber and wood polish	Deep copper	Light but still a bit chewy

GENERAL	PALATE	
Save for the lack of bees, this is like sticking your nose in a honeycomb. A surprisingly pleasant whiskey. Well-balanced, it would make a solid mixer.	An odd but not unpleasant mixture of dessert wine and Fritos	

PRICE	RATING

McCarthy's

Like Charbay in the Napa Valley and Koval in Chicago, Oregon's Clear Creek made its name as a European-style producer of small-batch *eaux de vie* and brandies. The distillery is the creation of Steve McCarthy, who fell in love with farmhouse distilling while studying in Alsace, where practically every French farmer has a personal still out back to convert surplus produce into potent potables.

McCarthy returned to his family farm outside Portland and began distilling under the label Clear Creek. He worked with a small still to make pear and apple liquors long before anyone else had an inkling of what American craft distilling could become. Along the way, he decided to branch out into whiskey, specifically the challenge of making a scotch-style single malt on the Pacific Coast.

Though by law unable to be called a "scotch," McCarthy's Oregon Single Malt is so peaty it might as well wear a kilt. McCarthy says that it is made in the "Islay tradition," and he gets his peat-malted barley from Port Ellen, a former distillery on the Scottish island of Islay that supplies Lagavulin and Laphroig. The barley is then fermented by Widmer Brothers, a nearby brewery, and pot-distilled by McCarthy. The whiskey goes through as many as three different barrels during its approximately three year aging process.

CLEAR CREEK DISTILLERY

2389 NORTHWEST WILSON STREET

PORTLAND, OR 97210

TEL: 503-248-9470

E-MAIL: steve@clearcreekdistillery.com

www.clearcreekdistillery.com

McCarthy's Oregon Single Malt Whiskey

AGE	PROOF
3 years old	**85**

NOSE	COLOR	BODY
Peat, iodine, geraniums, rubber tires, and leather	Pale straw	Medium and chewy

GENERAL	PALATE
McCarthy's is a patriarch of craft whiskey, and for good reason. This is a masterful interpretation of an Islay-style scotch; in a blind taste, would you know it's not from Scotland?	Smoke, iodine, saltwater, rubber, with tar, ash and clamshell on the end

PRICE	RATING
$$$	★ ★ ★

McKenzie

FINGER LAKES DISTILLING

4676 NEW YORK 414

BURDETT, NY 14818

TEL: 607-546-5510

E-MAIL: brian@fingerlakesdistilling.com

www.fingerlakesdistilling.com

BRANDS

MCKENZIE BOURBON WHISKEY

MCKENZIE PURE POT STILL WHISKEY

MCKENZIE RYE WHISKEY

Though it is located close to the center of New York State, Finger Lakes Distilling, the company behind the McKenzie line of whiskeys, is one of the leading lights in what has loosely been called the Hudson Valley distilling renaissance. Like Tuthilltown, Hillrock, Albany Distilling, and a passel of outfits in New York City, Finger Lakes makes a variety of liquors but focuses on whiskey, making a bourbon, a rye, and an "Irish style" pot-stilled whiskey (made with a mash of malted and unmalted barley).

Finger Lakes began after a 2007 conversation at a distillers' conference between Brian McKenzie and Thomas McKenzie, two men unrelated by blood but linked by a common interest in craft distilling. Two years later they opened shop outside Seneca, New York.

Taking advantage of the region's growing heirloom-agriculture industry, Finger Lakes sources almost all its ingredients locally. And the company makes full use of its location in New York wine country: after first aging its bourbon for 18 months in 10-gallon new oak barrels, it finishes the whiskey in used chardonnay barrels, collected from nearby vintners.

McKenzie Bourbon Whiskey

AGE No age statement		
PROOF **91**		
NOSE Butter, cardboard, Andes mints, acetone, and rye bread	**COLOR** Auburn	**BODY** Medium, smooth
GENERAL McKenzie's bourbon exudes a swirl of interesting notes that don't quite cohere. The rye notes exude a little too much funk to marry well with the mint and butter.	**PALATE** Pine tar and cedar on the tongue, finishing with an abrupt pop of spice.	
	PRICE **$$$**	**RATING** ★

McKenzie
Pure Pot Still Whiskey

AGE		
No age statement		

PROOF

80

NOSE	COLOR	BODY
Acetone and barley	Amber	Thin

GENERAL

The malted and unmalted barley used to make this "Irish-style" whiskey is hard to miss. McKenzie ages this expression in used bourbon and rye barrels.

PALATE

Simple syrup, citrus, spearmint, with a short finish

PRICE	RATING
$$$	**NR**

McKenzie
Rye Whiskey

AGE		
No age statement		

PROOF

91

NOSE	COLOR	BODY
Plum, wood, peaches, and rum raisin	Russet	Medium

GENERAL

A solid rye, this is easily the best of McKenzie's portfolio. The palate is interesting, if a bit odd, and at times oddly compelling. It's uncommon for savory/umami flavors to come into play in a whiskey, but it's definitely here.

PALATE

Pumpernickel, nuts, umami; finish is long and minty.

PRICE	RATING
$$	

Mellow Corn

HEAVEN HILL DISTILLERIES

P.O. BOX 729

BARDSTOWN, KY 40004

TEL: 502-348-3921

www.heavenhill.com

Corn whiskey is made with a mashbill of at least eighty percent corn and is aged in used or new uncharred oak. These requirements make it cheaper to produce than bourbon. But corn whiskey also has a shoeless, haystalk-in-its-teeth image that has probably scared off many a distiller and consumer over the years. Not Mellow Corn, from Heaven Hill, one of the few corn whiskeys on the market. It's certainly a novelty, though too bland and thin to be especially interesting.

Mellow Corn
Straight Corn Whiskey

AGE	**4** years old
PROOF	**100**

NOSE	COLOR	BODY
Chewing gum, corn, molasses	Pale gold	Thin

GENERAL	PALATE
Though Mellow Corn is bottled in bond, it still tastes like a young whiskey, perhaps because of the unusually high corn content. It's not a boring whiskey, but it's more a novelty than a serious drink.	Tons of burn, caramel, corn

PRICE	RATING
$	

Michter's

Michter's product lines may be the best sourced whiskey on the market. Which is to say, the company doesn't make its whiskey (at least not yet), but it does a damn fine job of picking it out.

There's a lot of misconception about what Michter's is and isn't. A lot of people confuse the current iteration, which opened in the late 1990s, with the historic Michter's Distillery, which operated in Pennsylvania from the 1950s through the early '80s. The only link between the two is the name, which the new owners, Chatham Imports in New York, bought from a bank years after the old operation went dark.

Interestingly, the new Michter's is almost definitely a lot better than the old. The brand was created by Louis Forman, a liquor broker in Pennsylvania. The distillery was bought by a group of investors in 1975, who poured money into a promotional campaign that included novelty decanters, t-shirts, and Christmas ornaments. Joseph Magliocco, the president of Chatham Imports, which now owns the brand, has a small collection of old Michter's decanters in his New York City office, including one shaped like the bust of King Tut. Eventually the investors lost interest and sold the distillery to what amounted to absentee owners, and it took a nosedive. It went bankrupt and its equipment was sold off.

Then came Magliocco and Dick Newman, the president of Austin Nichols (maker of Wild Turkey). Rather than start a distillery from scratch, the two decided to revive the Michter's name and attach it to a line of super-premium, sourced bourbons and ryes. Magliocco hired Willie Pratt, an industry veteran, as his master distiller, and the two went about selecting a small fortune in old barrels.

Michter's continues to source its whiskey and outsource its aging and bottling operations, but it is in the process of building a welcome center and small distillery in downtown Louisville, Kentucky. In late 2012 it introduced a twenty-year-old, single-barrel bourbon, which sells for about $450 a bottle, making it the most expensive new-release American whiskey currently on the market.

CHATHAM IMPORTS
245 FIFTH AVENUE
NEW YORK, NY 10016
TEL: 212-473-1100
E-MAIL: info@michters.com
www.michters.com

PRODUCER: UNKNOWN

BRANDS
MICHTER'S SINGLE BARREL
    STRAIGHT RYE WHISKEY
MICHTER'S SMALL BATCH BOURBON
MICHTER'S SMALL BATCH SOUR
    MASH WHISKEY
MICHTER'S SINGLE BARREL
    STRAIGHT RYE WHISKEY
MICHTER'S 10-YEAR SINGLE
    BARREL BOURBON
MICHTER'S 20 YEAR SINGLE
    BARREL BOURBON

Michter's Single Barrel Straight Rye Whiskey BARREL 13779

AGE
No age statement

PROOF

84.8

NOSE
Maple, butterscotch, and pepper

COLOR
Mahogany

BODY
Full and chewy

GENERAL
A great introductory rye—it's representative of the type, but not overly demanding. It deftly balances sweetness and spice, wood and cereal.

PALATE
Butter, cola, leather, and oak; smooth finish.

PRICE
$$

RATING
★ ★ ★

Michter's Small Batch Bourbon BATCH NO. 12LIB

AGE
No age statement

PROOF

91.4

NOSE
Brown sugar, cherries

COLOR
Auburn

BODY
Medium

GENERAL
The lesser of the Michter's pack, but the Small Batch is still fine whiskey. Like the ten-year-old Single Barrel, this one has full flavors, but they're not fully rounded and a little difficult to define.

PALATE
Orange, bitters; refreshing, quick finish.

PRICE
$$

RATING
★ ★ ★

Michter's Small Batch Sour Mash Whiskey

AGE		
No age statement		

PROOF		
86		

NOSE	COLOR	BODY
Juicy, vegetal, cocoa powder	Auburn	Medium

GENERAL	PALATE
Refreshing for a medium-bodied whiskey, and full of excellent, rounded flavors. It accomplishes something quite odd: it's robust, but the flavors are light and smooth. Well done.	Nuts and dry white wine; finishes long and spicy.

PRICE	RATING
$$	

Michter's Small Batch Unblended American Whiskey BATCH NO. 11-179

AGE		
No age statement		

PROOF		
83.4		

NOSE	COLOR	BODY
Cherries, dark fruits, polish, bubble gum, cola, toast, and grain	Mahogany	Light to medium

GENERAL	PALATE
Slightly sweet, but still balanced. It has power, but it's gentle, like Muhammad Ali petting a kitten. It's not quite a session whiskey, but close enough for a full evening.	Butterscotch, peanut brittle, vanilla and chili pepper; finishes with almond and anise.

PRICE	RATING
$$	

Michter's
10 Year Single Barrel
Bourbon BARREL NO. 11D-1

AGE
10
years old

PROOF
94.4

NOSE	COLOR	BODY
Candied cherries, strawberry, all spice, and light wood	Mahogany	Light to medium

GENERAL

A wonderful nose on this one, but the palate falls just a little short. The tastes never really define themselves. It's full-flavored, but not any particular flavor. However, treat yourself sometime to this good sipping whiskey.

PALATE

Chocolate, some indefinable spice, and a medium-length, subtle finish

PRICE
$$$$

RATING

Michter's
20 Year Single Barrel
Bourbon BARREL NO. 2368/BOTTLE 114

AGE
20
years old

PROOF
114.2

NOSE	COLOR	BODY
Maple, vanilla, teriyaki sauce, toffee, marzipan, white pepper, sweet wine, and root beer; some water brings out vanilla, soy sauce, soap/lavender, pine, fruit cake, and sherry.	Mahogany	Massive and chewy

GENERAL

Exquisite; this is one of the best whiskeys in the world, regardless of category. It has so many parts, but they all cohere, like a Mahler symphony (minus the sadness). The price is large and in this case, so is the whiskey.

PALATE

Giant red wine, with cream, cherry, walnut, and medicinal notes, finishing with a slight bitterness.

PRICE
$$$$

RATING

Noah's Mill

Noah's Mill is the most robust of Kentucky Bourbon Distillers' Small Batch line (the other's being Rowan's Creek, Kentucky Vintage, and Pure Kentucky XO). It is bottled at a barrel-strength 114.3 proof, which means it is not diluted after aging, as most whiskeys are.

It is also one of the most diversely blended whiskeys on the market. KBD sources all its whiskey, and for Noah's Mill it buys and mixes three whiskeys with three different mash bills, from a low-rye recipe to a wheated bourbon.

The whiskeys involved used to be at least fifteen years old, and Noah's Mill once came with a fifteen-year age statement. But KBD has since expanded the age range of its ingredient whiskeys, including one as young as four years old. This means that by federal law, KBD would have to put a four-year age statement on its label, or none at all. KBD opted for the latter, even though, according to the company, the bulk of the whiskey in each bottle is much older.

KENTUCKY BOURBON DISTILLERS

1869 LORETTO ROAD

BARDSTOWN, KY, 40004

TEL: 502-348-0081

E-MAIL: kentuckybourbon@bardstown.com

www.kentuckybourbonwhiskey.com

PRODUCER: UNKNOWN

Noah's Mill Genuine Bourbon Whiskey

AGE	No age statement
PROOF	**114.3**

NOSE	COLOR	BODY
Perfume, butterscotch, and geraniums	Mahogany	Full and syrupy

GENERAL	PALATE
A good mixer and a good high-proof sipper. The nose promises a lot but it lacks depth. Noah's Mill is a fun whiskey to figure out; there's something going on and you want to know more.	Chili peppers and salted nuts, finishing with a long, fiery spice.

PRICE	RATING
$$$	

Old Bardstown

KENTUCKY BOURBON DISTILLERS

1869 LORETTO ROAD

BARDSTOWN, KY, 40004

TEL: 502-348-0081

E-MAIL: kentuckybourbon@bardstown.com

www.kentuckybourbonwhiskey.com

PRODUCER: UNKNOWN

Old Bardstown is one of the brand lines from Kentucky Bourbon Distillers. Since KBD does not distill its whiskey, but rather sources it from other companies, there's no way to be sure where it comes from. Don't be thrown by the label saying it is made by the "Old Bardstown Distilling Co."; that's a front.

BRANDS

OLD BARDSTOWN KENTUCKY STRAIGHT BOURBON WHISKEY
(GOLD LABEL)

OLD BARDSTOWN KENTUCKY STRAIGHT BOURBON WHISKEY
(BLACK LABEL)

OLD BARDSTOWN KENTUCKY STRAIGHT BOURBON WHISKEY
ESTATE BOTTLED

Old Bardstown Kentucky Straight Bourbon Whiskey GOLD LABEL

AGE		No age statement
PROOF		**80**

NOSE	COLOR	BODY
Menthol, lacquer, almond, citrus	Chestnut	Thin to medium

GENERAL	PALATE	
Thin, simple, and inoffensive, with a good dollop of sweetness on the palate. It's nothing outstanding, but if you like a full-bodied yet uncomplicated whiskey, it's a decent choice.	Vague spice and metallic tinge	
	PRICE	RATING
	$	

Old Bardstown Kentucky Straight Bourbon Whiskey ^{BLACK LABEL}

AGE No age statement		
PROOF **90**		

NOSE	COLOR	BODY
Apricot, caramel, stewed fruit, some cinnamon candy, and cut flowers	Chestnut	Thin

GENERAL	PALATE
Candy toward the end, and there's some white wine. Still, the roughness at the finish is off-putting. (Not widely distributed in the United States.)	Butterscotch and salted nuts, with a developing burn on the finish

PRICE	RATING
$	

Old Bardstown Kentucky Straight Bourbon Whiskey ^{ESTATE BOTTLED}

AGE No age statement		
PROOF **101**		

NOSE	COLOR	BODY
Maple, honey, and pepper	Chestnut	Thin

GENERAL	PALATE
Despite the promise of "estate bottled" on the label, this is not a particularly individual drink. It's only a little more expensive than the other Old Bardstown expressions, likely because of the higher proof.	Bitter, sweet, and oaky

PRICE	RATING
$$	

Old Charter

BUFFALO TRACE DISTILLERY

113 GREAT BUFFALO TRACE

FRANKFORT, KENTUCKY 40601

TEL: 800-654-8471

E-MAIL: info@buffalotrace.com

www.buffalotrace.com

BRANDS

OLD CHARTER KENTUCKY STRAIGHT
    BOURBON WHISKEY

CHARTER 101 KENTUCKY STRAIGHT
    BOURBON WHISKEY

Introduced by the Chapeze Distillery in 1874, Old Charter is one of those used, abused, and only occasionally loved brands. After Prohibition the line and its remaining stocks were bought by Bernheim, which sold it a few years later to Schenley. It went to United Distillers when that company bought Schenley in 1987; a decade later United was swept into the multilayered, multinational merger that created Diageo, which then sold Old Charter, two years later, to Sazerac, which now makes it at its Buffalo Trace Distillery. Phew.

Over the years Old Charter has been released in higher- and lower-quality iterations, and today it falls somewhere just above the bottom shelf. There are three expressions on the market, two of which are reviewed here. All three—Charter 101, Old Charter 8 Year Old and Old Charter 10 Year Old—are made with Buffalo Trace's corn-heavy (about 80 percent) Mash Bill #1, which is also used to produce George T. Stagg and Eagle Rare, as well as the distillery's eponymous flagship brand.

Old Charter Kentucky Straight Bourbon Whiskey

AGE	**8** years old
PROOF	**80**

NOSE	COLOR	BODY
Pepperoni, cumin, some feinty notes, and a little wet fur	Chestnut	Light

GENERAL	PALATE
It's like the higher-proof Charter 101, but using its inside voice. At eight years old, Old Charter has more oak and less corn and has a smoother finish.	Oaky bitterness, finishing with a touch of fire.

PRICE	RATING
$	★

Charter 101 Kentucky Straight Bourbon Whiskey

AGE
No age statement

PROOF
101

NOSE
Fruitcake, dried fruit, butterscotch, and ethanol

COLOR
Tawny/auburn

BODY
Thin

GENERAL
Charter 101 is hot and fiery with fruit, leather, and a very slight woodiness on the palate.

PALATE
Dried apricots, wood and leather; finish is an Atomic Fireball.

PRICE
$$

RATING
NR

Old Crow

BEAM INC.

510 LAKE COOK ROAD

DEERFIELD, IL 60015

TEL: 847·948·8888

www.beamglobal.com

BRANDS

OLD CROW KENTUCKY STRAIGHT
    BOURBON WHISKEY

OLD CROW RESERVE KENTUCKY
    STRAIGHT BOURBON WHISKEY

James Crow was a Scottish doctor who settled in Kentucky in the 1820s and began making whiskey. He never owned his own distillery, but rather worked for a succession of employers, most notably the Oscar Pepper Distillery, located on the site of what is today Woodford Reserve, outside Frankfort. Crow's reputation was widespread, and the distilleries he worked for sold his whiskey under his name. Crow died in 1856, by which time he had set many of the standards for bourbon production: how to use set back, how to use measuring instruments—essentially divining the science of bourbon making. He did not, however, share his beloved recipe, and subsequent incarnations of Old Crow have been pale shades of the glorious progenitor.

The Old Crow Distillery opened in 1872, where a new version of Crow's whiskey was made under the ownership of National Distillers. Old Crow 2.0 supposedly wasn't bad, though the formula was changed in the late 1960s and the whiskey moved down several notches in quality. In 1987, National sold the brand to Beam.

There are two Old Crow expressions, one an 80-proof, three-year-old bourbon called simply Old Crow and the other, at 86 proof and four years-old, called Old Crow Reserve.

Old Crow Kentucky Straight Bourbon Whiskey

AGE	
3 years old	

PROOF	
80	

NOSE	COLOR	BODY
Corn mash, anise, wood, rose petals, and orange zest	Deep gold	Light to medium

GENERAL	PALATE	
Old Crow is a classic medium-bodied bargain bourbon. Corn, oak, and citrus dominate the profile.	Pepper, oak	

	PRICE	RATING
	$	★

Old Crow Reserve Kentucky Straight Bourbon Whiskey

AGE	
4 years old	

PROOF	
86	

NOSE	COLOR	BODY
Marzipan and apple juice	Deep copper	Light to medium

GENERAL	PALATE	
A slight improvement over the regular-line Old Crow, with a little more complexity and structure to the palate.	Mint, pepper; slightly minty finish	

	PRICE	RATING
	$	★

Old Fitzgerald

HEAVEN HILL DISTILLERIES

P.O. BOX 729

BARDSTOWN, KY 40004

TEL: 502-348-3921

www.heavenhill.com

Old Fitzgerald was created sometime in the late 1800s by a Milwaukee wine dealer named Charles Herbst. It was a fairly standard whiskey, first sold exclusively on passenger ships and in private clubs. During Prohibition it was one of the few whiskeys allowed to be sold for medicinal purposes. The whiskey gained its reputation from Julian "Pappy" Van Winkle, who added a "whisper of wheat" to the recipe and made it the headliner bourbon of the Stitzel-Weller Distillery. When Stitzel-Weller was sold to Diageo in 1992, the Old Fitzgerald brand went to Heaven Hill, which continues to produce it today.

The name Old Fitzgerald comes from a legend about a U. S. Treasury agent named—you guessed it—Fitzgerald, who had a key to the bonded warehouses around central Kentucky. He had a certain nose for good whiskey, and supposedly pilfered a bit whenever no one was looking. The same story lies behind Larceny, another wheated bourbon from Heaven Hill, introduced in 2012.

Old Fitzgerald 1849 Kentucky Straight Bourbon Whiskey

AGE	PROOF
No age statement	**90**

NOSE	COLOR	BODY
Almond, dark fruits, dirty flowers	Tawny	Light

GENERAL	PALATE	
An uninspiring whiskey; if the option is available, go for the similar but superior Larceny (see page 186), also from Heaven Hill. If not, though, you could do much worse than this for a bargain whiskey.	Bubblegum and black pepper	

PRICE	RATING
$	

Old Forester

First, what Old Forester is not: contrary to legend, its namesake is not Nathan Bedford Forrest, the Confederate cavalry leader who oversaw the Fort Pillow massacre during the Civil War and the post-bellum creation of the first Ku Klux Klan. Though the brand was initially spelled with two "r"s, and though no one knows for sure where the name comes from, the whiskey is most likely named for a doctor named William Forrester, who shilled for the brand's alleged medicinal properties.

Old Forester does, however, have two verifiable historic claims to fame. It was the first whiskey sold exclusively in sealed bottles—rather than dispensed to customers from a barrel—and it is the oldest continuously produced whiskey brand in America. Beginning in 1870 and plowing right through Prohibition and the dramatic decline in whiskey sales from the 1960s to the 1990s, and even as most of its fellow brands shuttered, Old Forester endured.

Both claims to fame go back to Forrester, and to the brand's half-brother founders, George Garvin Brown and John Thompson Street Brown. In the late nineteenth century the two men, whose name lives on in the Brown-Forman distilling company, strove to create a brand around consumer demand for unadulterated products—especially from the whiskey industry, which was infamous for adding coloring and flavoring agents to cheap booze, regardless of toxicity. To boost the brand's reputation, the Browns had a series of doctors, most notably Forrester, attest to its purity. That reputation stuck through to the onset of Prohibition, when Old Forester was one of only ten brands granted a medicinal exemption to the ban on alcohol production.

Today there are three Old Forester expressions, Old Forester, Old Forester Signature, and Old Forester Birthday Bourbon, a yearly release. They are all are produced at Brown-Forman's main distillery in Shively, Kentucky, using a mash bill of 72 percent corn, 18 percent rye, and 10 percent malted barley.

BROWN-FORMAN
850 DIXIE HIGHWAY
LOUISVILLE, KY 40210
TEL: 502-585-1100
www.brown-forman.com

BRANDS

OLD FORESTER KENTUCKY
    STRAIGHT BOURBON WHISKY
OLD FORESTER SIGNATURE
    100 BOURBON
OLD FORESTER BIRTHDAY
    BOURBON 2012

Old Forester Kentucky Straight Bourbon Whisky

AGE	
No age statement	

PROOF
86

NOSE	COLOR	BODY
Banana, almond, and cereal	Auburn	Light

GENERAL	PALATE
There are some nice fruit and nut notes here. The flavor is classic bourbon without a challenge to the palate or, unfortunately, much depth.	Cereal, brown sugar, and garam masala; abrupt finish.

PRICE	RATING
$	

Old Forester Signature Kentucky Straight Bourbon Whisky

AGE	
No age statement	

PROOF
100

NOSE	COLOR	BODY
Bit-O-Honey, Charleston Chew, boot leather, and plums	Auburn	Medium and chewy

GENERAL	PALATE
For once, an upgrade with a difference: in contrast with the regular Old Forester, Signature is complex and nicely balanced between sweet and spice. The definable candy notes on the nose are delightful.	Burnt caramel, chocolate chip cookies, and butter; a slightly spiced finish.

PRICE	RATING
$	

Old Forester Birthday Bourbon 2012

AGE
12
years old

PROOF
97

NOSE
Cherry cola, marzipan, and stewed fruits

COLOR
Mahogany/ burnt umber

BODY
Medium to full

GENERAL
A truly great whiskey for its price. There's a ton of rye in here, and it's obvious on nose and tongue. The forward malt and oak resolve into a silky smooth finish for a such a full-bodied drink. For under $50, you cannot go wrong on the 2012 expression.

PALATE
Atomic Fireball, pepper, and a little butter, resolving into a longish burn.

PRICE
$$$

RATING

Old Grand-Dad

BEAM INC.

510 LAKE COOK ROAD

DEERFIELD, IL 60015

TEL: 847-948-8888

www.beamglobal.com

BRANDS

OLD GRAND-DAD WHISKEY

OLD GRAND-DAD 114 KENTUCKY
     STRAIGHT BOURBON WHISKEY

Basil Hayden, Sr. is one of the few people in history with multiple whiskey brands to his name. Of course, there is Basil Hayden's, a part of Beam's Small Batch Collection. But many people aren't aware that the granddad in Old Grand-Dad is also Basil Hayden. Likewise a Beam product, Old Grand-Dad was created by Raymond B. Hayden in 1840; he named his distillery and its flagship product after his grandfather Basil, who led a group of Maryland Catholics to settle in Kentucky in the late eighteenth century.

At the end of the 1800s, Old Grand-Dad was sold to the Wathen distilling family, who later incorporated it into their American Medicinal Spirits Company and, then, National Distillers. That company, in turn, sold Old Grand-Dad to Beam in 1987.

Like Basil Hayden's, Old Grand-Dad is a high-rye bourbon, in keeping with the distilling fashions of Raymond and Basil.

Old Grand-Dad Whiskey

AGE		No age statement
PROOF		**86**

NOSE	COLOR	BODY
Cumin, wood, slight funk	Deep copper	Thinnish

GENERAL	PALATE	
Not bad for a stereotypical down-market whiskey. It exhibits decent wood, but it's lacking fruit and any real depth at all. A reliable stand-by as a mixing whiskey, but not for sipping.	Leather, cinnamon; fleeting finish.	
	PRICE	RATING
	$	★

Old Grand-Dad 114 Kentucky Straight Bourbon Whiskey

AGE	No age statement
PROOF	**114**

NOSE	COLOR	BODY
Cereal and Fluffernutter	Tawny	Thin

GENERAL

It's what non-whiskey drinkers think whiskey tastes like: aggressive and a tad sweet (thanks to its rye content), woody, and medicinal.

PALATE		
Butter and oak		
PRICE	**RATING**	
$$	**NR**	

Old Overholt

BEAM INC.

510 LAKE COOK ROAD

DEERFIELD, IL 60015

TEL: 847-948-8888

www.beamglobal.com

Best known these days as the rye whiskey of choice for *Mad Men's* Don Draper, Old Overholt is one of the last brands left from the old days of Pennsylvania rye distilling—though its recipe has long since changed and its no longer made in Pennsylvania. The whiskey has its roots in early nineteenth-century southwestern Pennsylvania. It was produced at the time by A. Overholt & Co. at the Broad Ford Distillery (originally called simply Overholt, the "Old" was added in the late nineteenth century to honor the company's founder, Abraham Overholt). The distillery fell into the hands of the industrialist Henry Clay Frick, who later sold it to his younger business partner Andrew Mellon. His ownership of the distillery during Prohibition, when it continued to produce whiskey for "medicinal" purposes, caused some amount of scandal during the 1920s. Mellon was for a time secretary of the Treasury and thus, officially, in charge of enforcing the ban on liquor production. (Old Overholt also plays a recurring role in HBO's *Boardwalk Empire*, with Mellon played by James Cromwell.)

Like many medicinal whiskeys during Prohibition, Old Overholt ended up in the ownership of the American Medicinal Spirits Co., which evolved into National Distillers after Repeal. In 1987, National became a part of the Jim Beam portfolio under Fortune Brands, which split into Beam, Inc. Along the way, production shifted to Kentucky, and today it is produced at Beam's plant in Clermont.

Old Overholt was said to be a classic, robust Pennsylvania rye, but today it is indistinguishable from the generic ryes on the market—in fact, it is largely the same as the standard Jim Beam Rye.

Old Overholt
Straight Rye Whiskey

AGE	**4** years old
PROOF	**80**

NOSE	COLOR	BODY
Floral, citrus	Chestnut	Light

GENERAL

There's a reason this whiskey has stood through the ages: it is affordable, versatile, and a perfect example of the rye category. That doesn't mean it's the best rye out there. But any serious bar will have a bottle; it tastes great on its own and will work in just about any cocktail that calls for whiskey.

PALATE

Butter, oak, cinnamon finish

PRICE	RATING
$	

Old Pogue

OLD POGUE DISTILLERY

716 W 2ND ST

MAYSVILLE, KY 41056

TEL: 317-697-5039

E-MAIL: ppogue@indy.rr.com

www.oldpogue.com

······································

PRODUCER: UNKNOWN

The Old Pogue label is one of the oldest extant brands in the world of bourbon, yet the Old Pogue Distillery is one of the newest in Kentucky. The original Pogue Distillery, founded by Henry Edgar Pogue in 1876 in Maysville, Kentucky, was one of the most fecund of the bourbon golden age, producing a portfolio of long-lost brands like Old Time, Old Maysville Club Rye, Belle of Maysville, and Niagara Whisky. The Pogue family shuttered and then sold the distillery during Prohibition; it reopened in 1935 and began producing Old Pogue Bourbon. The distillery couldn't survive the World War II whiskey ban and it closed for good around 1944.

The brand, however, was resurrected by descendants of Henry Pogue in 2004, at first as a sourced whiskey. In 2012, the family opened a new Old Pogue Distillery in Maysville and plan to have their own production of the old recipe on the market within a few years. The distillery also makes a white whiskey, called Limestone Landing Single Malt Rye.

Old Pogue Master's Select Kentucky Straight Bourbon Whiskey

AGE **9** years old		
PROOF **90**		
NOSE Black tea, oak, and peppermint	COLOR Chestnut	BODY Light
GENERAL Too many dry oak notes to work; it needs some sweetness for balance in the absence of florals and much fruit. Not a good balance, but not a failure.	PALATE Melons and a little spice; woody finish.	
	PRICE $$	RATING

Old Potrero

Produced since 1996 at the same San Francisco location as Anchor Brewing, Old Potrero comes in two expressions: 18th Century Rye and Straight Rye. Both are 100 percent rye mash bills made in pot stills and aged in lightly toasted oak barrels. The only real difference between the two is age: the former is under two-years-old, the latter just over three-years-old. (There is also an older expression, no longer in production but still on a few shelves, named Hotaling's.) The distillery touts its whiskey as "single malt rye," which, going by Scotch standards, means it is 100 percent malted rye and all made at the same location.

ANCHOR BREWERS AND DISTILLERS

1705 MARIPOSA STREET

SAN FRANCISCO, CA 94107

TEL: 415-863-8350

E-MAIL: info@AnchorSF.com

www.anchordistilling.com

BRANDS

OLD POTRERO SINGLE MALT
RYE WHISKEY

SINGLE MALT 18TH CENTURY
STYLE WHISKEY

Old Potrero Single Malt Rye Whiskey

AGE	No age statement
PROOF	**97**

NOSE	COLOR	BODY
Old hay, musty closet, some plum chocolate powder	Mahogany	Syrupy

GENERAL	PALATE
This whiskey has a peculiar profile, with a lot of funk, mixed with a syrupy sweetness; the sort of flavor that attracts lovers and haters in equal measure. But it's a good, unique expression, and worth sampling—just make sure you try it at a bar before shelling out for a whole bottle.	Citrus, cloves, and peanut brittle, finishing with a lingering pepper.

PRICE	RATING
$$$$	

Old Potrero
Single Malt
18th Century Style
Whiskey

AGE

No age
statement

PROOF

102.4

NOSE

Funky, rubbery, smoky, with some apples and dill pickles

COLOR

Chestnut

BODY

Medium

GENERAL

Unpleasant. Extremely feinty, but unlikely to appeal to scotch fans. The finish is interesting and easily the best part of the drink.

PALATE

Cinnamon and maple, finishing with a meaty, peppery burn.

PRICE

$$$$

RATING

NR

Old Rip
Van Winkle

For a whiskey widely regarded as the best America has to offer, Old Rip Van Winkle—and its more famous sibling brand, Pappy Van Winkle—has been in the limelight for a surprisingly short period of time.

The brand's history goes back to the late nineteenth century, when Julian P. "Pappy" Van Winkle, a traveling salesman, joined with a friend to buy the W.L. Weller and Sons wholesale company and the A.Ph. Stitzel Distillery. They combined the two into a new operation, the Stitzel-Weller Distillery, and proceeded to make some of the twentieth century's most iconic brands: W.L. Weller, Rebel Yell, Cabin Still, and Old Fitzgerald, among others. After Van Winkle passed away, control of the distillery passed to his son, Julian, Jr.

Stitzel-Weller was known for its wheated bourbons: instead of rye in the recipe alongside corn and malted barley, the distillery used wheat, which gave the whiskey a soft, bright flavor. A version of the recipe is used by Maker's Mark, whose founder, Bill Samuels, was a friend of Julian Van Winkle, Jr.

The decline of the American whiskey industry in the 1960s hit everyone hard, Van Winkle included, who sold the distillery in 1972. He also sold the rights to all its brands, save one relatively obscure label: Old Rip Van Winkle. Julian, Jr.—and, after he died in 1981, his son, Julian, III—retained the right to buy old Stitzel-Weller whiskey stocks, as well as some of the distillery's new products, which they bottled and sold.

In the 1990s Julian Van Winkle III decided to run against the flood of young whiskeys on the market by rounding up old barrels of Stitzel-Weller stocks and selling them at ages almost unheard of for American whiskeys: fifteen years, twenty years, even twenty-three years. He also created a new brand, Pappy Van Winkle, to use for his premium aged expressions.

Van Winkle's whiskeys began to gain acclaim in the late 1990s, and developed a rabid following. To

OLD RIP VAN WINKLE DISTILLERY
113 GREAT BUFFALO TRACE
FRANKFORT, KENTUCKY 40601
TEL: 502-897-9113
E-MAIL: info@oldripvanwinkle.com
www.oldripvanwinkle.com

PRODUCER
BUFFALO TRACE DISTILLERY
113 GREAT BUFFALO TRACE
FRANKFORT, KENTUCKY 40601
TEL: 800-654-8471
E-MAIL: info@buffalotrace.com
www.buffalotrace.com

BRANDS
OLD RIP VAN WINKLE HANDMADE
    BOURBON
PAPPY VAN WINKLE'S FAMILY
    RESERVE 15 YEAR OLD
PAPPY VAN WINKLE'S FAMILY
    RESERVE 20 YEAR OLD
PAPPY VAN WINKLE'S FAMILY
    RESERVE 23 YEAR OLD
VAN WINKLE FAMILY RESERVE RYE
VAN WINKLE SPECIAL RESERVE

meet demand, the company entered into a partnership with Buffalo Trace to make its whiskey, though giving Julian, III (and his own son, Preston) extensive access to the production process. Because of the advanced age of even the youngest Van Winkle whiskeys, those new, Buffalo Trace-produced barrels are only now being bottled.

Despite the new source of whiskey, Van Winkle only sells about 7,000 cases a year, or about 42,000 bottles—a mere rounding error for a mid-size distillery—with sales of $2 million. That's a big comedown from his grandfather's time, when Stitzel-Weller sold about 800,000 cases a year. But it may be more in line with Pappy Van Winkle's famous motto: "We make fine bourbon, at a profit if we can, at a loss if we must, but always a fine bourbon."

Old Rip Van Winkle Handmade Bourbon

AGE	**10** years old
PROOF	**107**

NOSE	COLOR	BODY
Model glue, lemons, beeswax, and caramel	Amber/ deep gold	Thin to medium

GENERAL	PALATE	
Measured, complex, and refined, it's the everyday Van Winkle, and an outstanding whiskey in its own right.	Cherry, salt, and bubble gum. Finishes hot.	
	PRICE	RATING
	$$$	

Pappy Van Winkle's Family Reserve Kentucky Straight Bourbon Whiskey

AGE	PROOF
15 years old	**107**

NOSE	COLOR	BODY
Currants, apples, caramel, and brown sugar	Red gold to tawny	Full and chewy

GENERAL	PALATE
A truly stellar whiskey, and better balanced than the twenty year old. Its sugary and woody notes, full body and chewy mouthfeel, make it a perfect glass for a cold winter night. The spicy candy finish is deeply satisfying and lengthy.	Butterscotch, oak, and cinnamon, finishes with a redolent of Red Hot candy.

PRICE	RATING
$$$$	

Pappy Van Winkle's Family Reserve Kentucky Straight Bourbon Whiskey

AGE	PROOF
20 years old	**90.4**

NOSE	COLOR	BODY
Lavender, sherry, and cherry	Red gold to tawny	Medium to full

GENERAL	PALATE
A lot of oak, not surprisingly, but a little too much. The mouthfeel is slightly lighter and more oily than its younger and older siblings, and the finish is a bit too harsh and abrupt. Still, a great whiskey if you can find it.	Salt, geranium, caramel, and Willy Wonka candies; finishes with spice and grape soda.

PRICE	RATING
$$$$	

Pappy Van Winkle's Family Reserve Kentucky Straight Bourbon Whiskey

AGE
23
years old

PROOF
95.6

NOSE
Fruity, mostly plum jam, with caramel, cinnamon, and cotton candy. A little water brings out a touch of menthol.

COLOR
Red gold

BODY
Full and chewy

GENERAL
There's a reason this whiskey is so sought after: simply put, bourbon doesn't get better. For a superannuated whiskey, there are very few obvious wood notes, though the influence of oak is everywhere.

PALATE
Grape juice, oranges, salt, sulfur, and grappa; the finish is spicy and longer than a Faulkner sentence.

PRICE
$$$$

RATING

Van Winkle Family Reserve Rye

AGE
13
years old

PROOF
95.6

NOSE
Cake, vanilla, marzipan, rosewater, woody; with a little water, cherry and cola notes emerge.

COLOR
Tawny

BODY
Medium

GENERAL
The nose is quite bourbon-like: sweet and floral, with little spice. The tannic edge on the tongue and the lack of any real sweetness make this a severe, serene sip; though atypical of most ryes, it's a beautiful drink in its own right.

PALATE
Cherry cola, floral, slightly tannic, with a pop of spice at the end

PRICE
$$$$

RATING

Van Winkle Special Reserve Lot "B" Kentucky Straight Bourbon Whiskey

AGE
12
years old

PROOF
90.4

NOSE
Spearmint, flowers, and fresh laundry

COLOR
Deep amber

BODY
Full and rich

GENERAL
An excellent drink, the Special Reserve is not to be overlooked in the Van Winkle portfolio. The dark, brooding notes set it apart as the rebellious younger brother in the family.

PALATE
Smoke, dark berry, salt, and plums finishing with a long spicy burn.

PRICE
$$$$

RATING
★ ★ ★ ✦

Old Whiskey River

DRINKS AMERICAS HOLDINGS

372 DANBURY ROAD

WILTON, CT 06897

TEL: 203-762-7000

E-MAIL: info@drinksamericas.com

www.drinksamericas.com

....

PRODUCER

HEAVEN HILL DISTILLERIES

P.O. BOX 729

BARDSTOWN, KY 40004

TEL: 502-348-3921

www.heavenhill.com

This six-year-old bourbon was "commissioned" (whatever that means) by Willie Nelson, and each bottle comes with an autographed guitar pick strung around its neck. The whiskey is made by Heaven Hill under contract for Drinks Americas Holdings, "a leading owner, developer and marketer of premium beverages associated with renowned icons" that also owns and markets Trump Super Premium Vodka and, no kidding, Kid Rock's American Badass Beer. Other than the celebrity affiliation, there's nothing particularly interesting about this whiskey.

Old Whiskey River Kentucky Straight Bourbon Whiskey

AGE **6** years old		
PROOF **86**		
NOSE Heather, black pepper, solvent	**COLOR** Tawny	**BODY** Thin
GENERAL It's a sad thought that when Willie is no longer among us, Old Whiskey River will still be sitting on shelves, a mediocre testament to his legacy.	**PALATE** Vague spice, cinnamon at back	
	PRICE **$$**	**RATING** **NR**

Old Williamsburg

Old Williamsburg is the Manischewitz of bourbon. Like the sickly sweet but religiously certified wine, Old Williamsburg is a bottom-shelf selection that is certified kosher, the only bourbon to receive such a designation. (Koval, a craft distiller in Chicago, also makes kosher whiskeys, but not a bourbon.) Old Williamsburg is made by Heaven Hill but owned by the Royal Wine Corp. of New Jersey.

What makes a whiskey kosher? Better yet, what would make a whiskey un-kosher? At the risk of getting Talmudic, there are a few obvious things: whether the whiskey is made by a company that follows kosher rules (including whether it observes the Sabbath), whether the aging barrels have been used previously to hold non-kosher foodstuffs (not an issue for bourbon, which must use new oak barrels, but certainly an issue for scotch), and whether it has any additives that might be considered un-kosher (again, not an issue for a quality bourbon, but when you get into blends, which can contain all sorts of additives, you run into trouble). Ultimately, the point of certifying a spirit as kosher is not to restate the obvious, but rather to assure observant Jews that a rabbi has reviewed the product and given his approval.

ROYAL WINE CORP.

63 LEFANTE WAY

BAYONNE, NJ 07002

TEL: 201-437-9131

www.royalwine.com

PRODUCER

HEAVEN HILL DISTILLERIES

P.O. BOX 729

BARDSTOWN, KY 40004

TEL: 502-348-3921

www.heavenhill.com

Old Williamsburg Kentucky Straight Bourbon Whiskey

AGE	No age statement
PROOF	**80**

NOSE	COLOR	BODY
Corn, Scope mouthwash	Amber	Thin

GENERAL	PALATE
Oy, gevalt. This is not good. The finish is, thank G_d, brief.	Vegetal, peppery, grassy; short at the end.

PRICE	RATING
$	**NR**

Peach Street Colorado Straight Bourbon

PEACH STREET DISTILLERS

144 KLUGE AVENUE

PALISADE, CO 81526

TEL: 970-464-1128

E-MAIL: info@peachstreetdistillers.com

www.peachstreetdistillers.com

Alongside Stranahan's, Leopold Bros. and Breckenridge, Peach Street Distillers is one of the leading names in Colorado's microdistilling movement. Since 2005, the company, located in the small town of Palisade, near the Utah border, has produced a wide range of spirits, but it has attracted national attention for its straight bourbon.

Made from corn harvested in Olathe, about fifty miles south, and aged for two to three years, the whiskey is available in limited quantities outside the state, though the company says that to meet growing demand it is building a second, dedicated still, and expects to greatly expand distribution by 2015. Thanks in part to the hype the whiskey has generated, in 2012 Peach Street was named distiller of the year by the American Distilling Institute.

Peach Street Colorado Straight Bourbon Whiskey

AGE		
2 years old		

PROOF		
92		

NOSE	COLOR	BODY
Slightly brackish, sulfur, menthol, dill, and, surprising for its youth, some vanilla	Russet	Medium-light

GENERAL	PALATE
One of the least bourbon-like bourbons on the market. More feinty scotch notes than you'd expect, with few of the sweet grainy notes bourbon fans crave. A compellingly original drink.	Spice, cherries, walnuts, and cough syrup, which continues through the finish.

PRICE	RATING
$$$$	★ ★

Pikesville Supreme

Whiskey drinkers should be forgiven for considering Pikesville a Maryland rye—it is sold almost exclusively in the Maryland area, it's named after a Baltimore suburb, and for a long time, it was, indeed, a product of the Old Line State. For at least the last thirty years, however, it has been made by Heaven Hill, in Kentucky, then trucked into Maryland for purchase.

Unlike their spicier, bolder cousins in Pennsylvania, classic Maryland ryes were smoother and brighter, and some were even blended with fruit liquors to give them even higher notes. Pikesville originated in the 1890s at the L. Winand & Bro. Distillery, and after Prohibition was picked up by the Monumental Distillery, later renamed the Majestic Distillery. As the century wore on, rye declined in popularity, and one by one the East Coast distilleries closed their stills. Majestic, the last of the Maryland whiskey makers, shut down distilling operations in 1972, but it bought rye in bulk and bottled it as Pikesville for another decade, before the brand moved to Kentucky.

HEAVEN HILL DISTILLERIES

P.O. BOX 729

BARDSTOWN, KY 40004

TEL: 502-348-3921

www.heavenhill.com

Pikesville Supreme Straight Rye Whiskey

AGE	PROOF
3 years old	**80**

NOSE	COLOR	BODY
Bright floral, pepper, stewed fruit, butter	Russet	Full and robust

GENERAL	PALATE	
Not bad for a mass-produced, lowest-common-denominator whiskey. Sadly, this is no longer "Maryland" in any sense save for its target market—it tastes like much like any ordinary rye.	Pepper, cream	

	PRICE	RATING
	$	

Pine Barrens

LONG ISLAND SPIRITS

2180 SOUND AVENUE

BAITING HOLLOW, NY 11933

TEL: 631-630-9322

E-MAIL: rich@lispirits.com

www.lispirits.com

Named for the scrub forests found along the North Fork of Long Island, this whiskey is made by Long Island Spirits, best known for its LiV brand vodka. Though the company calls this a "single malt," don't expect notes of Caledonian salt air or peaty smoke. Pine Barrens starts as a commercially produced barleywine—specifically, Old Howling Bastard, from Blue Point Brewing Co.—which is then distilled and aged for about a year. The role of the wood is minimal; instead, the beer's hops and malt dominate. Right now distribution is limited to the New York City area, but Richard Stabile, the founder and owner of Long Island Spirits, says that demand is such that coverage will probably expand over the next few years.

Pine Barrens Single Malt Whiskey

AGE	Less than **2** years old
PROOF	**96**

NOSE	COLOR	BODY
Tire rubber, solvent, wet grass, and black molasses	Amber	Thinnish

GENERAL	PALATE
Pine Barrens is a unique and surprisingly pleasing whiskey. Who'd have thought a distilled commercial beer could work so well as a whiskey base?	Mushrooms, beef bouillon, and water crackers, finishes with barley soup.

PRICE	RATING
$$$	★★

Prichard's

Phil Prichard has been in operation since 1999, making him an old-timer compared to the new crop of craft distillers. But, he's a relative infant compared to the twin giants of Tennessee whiskey, Jack Daniel's and George Dickel. Unlike his elders, though, Prichard produces a variety of spirits, including rum and liqueurs, alongside his range of whiskeys.

Prichard makes two of his three whiskeys—his single malt and his Tennessee—exclusively on site, using the water from a stream near his Kelso, Tennessee distillery (located in an old school house, of all places). Prichard's Tennessee Whiskey is not, strictly speaking, a Tennessee whiskey, as the term is popularly understood—it is not passed through sugar-maple charcoal, the so-called Lincoln County Process. Prichard, however, points out that by law, any whiskey made in Tennessee, whether it uses the Lincoln County Process or not, can be called a Tennessee whiskey. Anyone who says otherwise, he says, is just repeating Jack Daniel's marketing copy.

For his double-barreled bourbon, Prichard buys aged whiskey from a Kentucky distillery, dilutes it to 90 proof, then rebarrels it for another three to five years. The reason? These days, most American whiskeys are barreled at 125 proof, the highest level allowed by law. That's cheaper, for a variety of reasons, but it also makes for a less flavorful whiskey. By diluting and then rebarreling, Prichard says he can get a good approximation of how bourbon would taste, if, in his words, the big distilleries cared less about profits than taste.

PRICHARD'S DISTILLERY
11 KELSO-SMITHLAND ROAD
KELSO, TN 37348
TEL: 931-433-5454
E-MAIL: connie@prichardsdistillery.com
www.prichardsdistillery.com

BRANDS
TENNESSEE WHISKEY
DOUBLE-BARRELED BOURBON
   WHISKEY
SINGLE MALT WHISKEY

Prichard's Tennessee Whiskey

AGE	No age statement
PROOF	**80**

NOSE	COLOR	BODY
Oatmeal cookies, marzipan, and oak	Tawny	Medium

GENERAL	PALATE
Sweet, but not quite cloying, with some slight citrusy notes. This is a fine sipping whiskey taken neat or with a just a splash of water or ice.	Dark cherry and pepper; medicinal finish.

PRICE	RATING
$$	

Prichard's Double-Barreled Bourbon Whiskey

AGE	**9** years old
PROOF	**90**

NOSE	COLOR	BODY
Candy apple, bright floral, cinnamon, grass, cola	Auburn/ mahogany	Medium

GENERAL	PALATE
Sweet, but not overly so, with some slight citrusy notes. This is a fine sipping whiskey taken neat or with a just a splash of water or ice.	Citrus, Christmas spices, cigar; tart finishing.

PRICE	RATING
$$$$	

Prichard's
Single Malt Whiskey

AGE	No age statement
PROOF	**80**

NOSE
Peat, iodine, barley, mown hay, mushrooms

COLOR
Tawny

BODY
Medium to full

GENERAL
Prichard's Single Malt is full-bodied but not particularly flavorful. It has an intriguing nose, very barley and wood forward countered by sweetness that does not quite resolve itself properly.

PALATE
Corn flakes and cardboard; finishes with sweetness and a pleasant long tingle.

PRICE
$$$

RATING
★

Pure Kentucky XO

KENTUCKY BOURBON DISTILLERS

1869 LORETTO ROAD

BARDSTOWN, KY, 40004

TEL: 502-348-0081

E-MAIL: kentuckybourbon@bardstown.com

www.kentuckybourbonwhiskey.com

PRODUCER: UNKNOWN

Along with Noah's Mill, Rowan's Creek, and Kentucky Vintage, Pure Kentucky XO is one of Kentucky Bourbon Distillers' "small batch" bourbons, though what distinguishes those from other KBD products like Vintage, Johnny Drum, Willett, and Old Bardstown is unclear. "Small batch" is an undefined term, and KBD is notoriously opaque about what goes into its whiskeys (they are all sourced).

Until a few years ago, Pure Kentucky XO was labeled a ten- to twelve-year-old bourbon, but recent releases have come without an official age statement. Suspicion is that most of the whiskey in Pure Kentucky XO remains somewhere around that age. As with other KBD offerings without a specified age, it's thought that the folks behind the label want the flexibility to add younger whiskeys to the blend from time to time in order to round out the flavor profile.

Pure Kentucky XO Kentucky Straight Bourbon Whiskey

AGE
No age statement

PROOF
107

NOSE
Marzipan, orange chocolate, candy, meringue, truffle chocolate

COLOR
Russet

BODY
Light

GENERAL
It's spicy, for sure, but not enough else is in there to make it fun. Nevertheless, this is solid whiskey, one of the better expressions from Kentucky Bourbon Distillers.

PALATE
Curry, wasabi, and a little briny salt

PRICE
$$

RATING

(rī)1

If the diminutive rock star Prince drank whiskey, chances are he would prefer this rye (or perhaps not, given how well his own, short-lived sign-name went over). Released in 2008, (rī)1 is Beam's attempt to get a jump on the gentrification of rye whiskey, with a minimalist label and fussily baroque name. Unlike Beam's traditional ryes—Jim Beam Rye and Old Overholt—(rī)1 is a blend of different ages, with a minimum of four-and-a-half years old each. According to the company, it's aimed at "cocktail couture" and the "cocktail crowd." But no one who orders bottle service at a club orders rye, and no one who prefers rye would order bottle service.

BEAM INC.
510 LAKE COOK ROAD
DEERFIELD, IL 60015
TEL: 847-948-8888
www.beamglobal.com

(rī)1

	AGE No age statement	
	PROOF 92	
NOSE Butter cream, mint, high floral, citrus	**COLOR** Auburn	**BODY** Full
GENERAL The male model of ryes: all the right qualities are there on the surface, but there's no depth or individuality.	**PALATE** Butterscotch, oak, one-dimensional finish	
	PRICE $$	**RATING** ★★

Ranger Ceek

RANGER CREEK BREWING &
   DISTILLING
4834 WHIRLWIND STREET
SAN ANTONIO, TX 78217
TEL: 210-775-2099
E-MAIL: info@drinkrangercreek.com
www.drinkrangercreek.com

San Antonio's Ranger Creek Brewing & Distilling is best known for its beers. A few years ago, though, it joined a nationwide trend among craft brewers and started making a little liquor on the side, following the lead of places like Rogue, New Holland, and Dogfish Head. The move makes sense: whiskey is, more or less, distilled and aged beer, and most established craft brewers have already made a name for themselves as successful innovators.

Eventually, Ranger Creek plans to offer a regular-production, Texas straight bourbon whiskey. For now, it offers what it calls its Small Caliber Series, a limited annual release of whiskeys created with different ingredients under different conditions.

The 2011 release, reviewed here, is called .36 Texas Bourbon Whiskey. It is the same whiskey that will go into Ranger Creek's Texas straight bourbon, but was placed in smaller barrels, while the whiskey destined for regular release went into 53-gallon barrels. Like Garrison Bros. and Balcones, Ranger Creek makes particularly strong claims about the uniqueness of the Texas climate and its ability to accelerate whiskey aging. (In late 2012 Ranger Creek released another in the Small Caliber series, called Rimfire, a scotch-style whiskey in which the malt is smoked with mesquite.)

Ranger Creek .36 Texas Bourbon Whiskey

AGE	PROOF
9 months old	**96**

NOSE	COLOR	BODY
Cherry, wood, baseball mitt, barley	Burnt umber	Thick

GENERAL	PALATE	
Some nice cherry notes here, but they are hidden under a lumber yard's worth of oak. It's also over-burdened by a big bowl of barley soup funk on the nose that crowds out the more subtle notes lurking in the background. With some fine tuning, this could be a good whiskey.	Lemon, cherry, sour finish	

	PRICE	RATING
	$$$	

Rebecca Creek

Introduced in 2011, San Antonio's Rebecca Creek is a blended whiskey, similar to Seagram's 7 Crown—it mixes whiskey, in this case an eight-year-old sourced bourbon, with a neutral grain spirit to produce a lighter flavor profile. After blending the two, Rebecca Creek then redistills the blend and ages it in oak barrels.

REBECCA CREEK DISTILLERY

26605 BULVERDE ROAD

SAN ANTONIO, TX 78260

TEL: 830-714-4581

E-MAIL: info@rebeccacreekdistillery.com

www.rebeccacreekwhiskey.com

Rebecca Creek Fine Texas Spirit Whiskey

AGE		
No age statement		

PROOF		
80		

NOSE	COLOR	BODY
Apricot, banana candy, honeysuckle, and orange zest	Russet	Light

GENERAL	PALATE	
For a blended whiskey, there's a lot going on here, though all at the high end of the register. There's enough front-loaded flavor to make it decent for sipping, though it might really shine in a cocktail.	Cinnamon, banana, and floral notes, finishing with a numbing, sweet tartness.	

PRICE	RATING
$$	★ ⌐

Rebel Yell

LUXCO

5050 KEMPER AVENUE

ST. LOUIS, MO 63139

TEL: 314-772-2626

E-MAIL: contactus@luxco.com

www.luxco.com

....

PRODUCER

HEAVEN HILL DISTILLERIES

P.O. BOX 729

BARDSTOWN, KY 40004

TEL: 502-348-3921

www.heavenhill.com

....

BRANDS

REBEL YELL KENTUCKY STRAIGHT
        BOURBON WHISKEY

REBEL RESERVE KENTUCKY
        STRAIGHT BOURBON WHISKEY

Though its name might imply otherwise, and its quality is middle-of-the-pack, Rebel Yell has quite a pedigree. Its roots go back to the mid-nineteenth century, when William Larue Weller created a range of bourbons using wheat instead of rye as their small grain. Weller's wholesale business was later bought by Julian P. "Pappy" Van Winkle and merged with the A. Ph. Stiztel Distillery, which made Weller's whiskeys, to create the Stitzel-Weller Distillery.

Rebel Yell itself was rolled out in the late 1940s as a wheated bourbon for sale exclusively in the South (eventually its reach expanded nationwide). The Stitzel-Weller Distillery shut down in 1992 and its brands were sold off, with Rebel Yell ending up in the hands of Luxco, a St. Louis-based spirits marketing firm that also owns the Ezra Brooks brand. The whiskey is distilled, aged, and bottled by Heaven Hill in Kentucky.

Rebel Yell Kentucky Straight Bourbon Whiskey		AGE No age statement
		PROOF **80**
NOSE Nougat, orange, and a little oak	COLOR Amber	BODY Light
GENERAL The high wheat content makes Rebel Yell light and refreshing— a good summer whiskey with a splash of soda and a few ice cubes.	PALATE Spun sugar, oak, caramel cream, smooth finish	
	PRICE $	RATING

Rebel Reserve Kentucky Straight Bourbon Whiskey BATCH 1049/BOTTLE 52396

AGE

No age statement

PROOF

90.6

NOSE

Mossy, grassy, salty, and, honestly, porky

COLOR

Deep gold

BODY

Light to medium

GENERAL

Overall, a great balance. The meat and smoke notes intrigue the senses, complemented by the candy-cinnamon finish.

PALATE

Meat, smoke, Atomic Fireball at the finish

PRICE

$$

RATING

Redemption

BARDSTOWN BARREL SELECTIONS

1010 WITHROW COURT

BARDSTOWN, KY 40004

TEL: 203 226 4181

E-MAIL: ds@redemptionrye.com

www.redemptionrye.com

PRODUCER

MGP INGREDIENTS, INC.

CRAY BUSINESS PLAZA

100 COMMERCIAL STREET

P.O. BOX 130

ATCHISON, KS 66002

TEL: 800-255-0302

www.mgpingredients.com

The Redemption brand is owned by Bardstown Barrel Selections, a bottler in Bardstown, Kentucky, but distilled and aged by MGP's distillery in Lawrenceburg, Indiana. Redemption High-Rye Bourbon has, as its name implies, an unusually high rye content: 38.2 percent, to be exact, alongside 60 percent corn and just 1.8 percent malted barley. Redemption Rye is likewise cozy with the grain, coming in at 95 percent of the mash bill (the same as Bulleit Rye, also made by MGP). Both products are aged for two to three years and bottled at 92 proof. In 2011 Bardstown Barrel Selections introduced Temptation, a more traditional bourbon, with 75 percent corn, 20 percent rye and 5 percent corn, aged for four years and bottled at a relatively low 82 proof.

BRANDS

REDEMPTION HIGH-RYE BOURBON

REDEMPTION RYE WHISKEY

REDEMPTION TEMPTATION BOURBON STRAIGHT
BOURBON WHISKEY

Redemption High-Rye Bourbon

AGE	No age statement
PROOF	**92**

NOSE	COLOR	BODY
Floral, with pencil shavings and port	Tawny	Medium

GENERAL	PALATE
This is a full-bodied bourbon with a flavor swell in its middle. The dryness is remarkable—somewhat breathtaking—but with an ethereal, lingering sweetness. It's a solid introductory whiskey, and a good bourbon for rye fans.	Pepper, cloves, vanilla, quick finish

PRICE	RATING
$$	

Russell's Reserve

Produced by Campari's Wild Turkey Distillery, Russell's Reserve bourbon and rye are named in honor of Jimmy Russell, the company's master distiller, who has worked there since 1954. Jimmy's son Eddie works alongside his father and is an accomplished distiller in his own right. The original bourbon expression, released in the early 2000s, was a robust 101 proof limited-edition brand. In 2005 it was repackaged and rereleased at 90 proof, though still at the ten-year-old mark. The rye, introduced a few years later, is six years old.

AUSTIN NICHOLS DISTILLING CO.
1525 TYRONE ROAD
LAWRENCEBURG, KY 40342
TEL: 502-839-4544
E-MAIL:
    campariamerica@qualitycustomercare.com
www.wildturkey.com

BRANDS
RUSSELL'S RESERVE SINGLE BARREL
    KENTUCKY STRAIGHT BOURBON
    WHISKEY
RUSSELL'S RESERVE 10 YEAR OLD
    SMALL BATCH BOURBON

Russell's Reserve Kentucky Straight Rye Whiskey

AGE **6** years old		
PROOF **90**		
NOSE Maple syrup, anise, vanilla, geraniums, apricot, nougat	**COLOR** Russet	**BODY** Medium
GENERAL Russell's Reserve is surprisingly mild for a six year old. It exhibits a lot of typical rye notes on the nose and palate, with the addition of a touch of pipe tobacco. It errs a bit on the sweet side, but overall, a solid medium-bodied rye.	**PALATE** Vanilla, cream, spice; nutty, bitter finish.	
	PRICE $$$	**RATING**

Russell's Reserve Kentucky Straight Bourbon Whiskey

AGE
10
years old

PROOF
90

NOSE	COLOR	BODY
Honeysuckle, citrus, vanilla and apple	Auburn	Light and smooth

GENERAL	PALATE
A very enjoyable summer bourbon. For an older whiskey, it's quite light, full of floral and fruit notes.	Toasted bread, flowers, and minimum spice; more heat on finish.

PRICE
$$

RATING

Russell's Reserve Small Batch Single Barrel Kentucky Straight Bourbon Whiskey

AGE
No age statement

PROOF
110

NOSE	COLOR	BODY
Sandalwood, marzipan, apple, and corn (especially with some water)	Auburn	Light to medium

GENERAL	PALATE
The corn notes are almost overwhelming, but manage to balance with the fruit and spice. It's reminiscent of some of the better immature bourbons on the market. The toasted wood finish is excellent.	Tons of corn, umami, smoked meats, cumin; long, woody finish.

PRICE
$$$

RATING

Sam Houston

Walk into a well-stocked liquor store and you're likely to find two very different bottles of whiskey both bearing the name Sam Houston. One, squat with a black label, is a sourced bourbon made by McClain & Kyne, a marketing company that also oversees the Jefferson's brand of whiskeys. Where the underlying juice came from is unknown.

In 2009, McClain & Kyne sold the Sam Houston brand to a company called Western Spirits. That's why, alongside the squat black Sam Houston bourbon bottle, you'll also find a tall, slender bottle of "American straight whiskey," usually packaged in a cylinder similar to the traditional protective scotch tubes.

To be clear: these two whiskeys have nothing to do with each other. They're not even the same type of whiskey. They do, however, demonstrate the superficiality of brand names. For now, it's relatively easy to find either whiskey on the shelf, but the bourbon is steadily shrinking in population, so buy it if you see it.

WESTERN SPIRITS BEVERAGE
    COMPANY
2200 LAPSLEY LANE
BOWLING GREEN, KY 42103
TEL: 270-796-5851
E-MAIL: info@westernspirits.com
www.westernspirits.com

....

PRODUCER: UNKNOWN, FOR EITHER
EXPRESSION

....

BRANDS
SAM HOUSTON KENTUCKY STRAIGHT
    BOURBON WHISKEY
SAM HOUSTON AMERICAN WHISKEY

Sam Houston Kentucky Straight Bourbon Whiskey

AGE		
10 years old		
PROOF		
85.6		

NOSE	COLOR	BODY
Butterscotch and white pepper	Tawny	Light

GENERAL	PALATE	
Pleasant. It's very smooth on entry, with some sweetness up front and some rye bite toward the back.	Candy sugar, decent hit of pepper, spicy finish.	
	PRICE $$	**RATING**

Sam Houston
American Whiskey

AGE
No age statement

PROOF
86

NOSE
Vanilla, maple syrup, cola, white pepper, and wheat

COLOR
Chestnut

BODY
Medium

GENERAL
This is practically a mint julep on its own. Very sweet. Best as a mixer in a summer cocktail.

PALATE
Cola and hot peppers; fast, minty finish.

PRICE
$$

RATING
★ ⌐

Sazerac

The Sazerac story originates in a mid-nineteenth-century tavern in New Orleans called the Merchants Exchange Coffee House. The bar begat the cocktail, originally made with Peychaud's Bitters and a cognac called Sazerac de Forge et Fils. Eventually the bar changed its name to promote its flagship drink. In the 1870s the Sazerac recipe switched from cognac to rye, thanks to a phylloxera epidemic in French wine regions that decimated wine and cognac production.

Around the same time, the bar was bought by Thomas H. Handy; he and his descendants created the Sazerac company and steadily built it by widening its portfolio of brands and, later, distilleries. Today it makes whiskey at the Buffalo Trace facility and the Barton Distillery in Frankfort and Bardstown, Kentucky, respectively, and the A. Smith Bowman Distillery in Fredericksburg, Virginia.

Sazerac makes three rye whiskeys under its namesake brand: Sazerac 6 Years Old, Sazerac 18 Years Old, and Thomas H. Handy Sazerac, all three of which are made at Buffalo Trace. The latter two are part of the limited-edition Buffalo Trace Antique Collection.

BUFFALO TRACE DISTILLERY
113 GREAT BUFFALO TRACE
FRANKFORT, KENTUCKY 40601
TEL: 800-654-8471
E-MAIL: info@buffalotrace.com
www.buffalotrace.com

Thomas H. Handy Sazerac Straight Rye Whiskey, a limited edition bottle in the Buffalo Trace Antique Collection

Sazerac
Straight Rye Whiskey

NOSE	**COLOR**	**BODY**
High floral, wood, corn, caramel	Mahogany	Thin to medium
GENERAL	**PALATE**	
Sazerac is an exemplary rye whiskey, but a bit quirky, like the quarterback who also stars in high school musicals. If you like the flavor of rye but not the heat, choose this mellow rye.	Fruit juice, mint, minimal spice	
	PRICE	**RATING**
	$$	★★★

AGE
6 years old

PROOF
90

Seagram's 7 Crown

DIAGEO NORTH AMERICA
801 MAIN AVENUE
NORWALK, CT 06851
TEL: 646-223-2000
www.diageo.com

PRODUCER: UNKNOWN

Perhaps the best-known American blended whiskey, Seagram's 7 Crown experienced its heyday in the 1960s and '70s. Its light body and smooth flavor proved popular with consumers making the long-wave shift from harsher whiskeys to milder flavored white liquors like rum and vodka. In 1970 it sold 31 million cases. But the whiskey decline spared no one, and by 1993 it was down to 8 million cases per year. Then, when the whiskey boom picked up in the 2000s, Seagram's 7 Crown—widely seen as a down-market, *demode* vestige of shag carpets and chartreuse turtlenecks—got left behind. Today Seagram's, now owned by Diageo, is pushing a retro-chic marketing campaign, hoping to latch onto the same spirit that turned Pabst Blue Ribbon into a surprise hit a decade ago. It seems to be working: the brand was one of the fastest-growing in 2011.

Seagram's 7 Crown is blended from a variety of whiskeys, plus a heavy dose (75 percent) of grain neutral spirits.

Seagram's Seven Crown American Whiskey

AGE		No age statement
PROOF		**80**

NOSE	COLOR	BODY
Almost nothing, though there's a whiff of barley funk and wood.	Burnished	Light

GENERAL	PALATE	
At 75 percent neutral grain spirits, there's almost nothing "whiskey" about Seagram's Seven Crown. Still, it performs a function as one of the most common mixing whiskeys on the market and that's surely the only way to drink it.	Caramel cream, black pepper, acetone, barley, a touch of rye	
	PRICE	RATING

Smooth Ambler

Located just over the Virginia border, West Virginia's Smooth Ambler Spirits Distillery opened in 2009 offereing vodka, gin, and white whiskey; it soon added a young wheated bourbon, called Yearling, and a six- to seven-year-old sourced bourbon, called Old Scout.

The distillery's owners aspire to be a vertical operation, with everything from grain milling to bottling done on premises, so expect to see the profile of Old Scout change over the coming years as its production moves in-house. For now, Old Scout, made by MGP at its distillery in Lawrenceburg, Indiana, is heavy on the rye, at 36 percent, which makes it a nice contrast with the twenty-two-month-old Yearling, which has no rye at all. The company has also released, in very limited numbers, a fourteen-year-old "curated" (i.e., sourced) bourbon and a seven-year-old rye. Reportedly Smooth Ambler also has fifteen-, seventeen- and nineteen-year-old expressions on deck.

SMOOTH AMBLER SPIRITS
745 INDUSTRIAL PARK ROAD
MAXWELTON, WV 24957
TEL: 304-497-3123
E-MAIL: jlittle@smoothambler.com
www.smoothambler.com

PRODUCER
VARIOUS

BRANDS
OLD SCOUT STRAIGHT
    BOURBON WHISKEY
YEARLING BOURBON WHISKEY

Smooth Ambler Old Scout Straight Bourbon Whiskey

AGE		
5 years old		

PROOF		
99		

NOSE	COLOR	BODY
Shellac, apples, plums, and old oak	Tawny to amber	Full and viscous

GENERAL	PALATE	
A solid entry from a new distillery, even considering that it's sourced from elsewhere. It's very sweet, but not quite cloying; a real tightrope walker of a whiskey.	Pepper, boozy sugar, liqueur-like; spicy finish.	

	PRICE	RATING
	$$	★ ★

Smooth Ambler Yearling Bourbon Whiskey

AGE
1.5
years old

PROOF
92

NOSE
Vegetal, walnuts, dark bread

COLOR
Chestnut

BODY
Medium

GENERAL
Too young and out of tune, Yearling has a lot of potentially interesting moving parts— funk and nuts on the nose, sweet spice on the palate— but they don't cohere into anything compelling.

PALATE
Cinnamon and candies; finishes with a numbing acidity.

PRICE
$$

RATING

St. George Single Malt Whiskey

Founded in 1982, Alameda, California's St. George Spirits is among the oldest craft distilleries in the country. Like other early entrants—Clear Creek, Charbay—its early focus was on *eaux de vie*. Today, however, its best-known product is Hangar One Vodka.

Starting in 2000, St. George was also one of the first distilleries to release an American single malt. Like many American single-malt distillers, St. George gets its distiller's beer—the fermented, undistilled liquid—from a nearby brewery, in this case Sierra Nevada. The beer is made from a variety of malts, some light and bright, others toasted and dark, to give the resulting whiskey more complex flavors.

The latest release as of this writing, the so-called Lot 12, draws on a range of fifteen different whiskey barrels, from five to twelve years old, some of them first-fill, while some are reused bourbon, port, and sherry barrels. Using such a broad range of barrels gives the distillers a broader palette to work with. Keep in mind that each lot will be slightly different, as St. George aims for a slightly different flavor profile each time.

ST. GEORGE SPIRITS
2601 MONARCH ST.
ALAMEDA, CA 94501
TEL: 510-769-1601
EMAIL: lance@stgeorgespirits.com
www.stgeorgespirits.com

St. George Single Malt Whiskey

AGE No age statement		
PROOF **86**		
NOSE Light wood, honeysuckle, peat, acetone, citrus	**COLOR** Pale straw	**BODY** Light to medium
GENERAL A good but not exceptional interpretation of a classic single malt. Give it some time to open up after pouring a glass; it rounds out nicely.	**PALATE** Lavender, wood, citrus, charcoal, and sherry on finish	
	PRICE $$$$	**RATING**

Stranahan's

STRANAHAN'S COLORADO WHISKEY

200 SOUTH KALAMATH ST.

DENVER, CO 80223

TEL: 303-296-7440

EMAIL: info@stranahans.com

www.stranahans.com

Unlike many established craft distillers, Stranahan's, founded in 2003 in Denver, has always only made one thing: Stranahan's Colorado Whiskey. They blend scotch-style ingredients (four kinds of malted barley) and bourbon-style production (aged for two to five years in new, 50-gallon, charred oak barrels). And almost uniquely among American distillers, Stranahan's starts each mash wholly new, without backset—making it one of the only "sweet mash" whiskeys on the market.

Stranahan's reports that its production and distribution are in the process of expanding. Proximo Spirits, a New York-based distributor that also owns Kraken Spiced Rum, purchased them in 2010. Some of the whiskey's original partisans are concerned that the takeover will mean a decline in quality—especially after its original head distiller, Jake Norris, left in early 2012. Fortunately for fans of Stranahan's, its new distiller, Rob Dietrich, trained under Norris and has promised to hew closely to his teacher's methods and recipe.

Stranahan's Colorado Whiskey

AGE	PROOF
2 years old	**94**

NOSE	COLOR	BODY
Marsh gas, molasses, cabbage, wet ash, rubber, oranges, and peanuts	Burnished/ chestnut	Medium

GENERAL	PALATE	
There's far too much funk on this whiskey for it to rate highly, but it's sure to have its fans. Scotch partisans should take a sip, but don't expect too much.	Cabbage water, acetone, barley, spice on finish	

	PRICE	RATING
	$$$	

Templeton

Templeton is a frustrating whiskey. It claims to be a small-batch, authentic Prohibition-era Iowa rye whiskey, a favorite of Al Capone's and renowned as "The Good Stuff." But none of this holds up to much scrutiny. It's made not in "small batches" but at the sprawling MGP distillery—which is not in Templeton, Iowa, but rather Lawrenceburg, Indiana. Nor is there much evidence that the recipe is in fact "Prohibition era." It is almost completely rye, which is robust and flavorful and unlike most corn-heavy rye mash bills from the 1920s. Whether a whiskey called "Templeton" was ever enjoyed by Mr. Capone or not is almost beside the point. This is marketing, not heritage.

What matters, of course, is what's in the glass and how it tastes. MGP makes some very good whiskey, and only the most naive of consumers should be shocked that a company that sells a retro-friendly product would swaddle it in sepia-print legend. And if Templeton is more brazen than most in its refashioning of the past to suit its present needs, it's hardly alone—as a rule, the older and more established the "old-fashioned" distillery, the less likely its foundation myths will stand up to close scrutiny.

TEMPLETON RYE SPIRITS, LLC
206 EAST 3RD STREET
TEMPLETON, IA 51463
TEL: 617-233-4893
EMAIL: info@templetonrye.com
www.Templetonrye.com

PRODUCER
MGP INGREDIENTS, INC.
CRAY BUSINESS PLAZA
100 COMMERCIAL STREET
P.O. BOX 130
ATCHISON, KS 66002
TEL: 800-255-0302
www.mgpingredients.com

Templeton Rye Small Batch Rye Whiskey

AGE	No age statement
PROOF	**80**

NOSE	COLOR	BODY
Pine resin, mint, cakebread, bananas, vanilla	Mahogany	Light

GENERAL	PALATE	
A solid, well-built rye, if a bit one-dimensional. It's sweet and refreshing; light on wood and full of candy high notes. A nice summer sipper.	Cereal, cloves, finishes with heat.	
	PRICE	RATING
	$$	★ ★

Ten High

BARTON 1792 DISTILLERY

300 BARTON ROAD

BARDSTOWN, KY 40004

TEL: 502-348-3991

www.1792bourbon.com

The Ten High name refers to the whiskey's supposed position while aging in the rickhouse, ten ricks up, where it would be exposed to greater heat and thus develop a richer flavor in less time. Whether any Ten High ever came from such a prized location is questionable, though it was once good enough that people didn't think too much about the name.

Then, in 2009 Constellation Brands, which produced the whiskey at its Barton distillery, refashioned Ten High as a bourbon blend: a combination, usually half and half, of bourbon and "neutral grain spirits"—i.e., vodka. Some markets still get Ten High straight bourbon, but they are the lucky few. As one might expect, it's a ghost of its former self, a thin, one-dimensional whiskey. Sazerac, which bought the Barton distillery later in 2009, has continued the new expression, to the dismay of cheap whiskey lovers everywhere.

Ten High Kentucky Bourbon Whiskey

AGE No age statement		
PROOF **94**		

NOSE	COLOR	BODY
Banana, mango, and citrus candy	Russet	Thin

GENERAL	PALATE	
Ten High is too sweet to work on its own, though it might make a decent inexpensive mixer.	Almost no spice, nutty, bitter; bitter finish.	
	PRICE $	**RATING** ★

Town Branch

Many whiskey brands are owned by multinational spirits companies, but Town Branch may be alone in being owned by a multinational agriculture company. Town Branch is made by Lyons Spirits, which in turn is controlled by Alltech, an animal feed manufacturer that, thanks to its founder's interest in distilling, has a growing interest in the world of alcoholic beverages. It's not all that strange a connection—many distillers sell their spent mash to farmers for use as animal feed. So why shouldn't an animal feed company own a distillery?

Alltech isn't just dabbling in whiskey: in the fall of 2011 it broke ground on a 20,000 square-foot, $4.5 million distillery in Lexington, near where the company is headquartered. Eventually production will reach up to 80,000 cases a year. That's tiny compared to the big guys, but it's a large step in the direction of making Town Branch a major presence in the liquor store.

Town Branch, named for a river that runs through Lexington, has a unique mash bill: it has just 51 percent corn, with 49 percent malted barley. No wheat. No rye.

ALLTECH'S LEXINGTON BREWING AND
DISTILLING COMPANY
401 CROSS STREET
LEXINGTON, KY 40508
TEL: 859-255-2337
E-MAIL: kentuckyale@alltech.com
WWW.KENTUCKYALE.COM

Town Branch Bourbon Kentucky Straight Bourbon Whiskey

AGE No age statement		
PROOF **80**		
NOSE Pear, toasted barley, and toffee	**COLOR** Russet	**BODY** Light to medium
GENERAL Considering the mash bill (51 percent corn to 49 percent malted barley), it's not as unusual as one might expect. Still, Town Branch is very good whiskey. It has a wonderful nose and a pleasant combination of winey notes and spice at the end.	**PALATE** White wine, allspice; sweet, smooth finish.	
	PRICE $$	**RATING**

Very Old Barton

BARTON 1792 DISTILLERY

300 BARTON ROAD

BARDSTOWN, KY 40004

TEL: 502-348-3991

www.1792bourbon.com

BRANDS

VERY OLD BARTON KENTUCKY

STRAIGHT BOURBON WHISKEY

(86 PROOF)

VERY OLD BARTON KENTUCKY

STRAIGHT BOURBON WHISKEY

(90 PROOF)

Very Old Barton is regularly hailed as one of the best buys in whiskey—not great, but above average, and at an unbeatable price. Unfortunately, while it is one of the most popular brands in Kentucky, it has somewhat limited distribution outside the state and its neighbors.

The brand is made by Sazerac at the Barton 1792 Distillery in Bardstown, Kentucky. The name is also something of a misnomer: it's a six-year-old whiskey—aged, by some standards, but hardly old, let alone very old.

Very Old Barton Kentucky Straight Bourbon Whiskey

AGE	No age statement
PROOF	**80**

NOSE	COLOR	BODY
Caramel, cola, oak, cherries, tinge of resin	Russet	Medium

GENERAL	PALATE
A standard bourbon nose, but somewhat lacking in flavor. The forward sweetness is absent, and sorely missed, on the tongue.	Lots of mid-palate bitterness, with a bit of macadamia nut and wormwood bitterness; finishes quick and dry.

PRICE	RATING
$	

Very Old Barton Kentucky Straight Bourbon Whiskey

AGE
6
years old

PROOF
90

NOSE	COLOR	BODY
Vanilla, toasted nuts, and barley	Tawny	Medium

GENERAL

Very Old Barton 90 is a great example of a whiskey that hits above its price range. It has a good balance of dryness and slight sweetness.

PALATE

Cinnamon, jalapeno; finishes long and minty.

PRICE	RATING
$	★ ★

Vintage

KENTUCKY BOURBON DISTILLERS

1869 LORETTO ROAD

BARDSTOWN, KY, 40004

TEL: 502-348-0081

E-MAIL: kentuckybourbon@bardstown.com

www.kentuckybourbonwhiskey.com

Not to be confused with Kentucky Vintage, another product from Kentucky Bourbon Distillers, Vintage Bourbon is a seventeen-year-old, 94 proof whiskey sourced from an unnamed distillery. Vintage Rye is an even older—twenty-three years—expression, from a likewise anonymous producer.

PRODUCER: UNKNOWN

BRANDS

VINTAGE BOURBON

VINTAGE RYE

Vintage Bourbon

AGE		
17 years old		
PROOF		
94		

NOSE	COLOR	BODY
Pepper, leather, butter, port, marzipan	Auburn	Thick

GENERAL	PALATE	
Overall, considering the price and age, Vintage Bourbon is a bit underwhelming. The nose promises so much: caramel and vanilla, marzipan, orange, and freshly mown hay. The palate is oak heavy and slightly sweet. It begs to be tried again just to figure it out.	Grape juice, butter, caramel, squash; finishes fast.	
	PRICE	RATING
	$$$$	

Vintage Rye

AGE
21
years old

PROOF
94

NOSE
Marzipan, bright fruits, grass, peanut brittle

COLOR
Auburn

BODY
Full and robust

GENERAL
This is a superb older rye, if not exactly standard. It's woody and dark and full of funky feinty fruit and spice. Excellent to sip neat and savor.

PALATE
Muted spice, port, maraschino cherries; finishes with mint

PRICE
$$$$

RATING
★★★½

Virginia Gentleman

A. SMITH BOWMAN DISTILLERY

1 BOWMAN DRIVE

FREDERICKSBURG, VA 22408

TEL: 540-373-4555

E-MAIL: info@asmithbowman.com

www.asmithbowman.com

For years, Virginia Gentleman, made by the A. Smith Bowman Distillery in Fredericksburg, Virginia, was the only bourbon of any consequence produced outside Kentucky (nowadays, of course, there are bourbons popping up across the country). Virginia Gentleman was and remains only nominally non-Kentuckian: it is first distilled at the Buffalo Trace facility in Frankfort, Kentucky, then trucked to the Bowman facility where it is redistilled, aged and bottled. Until recently, Virginia Gentleman came in both the standard 80-proof expression and a higher 90-proof version; the 90-proof expression was discontinued when Bowman started releasing its own small batch and single-barrel whiskeys (see page 172).

Virginia Gentleman Straight Bourbon Whiskey

AGE	No age statement
PROOF	**80**

NOSE	COLOR	BODY
Maple, pepper, high floral, feinty	Russet	Light

GENERAL	PALATE
Solid and understated, Virginia Gentleman is a decent session whiskey for mixing.	Grape juice and cinnamon; cinnamon at finish.

PRICE	RATING

W.L. Weller

The Weller brand, currently owned and produced by Sazerac at its Buffalo Trace Distillery, traces its lineage to the mid-nineteenth century, when William Larue Weller, a Kentucky wholesaler, introduced the first wheated bourbon. Julian "Pappy" Van Winkle bought the W.L. Weller and Sons company and merged it with the A.Ph. Stitzel Distillery. The resulting entity, the Stitzel-Weller Distillery, produced a variety of wheated bourbons until 1972, when it went bankrupt. The brands were sold off, and the Weller name ended up in the hands of Sazerac.

BUFFALO TRACE DISTILLERY
113 GREAT BUFFALO TRACE
FRANKFORT, KENTUCKY 40601
TEL: 800-654-8471
E-MAIL: info@buffalotrace.com
www.buffalotrace.com

BRANDS
OLD WELLER ANTIQUE
W.L. WELLER KENTUCKY STRAIGHT BOURBON WHISKEY
W.L. WELLER SPECIAL RESERVE KENTUCKY STRAIGHT BOURBON WHISKEY

Old Weller Antique Kentucky Straight Bourbon Whiskey

AGE
No age statement

PROOF
107

NOSE
Menthol, bright fruits

COLOR
Tawny

BODY
Full

GENERAL
This is a very hot whiskey, and it needs water or an ice cube or two to mellow it out. Once tempered, it's a fine balance of flavors: sweet, spice, and citrus.

PALATE
Orange and other citrus, shellac, dark fruits; slow finish.

PRICE
$

RATING

W.L. Weller Kentucky Straight Bourbon Whiskey

AGE
12
years old

PROOF
90

NOSE	COLOR	BODY
Cedar, stone fruits, and old basement.	Russet	Medium

GENERAL	PALATE
A truly good whiskey, but not as fine as the Special Reserve. The spice pops up at the end and lingers with some sour notes at the edge, almost lemon. An excellent value for a twelve year old.	Restrained spice, lemon, salt; spice finish

PRICE	RATING
$$	

W.L. Weller Special Reserve Kentucky Straight Bourbon Whiskey

AGE
No age statement

PROOF
90

NOSE	COLOR	BODY
Salt, barley, oats, melon, and black pepper	Russet	Light

GENERAL	PALATE
An intriguing blend of scotch and bourbon notes. It's dry and spicy and slightly peppery, iodine, with quite a bitter aftertaste and a very faint sweetness on top.	Smoke, salt, pepper; quick finishing.

PRICE	RATING
$	★ ★ ⭙

Wathen's

Beam may be the best-known bourbon family in Kentucky, but the Wathens and Medleys are hardly less accomplished. Both families—though given how often they've intermarried, we're talking about two sides of the same coin—have been producing master distillers for well over a century. Charles Wathen Medley, the current patriarch, was the master distiller at the Glenmore Distillery, until it was bought in 1991 by United (now Diageo), which shuttered the plant and sold off the facilities, equipment, and brands. The company didn't want the whiskey itself, though, so Charles Medley bought it and set it aside. A few years later he began to hand bottle and sell some of it under the Wathen's label. When that supply ran out, he purchased new, sourced stock, which he continues to do today, though mum's the word on its age or provenance.

CHARLES MEDLEY DISTILLERY
10 DISTILLERY ROAD
OWENSBORO, KY 42301
TEL: 270-926-4460
EMAIL: info@wathens.com
www.cmdistillerskentucky.com

PRODUCER: UNKNOWN

Wathen's Kentucky Bourbon Single Barrel

AGE No age statement		
PROOF **94**		
NOSE Chocolate, toffee, wood, funk	**COLOR** Mahogany	**BODY** Medium
GENERAL An enjoyable, distinctive bourbon. The dark, chocolate and cream notes make it a real treat.	**PALATE** Cream, spiced chocolate, unsweetened tea; slight spice at finish	
	PRICE **$$**	**RATING** ★★

Westward

HOUSE SPIRITS DISTILLERY

2025 SE 7TH AVE

PORTLAND, OR 97214

TEL: 503-235-3174

www.housespirits.com

Westward is the first regular-production whiskey from House Spirits, a Portland, Oregon, distillery best known for its Aviation gin. The company was founded in 2004 in Corvalis, to the south, but later moved to downtown Portland to join the city's burgeoning craft distilling scene. Alongside House Spirits, one can find Eastside Distilling (maker of Burnside Bourbon), the New Deal Distillery, the Stone Barn Brandyworks, and the Vinn Distillery.

Westward itself is one of several West Coast malt whiskeys to appear in the last decade or so. Though it's too early, and the products are too varied, to speak of a regional *terroir*, House Spirits hopes that the area's distinct climate and locally grown barley will someday have people thinking of "Oregon whiskey" the same way they do Willamette Valley pinots or Columbia Valley cabernets.

Westward Oregon Straight Malt Whiskey

AGE		
No age statement		

PROOF		
90		

NOSE	COLOR	BODY
Caramel chews, salty chips, a touch of loam, and tons of malt, which comes even more with a bit of water	Russet	Light to medium

GENERAL	PALATE	
The nose is like a heady *schwarzbier*; the palate is surprisingly unsweet. Westward would go great in a beer cocktail.	Cola, ginger, malt, finishing with black and chili pepper.	

PRICE	RATING
$$$	

Whipper Snapper

The Whipper Snapper label proudly calls its contents "spirit whiskey." Which is what exactly? According to the U. S. Department of Treasury Tax and Trade Bureau, a "spirit whiskey" is "produced by blending neutral spirits and not less than 5 percent on a proof gallon basis whisky, straight whisky or combination of whisky and straight whisky provided the straight whisky is used at less than 20 percent on a proof gallon basis." Basically, it's an innocuous name for corn whiskey blended with neutral (i.e., above 190 proof) alcohol. Whipper Snapper, made by Oregon-based Ransom Spirits, is a mix of 79 percent unaged corn whiskey and 21 percent neutral spirits derived from barley; the blend is then aged in a combination of French pinot noir barrels and unused American oak barrels, for anywhere between six months and two years.

RANSOM WINE & SPIRITS

23101 SW HOUSER RD.

SHERIDAN, OR 97378

TEL: 503-876-5022

EMAIL: tad@ransomspirits.com

www.ransomspirits.com

Whipper Snapper Oregon Spirit Whiskey

AGE No age statement		
PROOF **84**		
NOSE Dill, fennel, barley, blue cheese	**COLOR** Amber	**BODY** Thin
GENERAL More of a *digestif* than a whiskey, but lacking full flavor. The strong herbal and spice notes are interesting.	**PALATE** Herbal, clove; dry finish	
	PRICE **$$**	**RATING** **NR**

Whistlepig

WHISTLEPIG FARM

2139 QUIET VALLEY ROAD

SHOREHAM, VT 05770

TEL: 802-897-7700

E-MAIL: info@whistlepigfarm.com

www.whistlepigwhiskey.com

BRANDS

WHISTLEPIG STRAIGHT RYE WHISKEY

WHISTLEPIG 111 STRAIGHT RYE
    WHISKEY

Whistlepig may be the country's most thoroughly hyped rye. It even made close-up appearances on AMC's *Breaking Bad*. Its backer is Raj Bhakta, a go-getter entrepreneur and former contestant on Donald Trump's *The Apprentice*. And its aggressive marketing and distribution teams make sure it is in all the trendiest whiskey bars across the country.

But if Whistlepig is hyped, it's not overhyped. It deserves all the accolades it can get. The whiskey is a 100 proof, 100 percent rye mash bill sourced from Canada, and it shares many of the bright, spicy pop of Jefferson's Rye and Masterson's, also made with rye from the Great White North. Bhakta says that the company is working on its own distilling facilities, under the command of Dave Pickerell, a spirit making consultant who has worked with so many start-up outfits that he's known as the Johnny Appleseed of whiskey.

In late 2012 Whistlepig released an eleven-year-old, 111-proof whiskey. Though only a few thousand bottles were produced, the company says to expect similar small, older and higher-proof expressions in the coming years.

Whistlepig
Straight Rye Whiskey

AGE **10** years old		
PROOF **100**		

NOSE	COLOR	BODY
Flower shop, with very little wood or cherry	Mahogany	Full and chewy

GENERAL	PALATE
A fantastic rye, with higher, more pronounced floral and fruit notes than usual, even for the style. It's also much smoother than a typical rye, though no less complex or interesting for it. The finish pleasantly leaves none of the usual rye bitterness.	Red Hot candies; dry finish.

PRICE	RATING
$$$$	

Whistlepig
Triple One
Rye Whiskey

AGE
11
years old

PROOF
111

NOSE
Bright floral, anise, apricots, faint woodiness

COLOR
Burnt umber

BODY
Robust and chewy

GENERAL
A perfect balance of wood, floral, and fruit notes, particularly in a rye. Rum-like in many ways with subtle sweetness and strong vanilla, tawny port, and oak in the finish.

PALATE
Lapsang souchong, black pepper, cinnamon, sherry; finishes with no spice.

PRICE
$$$$

RATING

Wild Turkey

AUSTIN NICHOLS DISTILLING CO.

1525 TYRONE ROAD

LAWRENCEBURG, KY 40342

TEL: 502-839-4544

E-MAIL:

wildturkey@qualitycustomercare.com

www.wildturkey.com

BRANDS

WILD TURKEY 81 KENTUCKY
   STRAIGHT BOURBON WHISKEY

WILD TURKEY 101 KENTUCKY
   STRAIGHT BOURBON WHISKEY

WILD TURKEY KENTUCKY STRAIGHT
   RYE WHISKEYWILD TURKEY
   KENTUCKY SPIRIT SINGLE
   BARREL

WILD TURKEY RARE BREED
   KENTUCKY STRAIGHT BOURBON
   WHISKEY

Wild Turkey may today be owned by the Italian liquor giant Campari, but its roots lie in two very distinctly American enterprises. The oldest is the series of distilleries owned by the Ripy family. Beginning in 1888, the Ripys made whiskey for a variety of wholesalers, who stuck their own brand names on the liquor and sold it retail. The distillery, known originally as Old Moore, went through a variety of ownership iterations, including, for a time, as part of the infamous Whiskey Trust (see pages 40–41), but always with a Ripy family member close at hand.

The second strand is Austin Nichols and Company, a Brooklyn-based grocery concern that began to source its whiskey from the Ripys. The firm was a classic urban retail grocer, except that, as many did when liquor regulations were more lax, it also packaged and sold whiskey. Originally, the whiskey was simply called Austin Nichols. But, legend has it, one day the company's president, Thomas McCarthy, was out hunting on Long Island and, perhaps inspired by his elusive prey, decided to change the name to Wild Turkey. Eventually, Austin Nichols bought the Ripy distillery outright, and, later, Austin Nichols itself was bought, first by Pernod Richard and then, in 2009, Campari.

For the last half-century, however, the Wild Turkey brand has been less associated with Brooklyn groceries or European mega-distillers than with a single, albeit very large man, Jimmy Russell. The legendary master distiller and his son, Eddie, have nearly 100 years of combined distilling experience, and even have their own line of eponymous whiskey under the Austin Nichols portfolio, Russell's Reserve.

Wild Turkey is a respectable, if not stellar distillery on the domestic scene. But like Four Roses, its real respect comes overseas—in Wild Turkey's case, Japan. There you will find a variety of export-only, ultra-premium expressions; bartenders who bring back a bottle or two have been known to sell two-ounce servings for upwards of $200.

Wild Turkey 81 Kentucky Straight Bourbon Whiskey

AGE		
No age statement		

PROOF		
81		

NOSE	COLOR	BODY
New oak, banana, and cereal	Chestnut	Light

GENERAL	PALATE
Light, refreshing, and nicely balanced. It's a thirst-quenching whiskey, with a snappy mouthfeel.	Chili pepper, vanilla, nutty

	PRICE	RATING
	$	★ ★ ✦

Wild Turkey 101 Kentucky Straight Bourbon Whiskey

AGE		
No age statement		

PROOF		
101		

NOSE	COLOR	BODY
Strawberries, smoked almonds, pencil shavings	Auburn	Thin

GENERAL	PALATE
Wild Turkey 101 has a good balance of sweet and bitterness with wood and an obvious touch of barley in the mash bill. At this proof, it's an excellent choice for mixing.	Pepper, light oak, simple sugar

	PRICE	RATING
	$$	★ ★

Wild Turkey Kentucky Straight Rye Whiskey

AGE
No age statement

PROOF
101

NOSE
Lots of high florals, saltwater taffy, and a bit of earthy funk, which really comes out with some water.

COLOR
Auburn

BODY
Medium

GENERAL
This is a very aggressive rye. Fortunately, a little water tames but doesn't break it. Wild Turkey has recently introduced an 81-proof rye and the 101-proof version is becoming more difficult to find.

PALATE
Grape; medicinal; a slight vegetal funk; finishes with a long, spicy burn.

PRICE
$$

RATING

Wild Turkey Rare Breed Kentucky Straight Bourbon Whiskey

AGE
6
years old

PROOF
108

NOSE
Butterscotch, oak, and mint

COLOR
Mahogany

BODY
Medium

GENERAL
Respectably complex, but it is too sweet and syrupy, even with water. The honey finish is a check in the plus column, though.

PALATE
Honey, pepper, long finishing

PRICE
$$

RATING

Wild Turkey Kentucky Spirit Kentucky Straight Bourbon Whiskey BARREL 51; RICK 32; WAREHOUSE

AGE
8½–9½
years old

PROOF
101

NOSE
Honey, geranium, grass

COLOR
Auburn/mahogany

BODY
Light to medium

GENERAL
Wild Turkey's single-barrel expression is selected by its master distiller Jimmy Russell. The whiskey is dry with a bitter finish and plenty of butterscotch and vanilla on the palate.

PALATE
Oak, peanuts, vanila; quick, bitter finish.

PRICE
$$$

RATING

Willett

KENTUCKY BOURBON DISTILLERS

1869 LORETTO ROAD

BARDSTOWN, KY, 40004

TEL: 502-348-0081

E-MAIL: kentuckybourbon@bardstown.com

www.kentuckybourbonwhiskey.com

....

BRANDS

WILLETT POT STILL SINGLE BARREL WHISKEY

WILLETT STRAIGHT RYE WHISKEY

For now, there are two iterations of the Willett name: first, a collection of sourced whiskeys bottled by Kentucky Bourbon Distillers, and second, a distillery that reopened in January 2012, after being shuttered for decades. Both KBD and the Willett Distillery are located in Bardstown, and both are owned by Even Kulsveen and his family.

The Willett Distillery was founded in 1936 by Lambert Willett, a local distiller. His son, Thompson, kept the family business going, but in his old age sold it to Kulsveen, his son-in-law. By then there wasn't much to sell, though—the operation had long since stopped making its own whiskey, and Kulsveen essentially took on a collection of outdated warehouses. But he had a vision, and reconstituted operations under the KBD name. Kulsveen created several brands, including Rowan's Creek and Noah's Mill, and at the same time relaunched the Willett line under the KBD portfolio. He used the proceeds from these whiskeys, which were all sourced from other distillers, to slowly modernize in the Willett Distillery itself.

Today the distillery has a 1,200 gallon pot still and eight rickhouses, and is reportedly now producing its own whiskey, though it will be years before any of it comes to market.

Willett Pot Still Reserve Kentucky Straight Bourbon Whiskey

AGE
No age statement

PROOF
94

NOSE
Oak, corn, teriyaki, black pepper

COLOR
Tawny

BODY
Light

GENERAL
Complex, refined, and refreshing. (And it comes in a truly great-looking bottle.) With a little water, the nose opens up to orange peel and flowers with only a bare hint of green wood.

PALATE
Rubber, tobacco, lemon, cinnamon; finishes hot.

PRICE
 $$

RATING

Willett Straight Rye Whiskey

AGE
4
years old

PROOF
110

NOSE
Candy apple, rye bread, citrus, and loam

COLOR
Tawny/ auburn

BODY
Light to medium

GENERAL
Rye lovers will adore this whiskey—it's like sticking your nose in a fresh, sweet loaf of caraway-studded bread. For all its rye roots, it is remarkably smooth with forward sweetness finishing in a slightly minty pop and lingering slight bitterness.

PALATE
Fruitcake, black pepper, tea

PRICE
$$

RATING
★ ★ ★

Woodford

WOODFORD RESERVE DISTILLERY

7855 MCCRACKEN PIKE

VERSAILLES, KY 40383

TEL: 859-879-1812

E-MAIL: info@woodfordreserve.com

www.woodfordreserve.com

....

BRANDS

WOODFORD RESERVE

    DISTILLER'S SELECT

WOODFORD RESERVE DOUBLE OAKED

Whiskey has been made on the site of the present-day Woodford Reserve Distillery more or less continuously for over 200 years. Located about halfway between Frankfort and Versailles, the location was first home to Elijah Pepper's distilling operation at the turn of the nineteenth century; his son Oscar took over the reins and, in turn, named the distillery after himself. The Old Oscar Pepper Distillery at one point employed Dr. James Crow, a Scottish immigrant who developed many of the foundational elements of modern bourbon making. The Peppers sold the distillery to Leopold Labrot and James Graham in 1878; their firm, Labrot & Graham, in turn sold it to Brown-Forman in 1941.

The facility was used on and off for the next fifty years, but in 1993 Brown-Forman reopened it as a home for its new small-batch expression, Woodford Reserve. Most Woodford whiskey is a blend of pot-stilled spirit made at its own distillery and column-stilled whiskey from Brown-Forman. In 2005 the distillery began its Masters Collection, an annual limited release series that utilizes inventive mash bills, woods, and finishes—the first two releases involved four-grain recipes, while others have used Sonoma-Cutrer Vineyards wine barrels and maple and seasoned oak barrels. In 2012 the distillery introduced a second regular-production whiskey, Double Oak, which involves a second round of aging in heavily toasted, lightly charred barrels.

Woodford Reserve Distiller's Select Kentucky Straight Bourbon Whiskey

AGE
No age statement

PROOF
90.4

NOSE
Toffee, boiled fruit (pears, plums), and cinnamon

COLOR
Auburn

BODY
Ligh to medium

GENERAL
Woodford is a good middle-of-the-road whiskey, solid but unchallenging. A fine standby whiskey by all measures.

PALATE
Bit-O-Honey, oak, and just a nip of a bite up front; the finish is long and spicy

PRICE
$$

RATING

Woodford Reserve Double Oaked Kentucky Straight Bourbon Whiskey

AGE
No age statement

PROOF
92.4

NOSE
Marzipan, oak, salted caramel, and apples

COLOR
Auburn/ mahogany

BODY
Medium

GENERAL
A well-done, well-textured whiskey, and a step up from the standard Woodford. The only possible fault is the intensity of the oak notes, but they end up complementing, rather than over-powering, the rest of the whiskey's well-rounded qualitites.

PALATE
Pepper, smoke, and barbecue sauce

PRICE
$$$

RATING

Acknowledgments

Clay Risen

While my name appears on the cover of this book, it is not mine alone. George Scott and Charles Nix originated the idea for a serious guide to American whiskey, and they had the crazy notion to bring me on as the author. Not only did they provide office space to store the several hundred bottles under review, but also their refined senses (scent, taste, and humor in equal parts) constituted the core of the book's tasting panel. Later, they did the heavy lifting involved in turning our notes and my text into a beautiful book. I cannot thank them enough.

Thanks to Nathaniel Marunas, formerly of Sterling, who acquired the book and to Carlo Devito, Diane Abrams and the Sterling Epicure publishing team who took over the reins. Their interest in the book and guidance on its development were invaluable.

Many thanks to Steve Ury for reading the galleys from cover to cover and providing thoughtful and thorough notes, suggestions, and corrections.

A shout out to Pitchaya Sudbanthad, another core member of the tasting panel—he has one of the most refined palates I've ever encountered. And thanks to all the other regulars and semi-regulars at the tastings. Their input was enormously helpful, almost as much as their friendship.

Though she is too young to remember the last year, my daughter Talia deserves a debt of gratitude. Our tasting schedule kept me away one, two, and on the rare occasion three nights a week, time I could, and perhaps should, have spent watching *Curious George* with her. Thanks, Bunny.

My wife Joanna, however, is certainly old enough to remember my frequent absences, and she had to deal with an occasionally well-oiled husband coming home late on a Tuesday night. She bore those months with humor and grace. I love you.

Scott & Nix, Inc.

George Scott and Charles Nix extend special thanks to Carlo Devito and Diane Abrams and the entire publishing group at Sterling Epicure. We thank Nathan Sayers for his beautiful photographs and good humor. We thank the local merchants who helped us acquire bottles, including Lakshmi Massand of Manor House Cellar and Jonathan Goldstein of Park Avenue Liquor Shop, and most of all, Michael Dolega of BQE Wine & Liquors in Brooklyn. Michael's vast and expertly curated selection of whiskey is a pilgrimage that we urge whiskey lovers to make. Many thanks to the distilleries that sent sample bottles to our offices for review. We also thank the many people from novice to expert who shared good cheer with us and whose impressions contributed to the whiskey accounts of the book: Christian Acker, Samantha Alderson, Michelle Brower, Peter Burr, Justin Burruto, Paul Carlos, Alexander de Voogt, Michael Duffy, Mark Franks, Stan Friedman, Gerry Gallagher, Luke Hayman, Beth Hertzog, Thomas Jackson, Scott Korb, Paul Lucas, Nathaniel Marunas, Abbott Miller, Andrew Morrow, Stephen Morrow, Michael Nix, Dean Olsher, Sanjay Rana, Mark Rotella, Jamie Ryerson, Ian Schoenherr, Patrick Seymour, Pitchaya Sudbanthad, Paul Sweet, and Alexandra Zsigmond. Most of all we thank Clay Risen for his exceptional mind, enthusiasm, and tireless work ethic.

We welcome comments, questions, and suggestions about this guide. Feel free to email us at whiskey@scottandnix.com.

Recommended References and Resources

Herewith a partial selection of books and other resources I have consulted in the writing of this book. I can recommend them all for more information regarding the fascinating history and culture of American spirits. Naturally, there are scores of excellent websites devoted to the interest and enjoyment of whiskey and other drinks. Listed below are the ones I follow closely along with several magazines and newsletters closely covering the world of whiskey.

Bell, Darek. *Alt Whiskeys: Alternative Whiskey Recipes and Distilling Techniques for the Adventurous Craft Distiller.* Nashville, Tennessee: Corsair Artisan Distillery, 2012.

Carson, Gerald. *The Social History of Bourbon.* Lexington, Kentucky: University of Kentucky Press, 2010 (reprint edition).

Cecil, Sam K. *Bourbon: The Evolution of Kentucky Whiskey.* Nashville, Tennessee: Turner Publishing, 2010.

Cowdery, Charles K. *Bourbon, Straight: The Uncut and Unfiltered Story of American Whiskey.* Chicago, Illinois: Made and Bottled in Kentucky, 2004.

Crowgey, Henry G. *Kentucky Bourbon: The Early Years of Whiskey Making.* Lexington, Kentucky: University of Kentucky Press, 2008.

Kosar, Kevin R. *Whiskey: A Global History.* London, Great Britain: Reaktion Books, 2010.

Lears, Jackson. *Rebirth of America: The Making of Modern America, 1877–1920.* New York, New York: Harper Perennial, 2010.

Lubbers, Bernie. *Bourbon Whiskey Our Native Spirit Sour Mash and Sweet Adventures.* Indianapolis, Indiana: Blue River Press, 2011.

Okrent, Daniel. *Last Call: The Rise and Fall of Prohibition.* New York, New York: Scribner, 2011.

Owens, Bill. *The Art of Distilling Whiskey and Other Spirits: An Enthusiast's Guide to the Artisan Distilling of Potent Potables.* Beverly, Massachusetts: Quarry Books, 2012.

Pacult, F. Paul. *American Still Life: The Jim Beam Story and the Making of the World's #1 Bourbon.* Hoboken, New Jersey: Wiley, 2003.

Rorabaugh, W.J. *The Alcoholic Republic: An American Tradition.* New York, New York: Oxford University Press, 1981.

Regan, Gary and Mardee Haidin Regan. *The Book of Bourbon and Other Fine American Whiskeys.* New York, New York: Houghton Mifflin Harcourt, 1995.

Scott, Berkeley. *The Kentucky Bourbon Trail.* Mount Pleasant, South Carolina: Arcadia Publishing, 2009.

Veach, Michael R. *Kentucky Bourbon Whiskey: An American Heritage.* Lexington, Kentucky: University of Kentucky Press, 2013.

Washburne, George R. and Stanley Bronner, eds. *Beverages De Luxe.* Louisville, Kentucky: The Wine and Spirit Bulletin, 1911.

Websites

Bourbon Blog | bourbonblog.com
Reviews and news, with a good sense for trends
on the craft end of the spectrum.

Bourbon Dork | bourbondork.blogspot.com
The name says it all.

The Chuck Cowdery Blog | chuckcowdery.blogspot.com
No one knows more about bourbon than
Chuck Cowdery.

Drink Hacker | drinkhacker.com
Not exclusively whiskey, but the authors know
from bourbon, for sure.

Drink Spirits | drinkspirits.com
Like Drinkhacker.com, not exclusive to whiskey, but
there are lots of news and reviews of brown spirits
to be found here.

*John and Linda Lipman's Adventures in
Bourbon Country* | ellenjaye.com
A breezy but encyclopedic tour of the places
and people behind the bottle.

K&L Spirits Journal | spiritsjournal.klwines.com
The official blog of California retailer K&L
Wine Merchants.

Kentucky Bourbon Trail | kybourbontrail.com
A wealth of information for planning a visit to the famous
distilleries around Lexington, Frankfort, Lawrenceburg,
Bardstown, and other locations in Bluegrass Country.

Lexington Convention and Visitors Bureau | visitlex.com
An information site for visiting Lexington, Kentucky and
surrounding areas.

Rowley's Whiskey Forge | matthew-rowley.blogspot.com
Matthew Rowley has a great sense of humor and a great
eye for the new and interesting in the whiskey world.

Scotch & Ice Cream | scotchandicecream.com
More scotch (and other whiskey) than ice cream, Tim
Read's blog combines extensive reviews with the occasional diatribe about what's wrong, and sometimes
right, with the world of brown spirits.

SKU's Recent Eats | recenteats.blogspot.com
   Despite the name, Steve Ury's site is chock-full of
   thoughtful information about American whiskey.

Sour Mash Manifesto | sourmashmanifesto.com
   Spot-on reviews of the latest bourbon and
   rye releases.

Those Pre-Pro-Whiskey Men |
   pre-prowhiskeymen.blogspot.com
   A great source on the history of American liquor.

The Whisky Advocate Blog | whiskyadvocateblog.com
   Editor John Hansell and Co. hold forth on all
   things whisk(e)y.

Periodicals

The Bourbon Country Reader. Made and Bottled
   in Kentucky, Chicago, Illinois.

*The Spirit Journal. The Independent Guide to Distilled
   Spirits, Beer, and Fortified Wines.* Wallkill, New York.

Mutineer. Wine Mutineer, LLC, Los Angeles, California.

Whisky Advocate. M. Shanken Communications,
   New York, New York.

Whisky Magazine. Paragraph Publishing Limited,
   Norwich, Great Britain.

Glossary
of Terms

ALCOHOL AND TOBACCO TAX AND
TRADE BUREAU (TTB): Better known by its
acronym TTB, this organization regulates alcohol
and tobacco production for the federal government.
Housed in the Treasury Department, it was a part of
the Bureau of Alcohol, Tobacco and Firearms until
2003, when that agency was dissolved and its law-
enforcement functions moved to the Justice
Department. The TTB today is focused almost exclusively on revenue collection, and to that end it
maintains extensive rules for the production and
labeling of alcoholic beverages. In other words, it's
the TTB that determines what can and can't be
called bourbon, rye, or scotch in the United States.

BARREL-AGING: Storing distilled spirits in a
wooden barrel. This imparts certain colors, aromas,
and flavors from the wood, while also allowing the
wood to draw out some of the less desirable
compounds found in newly distilled liquor.
According to the federal government, "corn
whiskey" does not have to be aged, but virtually
every other category of whiskey has to at least
touch the inside of a barrel. "Touch" is the operative
word: unlike scotch, which must sit in a barrel
at least three years, American whiskeys do not
have minimal age limits. However, in the case
of bourbon, rye, malt, and wheat whiskeys, they
must be stored for at least some time in new oak
containers—prohibitive to short-term aging,
since the expensive barrels cannot be reused.

BLENDED WHISKEY: In the United States, the
term "blending" can refer either to the combining of
different straight whiskeys or to combining at least
20 percent straight whiskey with younger whiskeys
and/or neutral grain sprits. If the type of whiskey is
specified—"blended rye whiskey," for example—
then at least 51 percent of the content has to be
straight rye. Blended whiskeys have a bad reputation in this country, since they have long filled the

ranks of the cheapest and unappetizing whiskey on the shelf. However, a few distilleries, most notably St. George Spirits and its Breaking & Entering bourbon, which combines whiskeys from some 80 different sources, are starting to change that image.

BOTTLED IN BOND: According to the 1897 Bottled-in-Bond Act, a bonded whiskey has been distilled by the same distiller at the same distillery in the same year, aged for four years in a bonded warehouse, and put in the bottle at 100 proof. These probably seem like pointless rules today, and indeed it's hard to find bottled-in-bond whiskeys any more. But at the time, these rules provided a federal gold standard for whiskey, a check against anyone trying to pass off adulterated or diluted liquor as a quality product.

BOURBON: A whiskey in which at least 51 percent of the mash bill is corn. It must come off the still at no more than 160 proof and be stored in new charred oak barrels at no more than 125 proof. Contrary to barstool wisdom, it does not have to come from Bourbon County, Kentucky, or anywhere in Kentucky. It does, however, have to be made in the United States.

CORN WHISKEY: This is a less-rigorous category of corn-based liquor than bourbon, with the one requirement that its mash bill be at least 80 percent corn, unlike bourbon's 51 percent. Like bourbon, it must come off the still at no more than 160 proof. But it does not have to be aged, and if it is, it must be stored in used or uncharred new oak barrels, at no more than 125 proof.

DISTILLATION: In the creation of whiskey, distillation is the process by which a mixture of water and fermented grain is altered through use of prolonged exposure to heat in a still. The fermented grain mixture is boiled and the resulting vapor is condensed and collected as liquid alcohol. This alcohol is a clear, highly potent liquid, which is then watered down, sometimes flavored, and/or aged in barrels, or whatever other finishing steps are intended. Distillation is about concentration: if the fermented grain liquid, such as beer, is mostly a combination of water and alcohol, then distillation is the process of removing a large amount of that water (which evaporates at a higher temperature than alcohol), leaving a higher percentage of alcohol behind. Distillation is also about removal: the process of taking out all sorts of unwanted compounds. These have different evaporation temperatures than either water or alcohol, and thus come off the still first (called the heads) or last (called the tails). The heads and tails are usually discarded, but they may also be used to distill once again to make the resulting liquor more palatable. Most whiskey sold in the United States is distilled twice to refine the quality of the distillate.

FINISHING: A whiskey is said to be "finished" when, after its normal time in the barrel, it is treated to a little something extra: either the distiller transfers it to a barrel that previously held something else—like wine or beer—or they add something to the whiskey barrel, like oak staves. The idea is to give the whiskey one little jolt of flavor at the end, the way a chef will add a squeeze of lemon or a dash of sea salt to a dish before serving. Finishing is still rare in the United States, but it is catching on, especially among craft distilleries. Probably the best known of the type is Angel's Envy, finished in port barrels.

MASH BILL: The ratio of different grains used to make whiskey. Every distiller claims to have found the perfect mash bill for their purposes, but most of them fall under a few broad categories: the traditional (or low-rye) bill for bourbon is about 70–80 percent corn, 15 percent rye, and the rest malted barley; high rye, in which the rye content is around 30 percent; and wheated, in which wheat, not rye, is the second-largest grain in the mash bill. Evan Williams and Jim Beam are typical traditional-mash bill whiskeys; Basil Hayden's and Old Forester are high ryes; and Rebel Yell and Maker's Mark are wheated.

PROOF: A beverage's "proof" is simply twice its alcohol content. If a whiskey is 40 percent alcohol, it is 80 proof. The term is said to originate in a primitive test of alcohol percentage, used in the eighteenth and early nineteenth century to demonstrate that a liquor hadn't been overly watered down. The liquid was mixed with gunpowder, and a flame was put to it. If the flame set off the gunpowder, it was said to be "proof" that the liquid was at least 50 percent alcohol (actually, closer to 57 percent).

RYE WHISKEY: A whiskey in which at least 51 percent of the mash bill is rye. Like bourbon and wheat whiskeys, it must come off the still at no more than 160 proof and be stored in new charred oak barrels at no more than 125 proof.

SINGLE BARREL: A term denoting that the contents of a bottle of whiskey have all come from the same barrel. Distilleries that take the term seriously will write the name and location of the barrel in the warehouse, and usually add information about when it was distilled and when it was emptied.

SINGLE-MALT WHISKEY: In Scotland, a single malt has been distilled and aged at a single distillery, in contrast to whiskeys, like Johnny Walker, that are the product of barrels bought from many different distilleries and blended. In the United States, the term is not defined by the TTB and therefore has no meaning. In any case, since most distilleries make all their own whiskey, it's safe to say that most every domestic malt whiskey is "single malt."

SMALL BATCH/VERY SMALL BATCH: Undefined terms, largely used for marketing purposes, implying that a whiskey was made in small volumes, presumably with more care than a "large batch" whiskey. Jim Beam produces more of its "small batch" whiskeys in a day than many craft distillers produce in a year.

SMOKED WHISKEY: There are very few smoked whiskeys on the market, but their numbers are growing. The term doesn't have a well-defined meaning, except that it denotes an American whiskey with a prominent smoky flavor. As with scotch, that smokiness is typically the result of cooking the grains over an open flame. In scotch's case, the fuel for the fire is peat, but in the United States it can be from a variety of sources, from wood to scrub brush.

STRAIGHT WHISKEY: A straight whiskey is one that has sat in a new charred oak barrel for at least two years. If a straight whiskey has been in the barrel between two and four years, the bottle has to reveal how long, to the year. In other words, if the bottle simply says "straight," with no age statement, you know it's at least four years old.

TTB: See Alcohol and Tobacco Tax and Trade Bureau

UNAGED WHISKEY: This simply means whiskey that has never been stored in a wood (most often oak) container. Unless coloring or flavors have been added, it will be crystal clear. Only unaged spirits made from at least 80 percent corn can be called whiskey. Keep in mind that whiskey won't age outside of a barrel: unlike wine or beer, whiskey does not develop further once it's in a bottle; the whiskey in a well-sealed bottle will taste the same in ten years as it does after a single year.

WHEAT WHISKEY: A whiskey in which at least 51 percent of the mash bill is wheat. Like bourbon and rye, it must come off the still at no more than 160 proof and be stored in new charred oak barrels at no more than 125 proof.

WHEATED BOURBON: Like all other bourbon, a wheated bourbon has at least 51 percent corn in its mash bill; unlike standard bourbons, though, "wheaters" have wheat instead of rye as their second-largest grain. Prominent examples of wheated bourbons include Pappy Van Winkle, Maker's Mark, and Rebel Yell.

American Whiskey, Bourbon & Rye Checklist

This alphabetical checklist reflects the whiskeys covered in this guide. It is by no means a complete accounting of American whiskeys available in today's ever-growing marketplace of special expressions and smaller distillery offerings. Feel free to give us your suggestions for what might be included in future editions via email to whiskey@scottandnix.com.

- [ ] Ancient Age
- [ ] Ancient Ancient Age
- [ ] Angel's Envy
- [ ] Baker's
- [ ] Balcones Baby Blue
- [ ] Balcones Brimstone
- [ ] Balcones Texas Single Malt
- [ ] Balcones True Blue
- [ ] Basil Hayden's
- [ ] Belle Meade Bourbon
- [ ] Bellows
- [ ] Berkshire Bourbon
- [ ] Berkshire Corn Whiskey
- [ ] Bernheim
- [ ] Black Dirt
- [ ] Black Maple Hill
- [ ] Blanton's
- [ ] Booker's
- [ ] Bowman Brothers
- [ ] Breaking & Entering
- [ ] Breakout Rye
- [ ] Breckenridge Bourbon
- [ ] Buck
- [ ] Buffalo Trace
- [ ] Bulleit Bourbon
- [ ] Bulleit Rye
- [ ] Burnside
- [ ] Cabin Still
- [ ] Charbay "S"
- [ ] Charter 101
- [ ] Collier & McKeel

- [ ] Colonel E.H. Taylor Barrel Proof
- [ ] Colonel E.H. Taylor Single Barrel
- [ ] Copper Fox Rye
- [ ] Corner Creek
- [ ] Corsair Triple Smoke
- [ ] Cyrus Noble
- [ ] Dad's Hat
- [ ] Dead Guy
- [ ] Dry Fly
- [ ] Eagle Rare
- [ ] Early Times 354
- [ ] Early Times
- [ ] Elijah Craig 12 Years Old
- [ ] Elijah Craig 18 Years Old
- [ ] Elijah Craig 20 Years Old
- [ ] Elmer T. Lee
- [ ] Evan Williams 1783
- [ ] Evan Williams Black Label
- [ ] Evan Williams Green Label
- [ ] Evan Williams Vintage
- [ ] Ezra B.
- [ ] F.E.W.
- [ ] Fighting Cock
- [ ] Four Roses
- [ ] Four Roses Single Barrel
- [ ] Four Roses Small Batch
- [ ] Garrison Brothers
- [ ] Gentleman Jack
- [ ] George Dickel Barrel Select

- [ ] George Dickel Cascade Hollow
- [ ] George Dickel No. 8
- [ ] George Dickel No. 12
- [ ] Hancock's
- [ ] Heaven Hill
- [ ] Henry McKenna
- [ ] High West Bourye
- [ ] High West Double Rye!
- [ ] High West Rendezvous
- [ ] High West Son of Bourye
- [ ] Hillrock
- [ ] Hirsch Selection
- [ ] Hirsch 20 Year Old
- [ ] Hudson Baby Bourbon
- [ ] Hudson Four Grain
- [ ] Hudson Manhattan Rye
- [ ] Hudson Single Malt
- [ ] Jack Daniel's Black Label
- [ ] Jack Daniel's Green Label
- [ ] Jack Daniel's Single Barrel
- [ ] Jefferson's
- [ ] Jefferson's 18 Years Old
- [ ] Jefferson's Reserve Very Old
- [ ] Jefferson's Rye
- [ ] Jim Beam Black
- [ ] Jim Beam Devil's Cut
- [ ] Jim Beam White Label
- [ ] Jim Beam Rye
- [ ] John B. Stetson
- [ ] John J. Bowman

- [ ] Johnny Drum Green Label
- [ ] Johnny Drum Black Label
- [ ] Johnny Drum Private Stock
- [ ] Kentucky Gentleman
- [ ] Kentucky Tavern
- [ ] Kentucky Vintage
- [ ] Kings County
- [ ] Knob Creek Rye
- [ ] Knob Creek Single Barrel
- [ ] Knob Creek Small Batch
- [ ] Koval Millet
- [ ] Koval Oat
- [ ] Koval Rye
- [ ] Koval Spelt
- [ ] Koval Wheat
- [ ] Larceny
- [ ] Liquid Dudlwa
- [ ] Maker's 46
- [ ] Maker's Mark
- [ ] Masterson's Rye
- [ ] McAfee's Benchmark
- [ ] McCarthy's Single Malt
- [ ] McKenzie Bourbon
- [ ] McKenzie Pot Still
- [ ] McKenzie Rye
- [ ] Mellow Corn
- [ ] Michter's 10 Years Old
- [ ] Michter's 20 Years Old
- [ ] Michter's Rye
- [ ] Michter's Small Batch
- [ ] Michter's Sour Mash
- [ ] Michter's Unblended
- [ ] Noah's Mill
- [ ] Old Bardstown Gold Label
- [ ] Old Bardstown Black Label
- [ ] Old Bardstown Estate Bottled
- [ ] Old Charter
- [ ] Old Crow
- [ ] Old Crow Reserve
- [ ] Old Ezra

- [ ] Old Fitzgerald 1849
- [ ] Old Forester Birthday Bourbon
- [ ] Old Forester
- [ ] Old Forester Signature
- [ ] Old Grand-Dad 114
- [ ] Old Grand-Dad
- [ ] Old Overholt Rye
- [ ] Old Pogue Master's Select
- [ ] Old Potrero Single Malt
- [ ] Old Potrero Rye
- [ ] Old Rip Van Winkle
- [ ] Old Weller Antique
- [ ] Old Whiskey River
- [ ] Old Williamsburg
- [ ] Pappy Van Winkle 15 Years Old
- [ ] Pappy Van Winkle 20 Years Old
- [ ] Pappy Van Winkle 23 Years Old
- [ ] Peach Street
- [ ] Pikerville Rye
- [ ] Pine Barrens Single Malt
- [ ] Prichard's Double-Barreled
- [ ] Prichard's Single Malt
- [ ] Prichard's Tennessee
- [ ] Pure Kentucky XO
- [ ] (rT)1
- [ ] Ranger Creek .36
- [ ] Rebecca Creek
- [ ] Rebel Reserve
- [ ] Rebel Yell
- [ ] Redemption High-Rye
- [ ] Redemption Rye
- [ ] Ridgemont Reserve 1792
- [ ] Rittenhouse Rye
- [ ] Riverboat Rye
- [ ] Rock Hill Farms
- [ ] Roundstone Rye
- [ ] Rowan's Creek
- [ ] Russell's Reserve
- [ ] Russell's Reserve Rye
- [ ] Russell's Reserve Single Barrel

- [ ] Sam Houston American Whiskey
- [ ] Sam Houston Bourbon
- [ ] Sazerac Rye
- [ ] Seagram's Seven Crown
- [ ] Smooth Ambler Old Scout
- [ ] Smooth Ambler Yearling
- [ ] St. George Single Malt
- [ ] Stranahan's
- [ ] Templeton Rye
- [ ] Temptation
- [ ] Ten High
- [ ] Town Branch
- [ ] Van Winkle Rye 13 Years Old
- [ ] Van Winkle Lot "B" 12 Years Old
- [ ] Very Old Barton (86 proof)
- [ ] Very Old Barton (UU proof)
- [ ] Vintage Bourbon
- [ ] Vintage Rye
- [ ] Virginia Gentleman
- [ ] W.L. Weller
- [ ] W.L. Weller Special Reserve
- [ ] Wasmund's Single Malt
- [ ] Wathen's
- [ ] Westward Malt
- [ ] Whipper Snapper
- [ ] Whistlepig Rye
- [ ] Whistlepig Triple One Rye
- [ ] Wild Turkey 101
- [ ] Wild Turkey 81
- [ ] Wild Turkey Kentucky Spirit
- [ ] Wild Turkey Rye
- [ ] Wild Turkey Rare Breed
- [ ] Willett Pot Still Reserve
- [ ] Willett Rye
- [ ] Woodford Reserve Distiller's Select
- [ ] Woodford Reserve Double Oaked

Index